THE FILMING OF *THE GREAT GATSBY*

HERE ARE THE PRINCIPALS IN A BEHIND-THE-SCENES DRAMA AS EXCITING AS THE FILM ITSELF

Robert Redford, hailed as the Clark Gable of the seventies, ready to fulfill his acting promise in a classic role, a man of few words on the set, aloof, distant, yet a presence that is always powerful . . .

Mia Farrow, proud possessor of the most coveted acting role since Scarlett O'Hara, mother of two with another child on the way, a condition that threatens to pose many a problem to the film's progress . . .

Karen Black, heroine of PORTNOY'S COMPLAINT and FIVE EASY PIECES, a disarming kook with a fierce determination underneath . . .

David Merrick, Broadway's legendary producer, now in film production, a power behind the scene with relentless dedication to make his picture faithful to the book, believing he is working on a film masterpiece.

Jack Clayton, noted British director of ROOM AT THE TOP, an enigmatic man being given the chance of his career . . .

Lois Chiles, beautiful young actress facing the self-doubts and fears of a difficult role, perhaps beyond her still-developing talents . . .

Bruce Dern, Sam Waterston, Francis Ford Coppola, Robert Evans, the fabulously wealthy socialites of glittering Newport . . . all figure in this fascinating exposé!

FILMING THE GREAT GATSBY

Bruce Bahrenburg

A BERKLEY MEDALLION BOOK
published by
BERKLEY PUBLISHING CORPORATION

To the Saturday Night Film Club
they know who they are and they
have my respect and friendship

International Famous Agency
1301 Avenue of the Americas
New York, New York 10019

SBN 425-02576-4

*BERKLEY MEDALLION BOOKS are published by
Berkley Publishing Corporation
200 Madison Avenue
New York, N.Y. 10016*

BERKLEY MEDALLION BOOKS ® TM 757,375

Printed in the United States of America

Berkley Medallion Edition, APRIL, 1974

Filming
THE GREAT GATSBY

Chapter I

The First Week

June 11

The production of *The Great Gatsby* began in Newport, Rhode Island, on the morning of June 11, 1973, under a state of siege: threatened with a strike by Local 644, the cameramen's union, and still affected by the Hollywood writers' strike which had prohibited Francis Ford Coppola from doing rewrites on his screenplay.

There was also a reawareness of the artist's mortality with the announcement in the morning papers that playwright William Inge had committed suicide in Los Angeles.

As the company assembled in front of Nick's cottage back from the cliff, the common boundary to the property along Millionaire's Road, Inge's death was noted by the crew. He had been considered an important playwright in the 1950s, mentioned often with Tennessee Williams and Arthur Miller, the two writers held most accountable for the last great renaissance on Broadway. He had won a Pulitzer Prize for *Picnic* in 1953 and an Oscar in 1962 for his original screenplay, *Splendor in the Grass*. Since then it had been a gigantic creative slide, and those in the crew old enough to have seen other writers take the same plunge into obscurity, tormented all the way by egos in despair, were sympathetic. Some remembered Fitzgerald had died in Hollywood, not dramatically in the front seat of a car in a garage filled with carbon monoxide, but from drink, equally effective.

Those who tried to be profound said Inge was an artist sacrificed in the pursuit of the American Dream. Newport is the ideal place for this observation. As America's last great public display of conspicuous consumption, it boasts mansions built from a reverie not of a country's future, but of a continent's past, when Europe's kings

7

and queens erected homes to the size of their personal treasuries.

Fitzgerald once told Hemingway the rich are different from the rest. Hemingway answered yes, they had more money. Still, Fitzgerald was correct in suggesting there was more to it. The rich do have money to build houses to match their dreams.

Around these tangible dreams, somber Tudor mansions and French chateaus defying the sea from their stronghold on the cliff, the crew goes about setting up lights and cameras to create another level of reality, the world of Jay Gatsby, knowing that at any moment word might come from New York that a strike had been called.

The tension on the set is evident in director Jack Clayton looking beyond his workers to the mist stagnating over the sea, nervously flicking off his neck the mane of long gray hair that circles his tanned, bald head; and it is there in the reluctance of anyone to speak about the possibility of a strike as if, visitors in the room of a patient dying of cancer, they are afraid to mention his disease.

To those not connected financially to the $6.5-million production it is amusing that the trouble comes down to two cameramen's jobs that have come to represent to the movie industry the threat of yet another runaway production, often the scapegoat for Hollywood's ills: the cutback in movie production, the empty studios—except for television film—the long lines at the unemployment offices.

Last week the Hollywood AFL Film Council charged that in planning to go to England to do the interiors of its multimillion-dollar production, Paramount had acted in bad faith by ignoring "the desperate employment situation of film craftsmen and artists in the United States."

The cameramen's union claimed it had a letter from Paramount promising that the camera operator and the first assistant cameraman would be Americans during the part of the *Gatsby* production done here. But the jobs were being done by Britishers Chic Waterson and Robin

8

Vidgeon while Americans Peter Powell and Robert Leacock were hired as standbys.

It seems an issue of no moment to a stranger in the jungle of theatrical unionism since the two Americans are being paid well for doing lesser work. But to union members the case represents another example of Hollywood companies fleeing to other countries to benefit from cheaper union costs. It is also a point of craft pride, they say.

"The men are on the set and should be working. Who wants to stand around doing nothing?" a union member said.

Meetings have been held in New York between the union and Paramount, and more are scheduled; still it does not prevent everyone from jumping when the telephone rings in the production office, a white mansion located across the street from Rosecliff and subdivided into apartments for the summer. The assumption of almost everyone connected with the production is that a prolonged strike will kill *The Great Gatsby*.

While the film is in production in the United States there will be only twelve British craftsmen working on it, among them Clayton; first assistant director David Tringham; script supervisor Annabel Davis-Goff, an Irish citizen; film editor Tom Priestley; director of photography Douglas Slocombe; and hairdresser Ramon Gow. Agreements reached between American and British unions require American standbys for the jobs done by Britishers here. Now there seems to be no hostility along national lines between the Americans and the British. On the set they eat together, and in the evenings after work they drink together, and the American standbys are almost always around the set ready to give a hand—their allegiance is to making a good picture. And on this first morning of production they sweat together as the heat wave that began a day earlier in New York worked its way to the rocky peninsula on which Newport is located.

For the film company, one of the greatest concerns is the weather. In June the fog rolls in at night, and this will be disastrous to the shooting schedule. Anyone who has driven in fog knows light is diffused by it, and the crew has visions of Fitzgerald's 1920s revelers dancing and drinking on the lawn, suddenly enveloped by a fog from the sea.

The first scene to be shot is of a chauffeur bringing Nick Carraway a formal invitation to a party to be held by Jay Gatsby at his mansion on the adjoining property.

Before the company's carpenters arrived in Newport in April there was nothing on the land next to Rosecliff, Gatsby's mansion in the film, except for what nature had put there: trees, inquisitive insects and tall, thick unattended grass. The last owner of Rosecliff, who had donated the mansion to Newport's Preservation Society, still owns the land. After he agreed to have Nick's cottage built on it, a contingent of eight carpenters, grips and painters arrived, and in six weeks put up a comfortable, one-story, three-room structure without a basement or bathroom but with a roomy veranda facing the sea. In labor and materials it cost under $100,000. It is sturdy enough to withstand almost anything but a violent hurricane, says its designer, John Box, a four-time Oscar winner from England, most famous for his work on two David Lean films, *Doctor Zhivago* and *Lawrence of Arabia.*

"I had to justify Nick's house in relationship to its proximity to Gatsby's mansion," he says. "When I came to Newport I saw the Breakers had such a cottage near the main building, probably a children's playroom. In designing Nick's cottage, using photos of similar homes on Long Island in the 1920s, I assumed Fitzgerald had it in mind as a place where the tutor lived and gave lessons to the children from the main house."

Though he is often the most visual of authors, Fitzgerald was not much help to a set designer about the cottage. In his book the only description of it is through Nick, the narrator, who calls it a "weather-beaten cardboard bungalow" and an "eyesore."

Though it is less than two months old, the cottage, because of the talents of its builders, looks weather-beaten and a sickly grayish white, as if it has long tried to withstand the assault from the sea air, the evidence of this struggle the flecks of paint missing from its surface. It has already started to settle unevenly into the ground.

The cottage is nearer to the cliff than is Rosecliff, and to make both visible to each other for the camera, the barrier of interlocking trees and bushes that separated the properties was thinned at one stretch and the section where the uprooting took place had been recarpeted with squares of new sod.

The first shot that morning is of the chauffeur walking into a close-up of Sam Waterston, who portrays Nick, in beige sweater and slacks standing in front of the cottage. Four tourists have taken positions in the shrubs by the red picket fence along the public's ocean walk at the edge of the cliff.

"You people in the bushes, please get out of the shot," says David Tringham, who as first assistant director has the often frustrating job of being a traffic manager around the camera. He can do nothing about the racket from the propellors of a Navy helicopter passing overhead.

Sitting on a chair under the largest tree in the front yard is the film's producer, David Merrick. His reputation as the scourge of Broadway critics and, in the only other film he has produced, *Child's Play*, as the man who fired Marlon Brando from a picture, has preceded him to Newport. Those who knew about him are anxious to see how he will react to the first day's shooting. Right now he is studying his fingernails and smiling inscrutably to himself.

In the rehearsals, the actor playing the chauffeur makes several adjustments to his line from the way it was written in the script, one time dropping the word "little" to describe the party, another time eliminating "tonight" in telling Nick when the party is going to take place.

The leaves are no protection to the heat of the morning sun, and Sam strips off his sweater during the rehearsals. The scene is played beyond the tree's shadows,

11

but to cast a shadow on Sam's face and shoulder a grip holds a branch of leaves over the camera.

A product of New England, a graduate of Groton and Yale, Sam Waterston has been in a number of movies, none of them artistically important or commercially popular, and he reacts somewhat defensively to the suggestion he might be inexperienced in movie work. He is still considered a stage actor with the potential to be a big movie star.

Actors are superb at disguises, often about their own selves, and can maintain them for extended periods off camera. There are, however, unguarded moments when a real self, or one approximating it, emerges, perhaps not the one they would like the public to see. At this Sam is still naive, not having learned the artifices of his trade. The person he is off camera is fairly consistent. He walks boyishly, hands dangling loosely, almost awkwardly at his side, the stride so forwardly pronounced that his weight lands on the balls of his feet, forcing his heels to slap at the ground. In his physical movements he strongly resembles Tony Perkins.

Sam is also polite, eager to be liked by his co-workers, and is almost a personality broker among them, using a smile and a few friendly words for the purposes of social cohesion. Yet he is somewhat distant, holding himself back from more personal encounters on the set, having devised a slightly jumpy, half-wink to signal the end of a conversation when it may have gone on too long.

In the book, Nick does not have a hobby, though there is at least one reference to his interest in flowers. In the movie, Nick likes birds, and to keep in character off camera, or at least to get to know him better, Sam reads books on birds and brings with him a pair of binoculars so he can scan the trees and fields.

At 10:51 A.M. Clayton calls for the first take of the scene, and he does it with a nod to Tringham who gives the command in a crisp, gentle bark that does not conceal the national origins of the accent.

The scene goes well and swiftly. The chauffeur in a uniform unbuttoned casually at the neck crosses the lawn. Sam smiles and accepts the invitation to the "little party." Clayton does three takes of the scene and then orders the lights and camera moved to the back of the cottage for the next scene.

In it a gardner comes to Nick's back porch and tells the bemused young man he has been sent over by Mr. Gatsby to cut the grass. At that moment a delivery truck arrives and two men begin carrying baskets of white roses, Daisy's favorite flower, into the cottage. Nick has agreed to let Gatsby hold his reunion with Daisy at his house, an event Gatsby has been looking forward to for eight years.

It has not rained in Newport for days, but the scene is supposed to take place after a shower, and two men are on the roof of the cottage running a hose so water drips off the eaves and flows into the gutter when the flower truck arrives.

The truck is a 1922 Model T Ford owned by Ed Smith, a young man with short blond hair and a pretty wife, Christy, who helps him manage their business, the Golden Retriever antique shop on a narrow street by the waterfront. According to Smith, the truck cost $295 in 1922; he bought it in 1972 for $2,200.

For the purposes of the picture, the sign painted on the cloth paneling on the sides of the car reads "Ed Smith Florist." He is not displeased by the advertisement. "But I wish they'd have let me paint on it 'The Golden Retriever Florist.' "

"I also hope we get underway soon," he added. "The old car isn't used to idling like this and it's starting to overheat."

Smith plays the driver of the van in the film, and through the first rehearsals, when he steers it from its hiding place behind a clump of bushes, his concern for the health of his car is apparent in the grimness on his round, flushed face. After a few coughs, the car's engine idles smoothly and Smith allows a smile to his wife, as if a child had performed well at a public function.

The gardener stands by his mower watching the men with the flowers. Because long hair and sideburns were

13

not worn by men in the early 1920s, the extras have been sheared, all except the gardener. "He's the only one in the film going to have his sideburns," hairdresser Ramon Gow says in his strong Cockney accent. "They felt the gardener should be old and careless enough to let his hair grow long."

Next to him, Annabel, the script supervisor, sits in her yellow canvas chair making notes on the script. She is dangling rainbow-colored heel-less shoes on the tips of her sun-browned toes. This action calls attention to the rest of her: the long blonde hair, pleasantly disheveled from the breeze; the slight curling down of her lips, giving her the innocent pout of a child; and the tall, full body in jeans and loose denim shirt.

Lights and cameras are tugged and pushed around her. A man kneeling on the roof plays the hose over the shingles. The grips gather at the coffee table, where coolers of lemonade and iced tea have been placed in deference to the heat wave.

"It's like an army ready to be moved by the call of a general," someone says to Annabel.

"Not precisely," she says without looking up from her script. "Each one here thinks he has the freedom to go his own way."

There is a break in the rehearsals, and Smith walks over to his wife who is sitting on an empty camera case. She is still new enough to a movie set to be fascinated by it, especially when she spots the film's star, Robert Redford, in a sleeveless blue T-shirt and jeans, talking with Clayton about the scene he will do in the afternoon; but she is already aware of the interminable amount of time needed to set up shots.

"If you're a movie fan, the greatest day of your life is the first day on the set," she is told, "and the second day is the dullest."

Six months earlier the Smiths had read an advertisement Paramount ran in a local paper requesting the use of old cars for the party sequence. The inducement was that the owners could be drivers in the movie. The Smiths responded, and when the company found out

14

about their antique business, sent them on a scavenger hunt for things needed in the film, some of which they already had in their store.

Old furniture catalogues and newspaper ads were consulted as the sources of authenticity for the interior decorations. Some of the things the Smiths found were oak ice-boxes, floor clocks, beat-up garbage cans, pocket watches and a $150 stove used in Nick's kitchen. "We had to go on a midnight raid in an old mansion for that one," Smith chuckles.

The popular furniture of the early 1920s, he says, was mission oak. "It was the working man's furniture, influenced by California. The most difficult thing to get, however, was old linoleum for Nick's kitchen. We finally found some in another attic in Newport." But they were unable to come up with thirty sets of 1925 car license-plates; these finally had to be made.

There is one more rehearsal, delayed a few minutes because the lawn mower won't turn over when the gardener pulls the string on the old contraption. Several grips surround it in a circle of deep concentration before someone suggests kicking it. The car's motor is also making threatening coughs from behind the bushes. But when Clayton, rubbing his hands on the sides of his faded blue jeans, calls for a take, both machines work on cue.

When the shot is finished, the company is given a half hour for lunch. It is served in a tent back up from Nick's cottage where catered hot and cold food is available, and it is a very democratic gathering, the social distinctions in a movie company erased before the hamburgers splattering on a greasy grill. Waterston, having changed from his clothes for the scene to a V-neck shirt and jeans, waits for his food next to the grip who has been on the cottage roof all morning playing the hose toward the drainpipe.

Bruce Dern, Tom Buchanan in the film, is not working the first two weeks of the production in Newport, but on the first day of shooting he begins his habit of coming on the set near the break to have lunch and pass a football with the grips. He is there now with his wife, An-

15

drea, and Benjy Rosenberg, the son of Stewart Rosenberg, who had just directed Dern in *The Laughing Policeman*. Benjy, a graduate of a progressive school in Los Angeles where it had been proposed the graduates play "Pomp and Circumstance" on kazoos, is a production assistant on the American part of *Gatsby*, a pleasant summer interlude before entering UCLA as a freshman in the fall.

Actors rarely photograph their real heights on the screen—everyone knows Alan Ladd had to stand on boxes to reach the lips of his leading ladies—and Dern is much taller than he appeared in his space suit in *Silent Running*. He walks with the commanding stride of someone who has used his body in athletics and works now at keeping it in shape. If anything, his body is now too well attended, squared and bulky for his narrow, sharply defined face. His speech is a collection of witty, often rabelaisian throwaway lines delivered in a soft, rapid voice, punctuated with an impish smile, especially after he says something particularly outrageous that makes the moustache he had grown for his role look like the trademark of a humorous rogue. He has a natural social grace one suspects might have been part of his aristocratic midwest upbringing. He possesses a spectacular amount of general information on subjects from baseball teams to old movies, and the way he rattles it off is convincing to the listener until he realizes some of the information is wrong. It is not an offensive trait, however, and Dern is very likeable.

After his meal, Dern remains at the long table as the crew files out of the humid tent back to Nick's cottage down the rutted car path next to a line of portable outdoor toilets, dark green and shaped like tank traps in the water at Normandy. He does not smoke or drink beer provided with the meal, which is surprising, considering his image as the debauched hero of dope and bike films. "Everyone thinks I'm a doper," he says with the smile of a cat licking its lips after a pleasing bowl of milk.

"Until *King of Marvin Gardens* I was about twenty-fifth on the list of actors getting offered the good parts. I got good notices for that picture, but getting this role has moved me up to about tenth," he says.

The man ahead of him on the list, close enough to being number one to claim the title, comes back to the set in late afternoon as Jay Gatsby. His red hair has been cut short and brushed back from his forehead, and each time he goes before the camera, it is touched up a darker shade of brown. He wears a white suit and vest, and walking across the lawn from the mansion to Nick's cottage, he pauses in the middle of the line of trees with the misty ocean to his right and the uneven, massive shape of Rosecliff behind him; he waits as if catching his breath before moving into the cluster of crew and cameras laying siege to Nick's cottage.

The next scene takes place in the living room of Nick's cottage. Gatsby has contrived for Nick to invite Daisy, without her husband, to his home. It is the culmination of his obsession to see her again, and he is anxiety-ridden while waiting for her, pacing the floor before the fireplace over which hangs a print of birds that reflects Nick's hobby. It is one of the more dramatic scenes in the book, an extremely difficult one, and Robert Redford has to do it on his first day of work.

Redford is on edge, which manifests itself in his tendency to withdraw into himself. Polite, he is nevertheless a person of great reserve which becomes accentuated when he feels surrounded and hemmed in by pressures and people. He stands by himself next to the fireplace waiting for a rehearsal of the scene.

The small living room, diminished further in size by the addition of camera and crew, is permeated by the nauseously sweet smell of roses. Great care has gone into the authentic detail of the room. The front page of *The New York Times* in the magazine stand is dated July 2, 1925. The inside pages are from yesterday's edition of the *Newport Daily News*.

Waterston is on the other side of the fireplace, his smile fleeting; after it is flashed his jaw is reset with the resoluteness of one used to keeping people at arm's length.

Clayton stands beside the camera studying the shot. Deliberately he steps behind the camera, peers through the lens. There is a meticulous conservatism in his actions around the camera as if he were conserving his energy, subduing motions, directing by gesture and soft voice rather than commands.

Dern, who is standing on the porch looking through the window, says Clayton is very much aware he is putting on film what is generally considered the best American novel. "He doesn't want it to bother him, but it does now and then."

Clayton calls for the first take and it goes flawlessly.

Outside Nick's cottage on the dirt road that separates it from Rosecliff, there is a young, good-looking man who had shown up earlier that day at the production office asking if he could get a job as an extra in the film. Told to apply at the nearby Catholic girl's college, Salve Regina, where casting and wardrobe have quarters, he is now back, having been turned down, but somehow having managed to get past the guard sitting on a chair at the end of the private road where it enters Bellevue Avenue.

"They said I'm too young," he says with the hurt of one who hasn't been rejected too often.

"How old did they want the extras?" he is asked.

"Twenty-five to seventy."

"How old are you?"

"Twenty-one." He looks three years younger.

"The set's closed to the public. How did you get in?"

"Through the fields, over there," he said, pointing in the direction of a dense wooded area around the food tent. He had parked his car by the production office and outflanked the guard by cutting through the woods.

"Did it mean that much to you to get on the set, to see a movie being made?"

"Sure."

"Why?"

"I want to be an actor more than anything else."

"Why don't you go back to school and study acting,

learn your craft in regional theater during the summer."

"I want to go into movies, that's all."

The guard did not look up when the young man with the ambition of an actor was escorted off the Rosecliff property.

Back at Nick's cottage, Clayton is into his third take. Between each, a grip dashes to the fireplace and turns back the hands on the mantel clock so that when the cameras roll it is always eleven.

When the hitch comes it is unexpected because the rehearsals have gone so smoothly.

"What's the matter?" someone shouts.

"The dolly on the camera won't work."

So ends the shooting on the first day.

That evening, Bernie Styles, casting director and veteran of many important films done in New York over the past several decades, Clayton and his assistant directors hold an open casting in the auditorium of Salve Regina for persons who might have the *Gatsby* look, a nebulous quality apparently having little to do with traditional concepts of good looks.

One of the first applicants is an attractive young Newport matron with a turban and pink underwear showing through her skin-tight white slacks. She is not chosen, but she gives it the Schwab's Drug Store try, making the simple mounting of the steps an exercise in eroticism.

A few days earlier a wire-service story had gone out that the production was looking only for WASP types. This was not accurate; a rereading of the book would have shown that Gatsby's parties, which the extras were to populate, were not a homogenous gathering of White Anglo-Saxon Protestants but a bizarre mixing of high society to Broadway bootleggers. None of the notices signed by Styles setting down the requirements for being an extra in *Gatsby* ever specified a WASP look.

"The period covered in our film is 1925," read the official letter given to the extras, "so obviously we must avoid a contemporary look among our 'extras.' All the

19

men must have short hair, no sideburns, and no beards. (A word of caution—please do not cut your hair until you are notified that you have been hired.)

"No one shall have a dark suntan. No one will be hired who must wear eyeglasses to see. The reason being that the eyeglass frames will not reflect the 'period' we are portraying. Women must not wear eye make-up. Women must be willing to work without bras or girdles. Women are not to bring purses or wear jewelry of their own. Modern handbags and jewelry will obviously conflict with the period wardrobe.

"Please do not bring valuables to the set. There are no facilities to safeguard them. Women will also be required to have short hair, or be willing to cut hair to a prescribed length. Some of the older women will be able to have buns on the back of their head.

"Everyone hired will be paid the minimum of $1.65 an hour, with a guaranteed minimum of 12 hours wages per day."

But the impression the company was hiring only WASP types persisted and made good copy. For several days the company was on the defensive.

On entering the school that evening, the several hundred hopefuls are separated by sex into adjoining auditoriums. Clayton, still in jeans and blue cotton shirt, his uniform on the set, stands in front of a blackboard next to Styles, his initial reaction to the male candidates hidden behind the dark glasses he wears. They study the variety of ages, shapes and sometimes ill-fitting toupees before them, occasionally huddling before singling out a man and telling him to go into the next room where he would get his casting instructions.

The two men provide a good contrast for a Gatsby party: Clayton, aristocratic, tightly controlled, using understatement and constrained physical response; Styles, short, rotund, exaggeratedly old New York by way of Damon Runyon and Lindy's, his favorite word "sweetheart" drawled on the first syllable to make it sound "shush."

Those selected are not always the young and handsome who fit an incorrect image that Fitzgerald only wrote about beautiful people. Some are fat with flushed faces, others bear the rough skin of those who battled acne unsuccessfully in their youth. Only 25 of the 100 in the room are chosen. It has become a matter of social prestige to get into the film, especially among the summer colony in Newport, and those rejected look as if they had been handed their walking papers from the Newport Country Club.

In the women's auditorium, Ramon Gow is circulating through the aisles, inspecting hair lengths and fingernail polish of women already selected. "Just the right dark shade, darling," he says to one young woman while holding her hand with the expert detachment of someone who is used to working over a woman's face to make it attractive.

There is another group of women to be inspected, and while Ramon, his silver-blonde, shoulder-length hair swaying as he walks, hands out instruction sheets that show the acceptable short 1920s hair styles to be worn at the movie parties, Clayton, sipping from a steaming container of coffee, inspects the new batch. One youngish woman, sitting by herself on an aisle seat, has obviously left her bra at home, which is revealed in the expanse of mounded flesh exposed by the wide-open plunge of her shirt towards the navel. She is the one of the first chosen. Other braless women are politely dismissed.

The women are given different colored tickets to indicate the costume to be worn in the party. Handing them out is John Farrow, Mia's brother, who has been signed on as assistant casting director, an uneasy job since there is apparent friction between him and Styles, who makes it obvious he thinks the only reason the brother is on the picture is because of his sister.

Styles tells the women, "Come next week at your convenience anytime between ten and five for your wardrobe fitting." The two thousand costumes to be worn by the men and women in the picture are hanging on racks in another part of the school.

He spots a woman handing Farrow a ticket. She has

come in through a back door. She had been selected earlier but failed to show up at her appointed time, and Styles is not forgiving. She pleads with him to be in the picture. He refuses. "You didn't come here when you were supposed to. Why should I expect you'll show up when we need you the nights of the party?" She retreats, somewhat humiliated.

Styles goes to his office, a laboratory on the first floor. Next to his desk on the shelf, sunk on the bottom of a jar filled with a yellowish liquid, is a human brain. "Yeah, sweetheart, one of those who didn't make it," he quips.

Styles is frustrated. Clayton is particular about the extras, making the final choices, selecting very few of the many who show up at the casting calls. Styles complains he no longer knows what the *Gatsby* "look" is, that the vision of it is contained within Clayton's head and he is not giving out too many clues. Nevertheless, Styles has resorted to newspaper ads and to radio and television, being a frequent guest on local talk shows to drum up attendance at the casting sessions. He has also made talks at the Rotary Club and Naval Base at Newport.

"In three weeks, I've seen about 4,000 people," he says. "We have a preliminary screening at which time we take a Polaroid picture of each of them, and then we make another cut from there. So far we have about 250 extras. The requirement for the party sequence is 400. We should have at least a thousand.

"Do you know what it's going to be like after the first few nights? They'll see how dull movie work is, remember that they're getting paid to work all night and they'll start taking off in droves."

Outside his office, four black women carrying cosmetic cases ask where casting is taking place. There is a crashing silence from the guard and wardrobe people in the hallway who are smoking cigarettes. The casting is for whites only. There are no references in the book that Gatsby invited blacks to his party, and in the social history of the 1920s, there is hardly any documentation that blacks were guests at the parties of the wealthy on Long

Island. It is not the time to explain this to the women. For legal reasons the ads for casting could not specify whites only; yet how to explain the truth to these women?

Styles takes an easy way out. He tells the women casting is finished for the evening.

"But we've come all the way from Boston," one says.

"I'm sorry, ladies, but casting was over at eight."

The women are disgruntled, almost furious. Complaining about the unfairness of the situation they back out of the door.

Later that evening, at a fish restaurant on the Newport waterfront, the conversation at many tables is about the arrival of the movie company. One woman, sitting with two men, both slightly younger than she, talks about Fitzgerald with a suspect familiarity. "I just love him, don't you? He's fantastic." She then begins discussing Gatsby, getting most of the book wrong.

Her face has not yet accepted the lines and loose flesh of her middle years—efforts would still be made to save it—and her hair has the brittleness of too many dye jobs. Being overly respective of her presence—she was probably going to pick up the check—her male companions listen to her forceful opinions, not correcting any of them.

"Oh, I so wanted to be an extra," she says with a voice that has known other disappointments, "but here I am, a genuine WASP, and they said I didn't look the part."

Chapter II

Background

The Great Gatsby persists while so many other novels, overreviewed, overpraised, have faded. In the year it was published to respectable, if not unanimously enthusiastic reviews, the Pulitzer Prize went to Edna Ferber's *So Big*. The sales of Fitzgerald's third novel were good, but not what his publisher, Charles Scribner's Sons, had expected, based on the reception to his first novel, *This Side of Paradise*, which had made him what ultimately destroyed him: a celebrity.

The book is not imposing in size, 182 pages in the popular paperback edition, nor is its story line complicated: Jay Gatsby, a young mysterious man of new wealth, living in a mansion on the North Shore of Long Island, who is famous for giving all-night parties, talks his summer neighbor, Nick Carraway, into arranging a meeting with Nick's distant cousin, Daisy Buchanan, a girl Gatsby still loves though his affair with her ended during World War I. She had jilted him, after discovering that he was poor, for Tom Buchanan, a wealthy midwesterner and Nick's classmate at Yale.

The Buchanans live across the Sound from Gatsby in a more fashionable area. Tom is having an affair with Myrtle Wilson, the wife of a garage owner who lives in a stretch of industrial wasteland separating Long Island from New York City that Fitzgerald calls the Valley of Ashes. The affair starts again between Gatsby and Daisy. He believes she will leave her husband for him. On returning from the Plaza Hotel, where, in front of Nick, Daisy's childhood friend Jordan Baker and Tom, Gatsby had forced Daisy into confessing she still loves him, Daisy, who is driving her husband's car, runs down and kills Myrtle. George Wilson, led to believe Gatsby was driving, kills him while he is floating on a raft in his pool and then commits suicide. Nick, who realizes that money and the pursuit of it have made the Buchanans moral criminals and that Gatsby was a better person, even if he was a bootlegger, returns home to the midwest to escape from those who are so careless with the emotions of others.

Though it is a beautifully crafted novel, divided into specific scenes of dramatic action connected by vividly poetic observations about man and society, it is seriously flawed in the middle section where the romance resumes between Daisy and Gatsby, but the reader never sees it happen in the present. Rather, it is reported sketchily by Nick, the narrator of the story, and Jordan. The absence of specific details about the affair, how the lovers feel and what they say to each other, robs the story of a sensual passion which would go further in explaining the motivations of Gatsby, and leaves Daisy less well-defined than she should be.

Even after the book was published, Fitzgerald was aware of this, and in a letter to Edmund Wilson, his intellectual mentor since they were both undergraduates at Princeton, he wrote, "I gave no account (and had no feeling about or knowledge of) the emotional relations between Gatsby and Daisy from the time of their reunion to the catastrophe. However the lack is astutely concealed by the retrospect of Gatsby's past and by blankets of excellent prose that no one has noticed it—I felt that what (H. L. Mencken) really missed was the lack of any emotional backbone at the very height of it."

Yet how many other books in the twentieth century have a legitimate claim on being the Great American Novel, as mounds of scholarly monographs pile up in college libraries to chart minute symbols and obscure philosophical implications in it? Since it was published in the spring of 1925, *The Great Gatsby* has sold almost two million copies in both hardcover and paperback in the United States, and has been published in Sweden, Yugoslavia, Holland, Spain, Norway, Denmark, France, Japan, Germany, Israel, Italy, Bulgaria, Rumania, Hungary, Pakistan and India.

It sold an estimated 300,000 copies in paperback last year in the United States, primarily to a young student audience, and maintains a high level of sales each year.

Its appeal changes depending on the age of the reader. When young, it appears primarily a bittersweet love story of a doomed affair, poignant in its implication that not all dreams come true in America where one is conditioned to believe in achieving the impossible. When the reader is older, the love story recedes in significance, and it becomes a novel searingly critical of the materialism that leads Gatsby into believing what he has no right to: that accumulation of great wealth will get him what his drive alone has failed to do. As one's response to the novel's many themes varies, so does one's sympathy for the characters. After many readings, Daisy becomes bitchier, Jordan more cunning, Tom his own man, and Nick a noninvolved moralist comparable to Marlowe in Joseph Conrad's tales. It is Gatsby who gains stature. He is heroic in resisting failure, and in defeat his grace is almost majestic.

Immediately after its publication, the book was brought to the Broadway stage, and it did well there and on tour. In 1926 there was also a movie version with Warner Baxter as Gatsby and Lois Wilson as Daisy. It was directed by Herbert Brenon from a screenplay by Owen Davis. *Variety* called it "quite a good entertainment" while carping that the characters were not well developed and the direction not overly imaginative. The prints of this silent version are lost, though one is reportedly in Moscow.

In 1949 Paramount did another screen version, this one directed by Elliot Nugent with Alan Ladd as Gatsby, Betty Field as Daisy, Barry Sullivan as Tom, MacDonald Carey as Nick, Ruth Hussey as Jordan, Shelly Winters as Myrtle and Howard da Silva as Wilson. *Variety* found it emphasized the "sentimental romance." Except for a few pictorial tracings of parties and brittle high life, the flavor of the Prohibition era is barely reflected. Indeed there are reasons for suspecting that Paramount selected this old tale primarily as a standard conveyance for the image of its charm boy, Alan Ladd."

It was hardly a favorable review, but it didn't discourage other producers from seeking rights to it. For years there has been talk of practically everyone wanting to do it on film, and even as a Broadway musical comedy. When it came time to be done again, it was not surprising Paramount would do it since the company held the international rights to the novel.

The impetus came from Robert Evans, executive vice-president in charge of worldwide production at Paramount. In the early 1970s he was married to Ali MacGraw, a model who came rather late to movie acting bringing minimal skills to the craft. She had always wanted to play Daisy, and Evans went about getting the property for her. This was after Miss MacGraw's commercial triumphs in *Goodbye Columbus* and *Love Story*, both Paramount pictures. She probably could have had the world if the studio found it was up for sale.

David Merrick came on the picture as producer for good reason: his reputation for producing quality works and he is a good friend of Fitzgerald's daughter, Scottie Smith, who still holds the rights to her father's works. Having seen his books mangled by Hollywood before—the 1949 version of *Gatsby* was a masterpiece compared with the 1962 version of *Tender is the Night*—Mrs. Smith was reluctant to sell the rights until she felt she could trust someone with her father's books. Finally, she sold the domestic rights to Merrick, who then was producing his first film, *Child's Play*, which he had presented on Broadway. Mrs. Smith received a nice sum for the rights, an estimated $325,000, and she will get a percentage of the film over a certain gross. If Paramount had waited longer, the fifty-six years would have been up and *Gatsby* would have come into the public domain.

So at the start there were Evans, Miss MacGraw and Merrick. A budget was prepared, the figure set at $6.5 million. The cost did not vary much, Merrick said, although almost everything else about the production did in 1972.

Next to come on was Jack Clayton, a curious choice, a Britisher to direct the very American property. Clayton works, to put it mildly, at a deliberate pace. From 1959, when he directed *Room at the Top,* his first feature film, he had done only four movies, hardly a breathless speed, and he is known for working slowly during shooting. No one now is really sure who was responsible for Clayton. It is believed Miss MacGraw was impressed with his films, in *Room at the Top* and *The Pumpkin Eater* for his adroit handling of social themes, and in *The Innocents* (based on Henry James's *The Turn of the Screw*) for bringing a classic faithfully to the screen. Others say it was actor Warren Beatty, wanting to play Gatsby, who told Miss MacGraw about Clayton.

Once on the film, and with a contract that gave him approval of cast, principal crew, and script, Clayton made the decision to bring in Truman Capote, who had been the scriptwriter on *The Innocents.* As it turned out, it was not a wise decision. Capote's script, if it was ever finished—and that is still debated—was unacceptable. Some claimed it was too literary, better read from a lectern than in front of a movie camera.

At that time Capote was not physically well, and it was decided to bring in Francis Ford Coppola, who had just done both the screenplay—with Mario Puzo—and direction of *The Godfather* for Paramount. Known primarily as a director, Coppola had won an Oscar for his *Patton* screenplay.

Capote did not accept being relieved from *Gatsby.* He took to television and the courts to present his case. Paramount reportedly offered to pay one-third of the original price for his screenplay. Capote promptly brought suit for the full amount, $125,000, and received it after an out-of-court settlement.

"Truman was very ill," Clayton said, "and I refused to testify against him."

Everyone was eager now to get the film into production. Coppola wrote a screenplay in five weeks, and Clayton went to San Francisco to work with him on it.

"From the start I got on very well with Coppola. The script is really his, but it was terribly long. I had to tighten it. I took out about thirty pages. It was also my decision to have the romance between Daisy and Gatsby fleshed out in the script. The resumed romance was only implied in the book. It would be acceptable there but not on film," Clayton said.

If Daisy was the most sought-after role since Scarlet O'Hara, then Gatsby was Rhett Butler. Almost everyone connected with the production would have liked Marlon Brando for the role if he were ten years younger and several stones lighter.

"I went to Rome to see rushes of *Last Tango in Paris*," Clayton said. "He's the most wonderful actor in the world, but he would have been too old. I met him in California, and we laid down a ground rule that we would not talk about Gatsby.

"Warren Beatty was then being mentioned, but he would not have been right. He is too pretty."

Jack Nicholson was considered and rejected. Merrick then brought Redford's name to the attention of Paramount's president, Frank Yablans. It is one not mentioned too loudly in the corridors of Paramount since the studio and Redford had a monumental battle several years ago over his refusal to do a stinker of a western called *Blue*. But Redford was now hot, and animosities in the movie industry are soon forgotten when a star means money at the box office. Clayton, not an avid moviegoer, was unfamiliar with Redford's work. He met with him for fifteen minutes in London's airport and agreed he would make an excellent Gatsby.

At this point everything should have gone smoothly. The money was available, the stars selected, the director signed and the screenplay done. Unfortunately, Miss MacGraw went to work with Steve McQueen on *The Getaway*. Rumors started, later to be confirmed, that she was having an affair with him. Hollywood is not known for its moral discretions, and stories soon began appearing in newspapers that Miss MacGraw thought McQueen would be splendid as Gatsby, though by now everyone else believed Redford would make the better choice. McQueen was vetoed by Charles Bluhdorn, head of Gulf and Western, according to Merrick, because he did not want to do anything to embarrass Evans during his period of matrimonial distress.

Miss MacGraw stayed with the picture until her position, to say the least, became untenable. When she dropped out in the spring of 1972, the film, which was to be shot that summer, was postponed, with the reason given that the costumes were not done, a dubious cover story that passed the inspection of a gullible press.

Up to the end of 1972, the production was on and off. Eventually it was Yablans who went to bat for *Gatsby* with Paramount's parent corporation, Gulf and Western, ensuring them the film would be made. Both Merrick and Clayton still praise Yablans for the support he gave the film at that crucial time.

At 36, Yablans is one of the few success stories in an industry on the skids. He is credited with being the genius behind the marketing of *The Godfather* and *Love Story,* the films which have made Paramount the most successful Hollywood studio today.

The picture was on again without a female star for a role lusted after by every actress who could pass muster at being twenty-five or thirty. Press reports said 150 girls were being considered, but to be accurate this would have had to include girl friends and mistresses of almost every agent and producer in Hollywood. There were only a few serious candidates, and dutifully each—except the one who got the part—came to New York to do a screen test with Redford. They were Candace Bergen, Faye Dunaway, Katharine Ross and Lois Chiles.

"I wanted to test Tuesday Weld, but she wouldn't do one," Clayton added.

Mia Farrow did her test in London with a temperature of 103 degrees and promptly passed out in the middle of it. Nobody at the studio really wanted her for the part, but the search was over.

Clayton, whose idea it had been to test Mia, said, "I literally forced Andre Previn to bring Mia in for the test, promising that we would run it for her and destroy it if she didn't like it.

"But the moment I saw it, I called her up and said, "Look, don't worry about seeing the test, it's absolutely marvelous.

"All of the tests were good. There's not one of those actresses who couldn't have played Daisy. Mia Farrow got the part because she is more like Daisy than the others."

Yablans approved of the Farrow casting. He told executives of the company that he loved the way Mia handled the glass of champagne in the test with a femininity that quickly established Daisy's character.

The rest of the casting was largely Clayton's. The only other person he really had in mind for Nick Carraway, other than Sam Waterston, was Scott Wilson, whom he cast as George Wilson. "Tony Perkins would have been fine for Nick if he were also ten years younger," Clayton said.

Somebody suggested Bruce Dern for Tom Buchanan. Clayton saw his work and wanted him against the wishes of the studio, who thought his overexposure in bike and drug movies would not make him a credible aristocrat. "I had to sell him to Paramount by going into his family background, showing them who he is and where he comes from," Clayton said.

No one was astonished that Lois Chiles ended up in the film. She was never really in the running for Daisy, but when she tested, everyone believed she was Bob Evans's new girl friend. "It is not saying anything against Lois to say any six actresses could play Jordan," Clayton said.

Chapter III

Newport Revisited

June 12

MEMO FROM PRODUCTION

After discussing problems with two local lobstermen, both said they would not pull the lobster pots or buoys because as soon as they do other lobstermen would move into their area. However, there is a good possibility that they might replace the Clorox bottle buoys with cork we would supply. Will discuss this further with one of the lobstermen tomorrow.

The haze crushed down by the hot sun is there over the water, obscuring the finger of land in the distance, and the lobster buoys, squares of white, bob undisturbed in the swells. If the camera is going to scan the water's surface, as it must in the close-up shots of Nick with the sea as a background, they must go or be replaced by something less bulky and less visible.

The scene to be shot is one of the more important in both book and script, the meeting of Gatsby and Daisy at Nick's place eight years after their romance was displaced by other passions generated during World War I. Nick and Gatsby are now on the steps of the porch facing the sea. Nick asks Gatsby about his background and how he made his money, and Gatsby is evasive. Joined by Daisy, they proceed across the lawn toward Gatsby's mansion with Daisy exclaiming how huge it is.

It is Mia Farrow's first day of work in the picture, and everyone is politely determined to make it as pleasant as possible for her. A reputation has preceded her, not a clearly defined one since she is called everything from difficult to lovely. She arrives followed by Ramon who has worked on her wig, and Erica Eames, the British wardrobe mistress who has helped the star into her beautiful lavender dress and hat. Mia is affectionately received by everyone.

The contrast of Mia off camera and now on as Daisy is startling. In the food tent, where she eats with the crew, wearing loose, comfortable caftans, her twin sons tugging on it, her adopted Vietnamese daughter on her lap, Mia is the picture of young motherhood. Now, in her costume, she is riveting, transformed by wig, makeup, dress and the way she sits on her chair talking with the crew. Her voice is a studied accent, almost English, different from what she had in *Peyton Place*. She is a reasonable approximation of one of the most famous women characters in American literature, and those who say she could not pull it off physically—jealousy in show business being a common virus—already have seconds thoughts.

Before shooting began, a few days earlier, Mia had been sitting in the makeup room on the third floor of Rosecliff getting a wig fitted by Ramon. Someone said Lord Snowden, who had taken many stills of Mia in the clothes of Daisy, must have read the book because he had certainly gotten the essence of her character into his pictures.

Ramon, tugging the wig over Mia's real hair, both faces close in the mirror of the dressing table framed by bright lights, said with his voice shaking vibrantly, "She is Daisy!"

Now, seeing her on the set, how right Ramon seemed in his slightly theatrical judgment.

Work progresses in getting the shot ready. Douglas Slocombe, the British director of photography who is called "Dougie" by everyone, checks the sky for light with a round, dark filter, his head tilted back, the glass to his eye. The grip is back on the roof hosing it down with water. Redford's hair needs to be darkened further, and he returns to his room in Rosecliff. The water erupting from the drain splatters Waterston's pants. He is unaware of it, preoccupied, giving his nervous half smile to questions about inconsequential things.

Clayton is quite nervous, playing his hands in a variety

of motions over his faded jeans. The labor problems keep everyone tense. He calls for a rehearsal after Redford returns, his hair freshly slicked back from his forehead.

Mia has difficulty walking in her purple high-heeled shoes. She is particularly bothered by the right one, concerned the audience will see her favoring it in her walk across the lawn to Gatsby's mansion. Erica wedges something into the heel to keep the shoe from flopping. Mia is also troubled by her colored stockings which are knotted above her knees, well concealed by the long dress. The stockings keep wrinkling, and when she stands, Erica tugs them up.

Between rehearsals, Redford sits on the porch reading accounts of the Watergate hearing in *The New York Times*. Sam reads his book on birds. Mia wonders aloud if the Auchinclosses liked them. She is referring to a party given for the cast two days earlier at Hammersmith Farm by Mr. and Mrs. Hugh Auchincloss, mother and stepfather of Jacqueline Kennedy Onassis, who, along with her sister Lee, was in attendance at the affair.

By her question, Mia reveals some of the bedrock insecurity of actors, especially when they move outside their own world into other levels of society.

Mia also confesses she has lost three pairs of glasses since coming to Newport. "I can't see beyond my knees without them," she says, and is concerned she should be saying good morning to people she cannot see. "I'd bite my nails," she laughs, "but it would be out of character."

She also talks about parts offered to her now that she has worked on the London stage, among them several plays about Joan of Arc. When she stands to go before the camera for the first take, she describes her lovely dress as butterfly wings, and the touch of the poetic seems entirely natural to her.

David Merrick, unobtrusive as ever, the only one who consistently wears a suit and tie on the set, is by himself under the tree. He expresses his liking for the short hair on the men in *Gatsby* and hopes it will start a trend.

"The long hair started with my musical *Oliver*," he says. He suggests a good publicity release would be about the tons of hair sheared from male scalps for the movie.

One take of the scene follows another with Daisy running from the house, swirling lavender, her eyes rounded ovals of surprise over the massiveness of Gatsby's mansion. She has the look of wealth contemplating wealth, and it is a look without judgment; she is unconcerned how the wealth was made, its presence in sufficient quantity eliminating any need to explain the morality of its acquisition.

Who cares in the age of Watergate about the money acquired by those who made Newport a playground of toy castles deposited on cliffs near the sea? After a suitable lapse of time, money justifies itself; only a few moralists worry about the ethics surrounding its accumulation. The tourists come to see what wealth can buy. And these houses, silently guarding the stories of what was lost to acquire them, are so right for *Gatsby*, a story about what being rich does to people.

Daisy, exuding the coldness inherent in Fitzgerald's rich who play indecently with human emotions, as she does with Gatsby, is attended to now by hands pinning up her dress, drawing the strings of her hat around her neck, running a comb through the wig. Her face is half in shadow.

Clayton has been standing by himself, his face to the sea mist which still makes invisible the distant point of land. When he turns, as if he has resolved what must be done, he says to his first assistant, "David, I feel like shooting," and serious preparation begins.

At lunch break, Mia, in her flowering caftan, stands momentarily at the tent's entrance, pulling herself together for the long walk to the food table. When she passes the first group of diners, without her glasses, she says, "Hi, kids" to two men well into middle age.

The chronology is again rearranged in the afternoon's shooting. Daisy is now arriving at Nick's for the fateful meeting with Gatsby. She drives a 1925 Studebaker convertible. She stops at the back door where she is met by

35

Nick. They exchange a social kiss, a formality made common by the rich. She asks her distant cousin if he loves her. He says yes. Why did I have to come alone, she asks. He replies it is the secret of Castle Rackrent.

Behind the cameras, someone asks a pertinent question. "If it was just raining out, how come she arrives with the top down?"

"Because it's a fairy tale," someone says.

That night at a staff meeting in the production office, enraged by the uncertainty of production caused by the labor unrest, Clayton smashes a window, and a woman must be brought in the next morning to sweep up the pieces.

June 13

Everyone remains tense; it is there, unspoken, like the persistent mist over the sea. There is nothing new in the negotiations with the cameramen's union in New York. Steve Schapiro, who has been hired as a special photographer, is not allowed on the set until the trouble is resolved. The production is fearful that having another man with a camera on the set will give the union one more issue, although it is difficult to comprehend any connection between having Schapiro in Newport and the union's complaint that Paramount is not living up to its commitment to employ Americans in the two cameramen's positions. Schapiro remains in New York, unhappy that he is not on the set photographing what are some of the most important scenes in the picture.

If *The Great Gatsby* is a classic romance as well as one of the more devastating literary comments on American materialism, one of the book's great moments is the meeting of Gatsby and Daisy in Nick's cottage, and on the third day into production this scene is shot.

From seven A.M., trucks have been bringing workers and equipment into the cleared field behind Nick's cottage. The activity has produced one casualty. There is a dead sparrow in the road, struck by a truck, and drops of blood are congealing on its crushed wing.

Clayton's ever-present anxiety is there in his motions rather than any elevation of his voice. He walks as if trying to pass through a field of eggs, and he touches deliberately and sensitively objects around him: a camera's surface, the cover of a magazine, the knob on a door. He also rhythmically fluffs the gray hair off his neck.

Gatsby, too, is anxiety-stricken. He has waited hours for Daisy's arrival, and is convinced now he has made a mistake, that she will never come. When the car is heard in the driveway, Nick goes to the door. In the book, Nick stands outside the living room so the reader does not know what immediately passes between Daisy and Gatsby. The scene is played through Nick's ears, and there is a pause before he hears Daisy speak, saying how glad she is to see Gatsby again. In the film, the audience sees the memorable confrontation.

Daisy bursts into the living room and gasps excitedly, childishly, about the lovely bouquets of white roses scattered about. She does not see Gatsby standing by the fireplace near the steps to Nick's bedroom until she looks up from a vase of roses into a mirror and there is the image of a lover last held in Louisville, Kentucky, he then in the Army on leave before going to Europe.

The camera is directed on the mirror, and the first recognition is in Daisy's eyes. The camera remains on her face as she turns from the mirror, stares at Gatsby and walks slowly toward him.

To control the lighting inside the cottage, strips of auburn plastic have been placed over the front-porch windows. It is bright and cramped inside the living room with space only for the three actors and six crew members, among them Clayton, Slocombe and Annabel, who sits on the floor in the corner, the script open on her lap, a stop watch to time the scene in her hand.

Clayton seems to be a director who leaves a great deal of the acting to actors. He does not tell them to do specific face gestures or body motions, only where to stand and when to move. His camera is very fluid, constantly moving, tracking the actors as they walk so that the film has great mobility. His scenes will be fleeting moments, fragments of a dream.

Mia discusses the scene with Clayton. Should she cry

when she first sees Gatsby? Should the scarf around her neck be tied or untied when she enters? Waterston also has a question. When should he walk into the shot from the hallway?

It is a troublesome scene for Redford. In the book Gatsby's wait for Daisy in Nick's cottage is interminable, and just when he gets up to leave, convinced she is not coming, Daisy arrives. "Gatsby acts like a ten-year-old here," Redford says. "There's too much hand fluttering, schoolboyish things going on."

The physical signs of his impatience will be played down in the scene.

An essential of any good film is its rhythm, and Clayton is trying to establish it for this crucial scene. Before he orders a take, he goes through several rehearsals, standing behind the camera tapping his fingers against his jeans as if trying to locate a rhythm from within on how the scene should be paced before trying to transmit it to his actors and his camera operator, Chic Waterson.

(Somewhat differently from the American system, the British director of photography primarily does the lighting while the operator works with the director on angles and the operation of his camera.)

There is not much discussion among the principals. Redford and Mia stand at opposite ends of the room. It is a heavily dramatic moment very early in production, and they are almost totally within themselves.

After one rehearsal the sound boom knocks over a vase of flowers. When the lovers meet in front of the fireplace, the boom is incongruously below Mia's backside where it is to pick up her voice.

There are other distractions, some of them reasonable as the grips make adjustments to their equipment. Clayton becomes impatient. "Are we waiting for a good purpose?" he asks sarcastically.

The director has decided on the timing of the scene. He will snap his fingers when Mia should turn from the mirror to face Redford. The technique works well in the first rehearsals. Then Mia fails to heed the snap. "Did you hear me?" Clayton asks quizzically. Mia says yes, she had, without elaboration. It is her way of going further into her character, finding new responses, getting temporarily lost in the development of Daisy. Clayton is not displeased.

After an hour the rehearsals are over, and at 11:20 A.M., Clayton orders the first take. Mia stands in the doorway, shaking her arms to stay loose, much as runners do on the starting line for a track meet.

The scene begins. The camera turns. Daisy dashes up the steps into the living room, her eyes opened by the flowers, a tribute from an adoring distant cousin. And then the eye contact in the mirror and the sense of being hurtled back to her youth.

Clayton does the scene in five takes, and after the last he gallantly holds Mia's hand to his lips and kisses her fingers.

While this scene is being shot in Newport, Peter Bankers, a young publicity writer for Paramount Pictures, leaves his New York office on the twenty-ninth floor of the Gulf and Western building at Columbus Circle and goes to Cartier's on Fifth Avenue to pick up close to $1 million in jewels to be used in the film.

There are fifty-eight pieces, from cuff links and cigarette cases to bracelets and earrings. The single most valuable item is a $130,000 necklace. Bankers finds the jewelry has not been inventoried, and he does it there, finding that there is one less piece than Cartier's said. It is found and added to two boxes which are taped and marked "fragile, handle with care." The total value of the two packages is $895,000.

Bankers is joined by a guard from a private detective agency, and by taxi they go to La Guardia. They are whisked through security without having to be checked. The two men take their seats in first class, the jewels on the armrest between them.

At Providence, Bankers is met by two new guards, and in separate cars, Bankers in the first with one guard and the jewels, they are driven to Rosecliff where the treasure is placed in a guarded safe.

In late spring and early summer, the weather of Newport is usually bad. This had always been a factor in planning the production. The Preservation Society, a nonprofit organization set up to run those mansions that have been made public, obtained for Paramount the weather history of Newport for the past fifteen years from a federal agency in Kentucky. David Merrick read it and thought about postponing production for two weeks. The forecast was not promising. June was the month for fog and rain, and it usually began after lunch as a shower squall, sweeping across the green lawn of Gatsby's mansion past the artificial arch built by the movie company into the real marble wall at the end of the Rosecliff property near the cliff.

The sky is somber now where it touches the sea, an indication the bad weather will stay for the day. It will not disrupt the afternoon's shooting since the scenes are interiors, nor does it stop the workers coming in and out of the basement of Rosecliff where many of the props are kept and the painters work in damp, ill-lighted rooms.

Rosecliff is one of the six mansions along Bellevue Avenue that were made public as the rich found them too expensive to maintain. Rosecliff was designed by Stanford White, modeled on the Petit Trianon Marie Antoinette had built at Versailles for her private infidelities away from King Louis XVI. It was built in 1902 by Hermann Oelrichs, and many a splendid party was held in its ground-floor ballroom, the largest in any Newport mansion, before it was turned over to the Preservation Society several years ago.

One of the more popular tourist spots that gets its share of the 200,000 visitors Newport has in a season, Rosecliff is on the swing from the Breakers, built by Richard Morris Hunt in 1895 for Cornelius Vanderbilt and considered the jewel of Newport summer residences, to Marble House, built by the same architect in 1892 for William K. Vanderbilt.

Paramount worked out contracts in May, 1972, for renting Rosecliff from the Preservation Society. The sum was not disclosed by the Society, but a spokesman for it indicated the money was sufficient to cover the admissions lost by having the mansion closed from April to November, 1973. The reported price is $50,000.

"Considering everything," he said, "the economics of having the movie company here is terrific. Think of the money being spent in bars, restaurants, shops and golf courses."

The 160-member company arrived at the right time for Newport, which had just received bad news from the federal government that it was closing the naval base, and taking away an annual payroll estimated in the millions. The movie company would not be in Newport long enough to make any appreciable difference in the economy over the long haul, but it gave officials hope that for some obscure reason producers would seriously consider Newport, with its dense fogs and days of rain, an ideal location for movie production, a dream nurtured the previous year when a television movie, *The Man Without a Country*, had been shot here.

More realistically, Newport planners see their town as an ideal vacation resort for Middle America. There are the charming narrow streets by the waterfront and the renovated, freshly painted colonial homes. It may once have been the exclusive domain of the rich, but Newport's future would seem to be in the past, in the Revolutionary War and the public's interest in the bicentennial anniversary of the United States.

There are those who have other ideas, such as making Newport into the Las Vegas of the East, and there have been attempts to get gambling legalized.

In one important aspect, Newport is ill-suited for any serious influx of tourists. It has very inadequate housing, as the movie company discovered. Most of the company was put up in the Viking Motor Inn near the center of town. Its only attraction is a number of eager, young college students who work for the summer at a job comparable to plugging a dike that has more holes than available fingers. It is the kind of hotel where when a door is opened the knob falls off, or the lights do not work, or the television set has been taken out to be

41

repaired and never returned, or the swimming pool and sauna are separated so that a patron must walk through the ballroom in soggy trunks to get from pool to sauna.

It became an impossible situation for some of the crew, who moved out the first week. Others stayed and found it a hardship. A grip had his stereo tape recorder stolen. A driver looked out his motel window, saw some young men fooling with his car, and when he went out to check was hit in the side of the head with a two-by-four plank. The company immediately hired a guard to patrol the parking lot all night. The thieves are suspected to be sailors or college students, drug-crazed and needing quick money.

Though famed for its wealthy summer colony of four hundred, it is the Navy and its ancillary civilian personnel who make up 70 percent of Newport's population. The shops around the main square reflect the financial investment in the military: Army and Navy surplus clothing and X-rated films—as if all sailors are sexually inflamed.

The sailors will not be here much longer, and they stand on the steps of the YMCA or in front of the dirty bookshop looking already like those who have said a thousand good-byes in bus terminals.

Newport once had the jazz festival, but that is gone, along with many of the rich and soon the Navy. "Maybe we'll get some engineering companies to locate here," the Preservation Society spokesman said wistfully.

Newport remains new money, in part the beneficiary of the military-industrial complex, versus the old, established wealth of the few who built the mighty homes on Bellevue Avenue at the turn of the century. Fitzgerald would have understood the scene. He wrote about a similar social situation in *The Great Gatsby*. East Egg versus West Egg: new, slightly tarnished against old, more secure money, each making for differing social distinctions and sets of manners; everyone getting corrupted when the pursuit is for money and nothing else, with only the Nick Carraways, who stand aside to make the final judg-

42

ments, surviving with a trace of original innocence, having nibbled but not eaten the whole apple before the fall.

June 14

F. Scott Fitzgerald's only child, a daughter, Scottie, now a gray-haired matron wearing fashionable slacks, arrives at Nick's cottage with Mrs. Janet Auchincloss, the wife of Senator Claiborne Pell, a Rhode Island Democrat, and several teenagers. It is sunny and humid, and they have come to watch Nick leave the lovers alone in the living room. He goes to the kitchen, takes a boiling teapot off the stove and walks outside to sit under the tree. It is a tracking shot and the camera follows Nick the length of his walk along the kitchen porch from where he can look through the window at the couple.

The sea will again be the background for a close-up of Nick under the tree. Clayton asks that the thicket of trees and shrubs by the cliff walk be thinned out so the water can be seen. The men dutifully hack and dig at the growth.

When the three actors in the scene arrive on the set from their dressing rooms in Rosecliff, Mia is still having difficulty walking in her high-heeled purple shoes. She wobbles across the lawn, eager to thank again Mrs. Auchincloss for the party. Sam also joins the visitors under the tree, but Redford goes immediately into the cottage.

"Shall we go?" Clayton says. The rehearsal begins. It is very quiet when Sam comes out of the kitchen on the porch. The only sound is Scottie coughing.

It is not a particularly interesting scene for visitors to watch. Some of the teenagers in the party get restless and want to go back to the beach. Mrs. Auchincloss asks one boy if he doesn't want to see the stars work. The boy is uninterested if it requires a longer wait. Mrs. Auchincloss is quite star-struck. She has rented out quarters on her Hammersmith Farm to Redford, Clayton and Hank Moonjean, the assistant producer. Her son James, a young photographer, says she would be on the set everyday if the production would let her. She refuses to take shelter from the broiling sun, or to sit in the canvas chair offered her. She wants to stand as close to the camera as possible.

Scottie Smith is also quite attentive. Watching her watch the filming of her father's classic, one wonders what she has had to do to survive the legend of her self-destructive parents, the Golden Couple who defined an age.

The party leaves before the lunch break, and later Scottie, who is protective about the film and is against commenting on it before the shooting is completed, is reported to have said Sam is the perfect Nick, that he looks so much like her father when he was a young man.

To those who know Fitzgerald's appearance only by old photographs, there does not seem to be a strong resemblance between the actor and the author. Fitzgerald has a much more pained sensitivity in his eyes, and the haunted look of one who cannot prevent his self-inflicted ruin. Sam gives off the certainty of having his emotions under control.

June 15

There is a cloud covering over the sky, yet the mist above the sea has lifted and the peninsula is a clearly defined outcropping of rock hugging the water. The heat wave has broken.

The morning's work is a continuation of yesterday's scene. Sam leaves the porch and sits on a chair under the tree. Down by the ocean walk, the crew continues hacking at the underbrush, clearing a lane for the ocean to be in Sam's close-up. The hard work is watched by several tourists with Instamatic cameras. There have been so few outsiders trying to sneak on the set, contrary to earlier fears about a deluge of sightseers, that they are not chased away; and when they see how boring filmmaking can be, with the endless tugging and pushing of lights and cameras, they drift away.

Perhaps Newporters are a different breed of movie fan, more reticent if not any less curious. A few nights earlier Redford had dined with two friends at a waterfront restaurant. Possibly to ingratiate themselves with their girl friends, the waiters had reported the star's presence, and suddenly at the windows appeared scrubbed, pretty faces. To leave the restaurant, Redford had to pass through a gangwalk connecting the dining room with the bar. The girls were pressed against the wall. Rather than ask for his autograph or even speak to him, they released squeals in varying tones, making it sound as if Redford was passing an organ going out of control.

Under the tree, Sam waits for the first shot. His stilted graciousness with everyone and the recurring nervous half smiles make one think of a young, ambitious lawyer in the Nixon administration.

In the scene, Sam sits down, opens a case, takes out a cigarette and taps it before lighting it. Clayton suggests he tap it five times. In the first rehearsal Sam stops at four and Clayton quietly suggests he do five.

"Don't you ever smoke?" Clayton asks Sam.

Behind them men are pulling a hose down the rutted road from a fire truck parked opposite the food tent. The ritual of watering down the roof and trees begins.

Sam, who does not smoke off camera, smokes with authority during the rehearsal. "Once I needed to prove to myself I could do something," he says, "so I gave up smoking when I was up to three packs a day. I've given up about ten times. The first time was when I was ten, and my father caught me. He said he'd give them up if I did. His resolve lasted four years."

Suddenly the sun refuses to cooperate. Having broken the cloud covering into layers of dingy balls, it has now retreated behind the biggest.

"Missed by a millimeter a lovely patch," Slocombe says, holding the light filter to his eye. "The clouds are changing all the time."

Clayton sits down and talks with Annabel about strip mining and bird migrations, and he does it knowledgeably, as if they are subjects worthy to be studied, the world being filled with things to expand one's awareness of life.

45

A decision is made to do a cover scene in the ballroom of Rosecliff. As soon as most of the workers go there, the sun comes out, and the crew is called back to get Sam's close-up. Water is again sprayed on the leaves, and a piece of plastic is held over Sam's hair while Ramon attends to it, pressing down a stray lock.

"Be careful of Sam," Tringham calls to the hose bearer.

In a race with the sun that floats towards another group of stringy clouds, Clayton calls for a take, and when Sam is finished and gets up from the chair, the director holds the camera on the tree. The sun is out, the water is dripping off the leaves, which are gold ringed by the sun behind them. It is a lyrical shot, an example of the beautiful visual style Clayton wants for his picture.

Clayton has been less successful getting usable shots of the famous green light, which in the book is the symbol of what Gatsby has pursued, the dream of a great love to be obtained through the accumulation of wealth. It is the light on the end of Tom and Daisy Buchanan's dock on Long Island Sound, and when Nick first sees Gatsby, he has come from his mansion at night to stand on the lawn and stare at the light across the sound. It is a light that goes through dozens of literary interpretations each year.

The green light is now on top of a metal pole beyond the false arch at the end of the Rosecliff property. Each time Clayton has tried to photograph it, the pole shows up distinctly. It is one time fog might come in handy to block out the pole and leave the light a blurry green.

After lunch, the first scene is of Gatsby and Nick arriving in front of Rosecliff in Gatsby's yellow Rolls Royce. Redford, wearing a big hat, is driving, and the camera picks up the car halfway up the graveled road and follows it as it passes the entrance to Rosecliff. The first time everything goes well, and Annabel sighs, "Beautiful!" On the second take the car stalls before Redford can shift the gears. It backfires crazily and expires in one desperate cough. The crew applauds.

Men huddle around the car, including the owner of

the 1926 Rolls Royce, who says the trouble is that the water gasket has blown.

"My car cost $150 and doesn't do that," a grip says.

The ballroom of Rosecliff, which is the dimension of the Palace of Versailles, suitable enough for the signing of treaties to end wars, is being rearranged to make it Gatsby's home. It is hot again, and a number of the men —most of them British—who seem unable to get enough sun, take off their shirts. The crew goes about replacing stodgy panelings on the doors with mirrors, and putting up a new painting, filled with people on a lawn in pale blues and pinks, over the fireplace. A long plank has been put down on the side of the room over which the camera will move in on Gatsby and Nick, together the morning after Daisy has killed Myrtle with Gatsby's car. He has stayed up all night waiting for Daisy to call him, needing to believe she will.

The actors are being wired with microphones: Sam's is under a beige sweater on his waist at the back as is Redford's, which is under the vest of his pink suit. Clayton is eventually displeased with the lining of the suit, and a tailor must work through the night to put in a new one.

In the first rehearsal the tires on the camera make a growling sound as they move over the board. One of the grips thinks it is his shoes and he takes them off. The sound persists. Clayton stands with his arms folded over his chest, his fingers tapping his rib cage. He calls for a take and the camera is pushed forward too quickly. "Cut it," he says, "a bad start."

Gary Liddiard, who is Redford's makeup man and has been with him on most of his recent pictures, puts something under Redford's eyes. Clayton paces, his concentration restricted to the scene of Redford standing at the terrace window holding back the curtain so he can look towards Daisy's home across the Sound and on Nick, the friend, standing close to him, knowing what Gatsby cannot accept—that Daisy is a destructive, selfish person who will not call him for help.

Between takes, the people behind the camera come

forward to function within domains established by union rules and regulations, each jealously guarding his prerogative. Hair is combed. Lights are adjusted. A step ladder is moved. A board is picked up. A shirt is smoothed out.

Rocking on the balls of his feet, Clayton, his teeth clenched, hisses, "Quiet!" It takes no more than that. He is the director and has the authority, though some have noticed that when he sits down and his pants leg is hiked, a knife is visible in the side of his boot; they wonder about what he did in the war—whether he had really been in the secret service and killed men, as reported.

The workers retreat behind the line of defense, the camera being the furthest outpost. On cue, it is pushed forward, with Clayton, Slocombe and Jim Dalton, the boom man, walking at its side, as if it were a mine detector and they were going into battle with it.

The camera moves closer to the face at the window. Gatsby's ordeal must be revealed to the audience as he looks toward the green light getting dimmer.

June 16

Redford sits alone on the couch at the end of the ballroom away from the workmen. His back is reflected in many mirrors. The size of the room does not diminish him. He dominates it, and it is not just because he is a singular, impressive presence in *any* room. It is what everyone brings to him, the image they have of him. He is the star, the muscle on the picture, and the grips have already seen how the different departments cater to him. Some say they have seen Waterston trying to get the same treatment, without success. While Redford, unlike Waterston, stands back from any real social involvement with the company—he does on a rare occasion pass a football on lunch break—he is well regarded by the crew. He is distant enough with them to remain mysterious, and these men are not without their snobbery. If Redford mingled freely among them, how could he be a star?

Redford has been inundated with requests from the Newport rich to be this season's prized adornment at their social gatherings, and he says he has accepted some of the invitations because he is bemused by the rich, trying to find what is important to them. He thinks a leveling process has been going on among the young that is removing the artificial distinctions based on wealth.

As he talks, it is easy to believe the sons of Gatsby are no longer standing with their noses pressed to the windows of country clubs that are out of bounds to them. They are now inside smoking a joint with the children of the rich, long hair and rock having created the classless society that Marxism could not.

Redford stands, leaving the person to whom he has been talking in mid-thought, and goes forward into the throng around the lights and camera. Once there, he loses his identity.

Redford and Waterston are called to the terrace of Rosecliff for the single most important scene in the picture and book, the moral summation Fitzgerald gives his fable. Daisy has not come. It is dawn. Nick decides to go home. Gatsby stands at the top of the steps overlooking his pool and says, wishing he could hold back its demise, that summer is almost over. He asks Nick to come over later for a swim.

Halfway across the lawn, Nick stops, turns to Gatsby and says, "They're a rotten crowd. You're worth the whole damn bunch put together," which are the same words that appear in the book. In Nick's eyes, Gatsby's quest has been a transcendent experience: he is now above the rich who have corrupted him with their false dreams.

Sam is worried about having to squint into the sun at the beginning of the scene. Redford says he feels uncomfortable playing the scene without the vest to his pink suit. Sam asks Clayton if he should make a gesture, possibly a hand wave, when he says his famous line. Clayton agrees, and in the first rehearsal, after he speaks, Waterston turns his back on Gatsby and waves. It looks appropriate, though Redford claims he has no idea what Waterston was trying to do.

Gary Brink, a young prop man from New Jersey, is

using a shovel to stir up the water in the pool. If photographed without some ripples, he says, the water would have no definition on the screen and would be just a dull, flat surface. Clayton nods for him to stop. Tringham shouts into his megaphone, "All ready, boys!"

In the first take, the sound boom is too close to Sam and casts a shadow over his face.

After a few takes, the sun goes behind the clouds and Dougie scans the sky with his filter lens for five minutes until he sees a few weak rays and a patch of pale blue. Another take is called. Redford does each one slightly differently. One time he will come on the terrace, look to the sky and walk to the steps. Then he reverses the motions, going to the steps before looking to the sky.

As soon as the scene is finished, the lunch break is called. Some of the grips on the lawn begin hitting golf balls in the direction of the green light which has been moved closer and is now directly over the false arch in the marble wall.

The labor tensions are pervasive. Everything is suspect. Directions become shouts, the slamming of a door the impetus for people to jump from their seats. Executives are flying between New York and Newport. Lawyers are working overtime. There are threats of court action. Both sides are adamant and charge each other with lying and bad faith. The victims are those who are supposed to be making a movie. Associate Producer Hank Moonjean's day is taken up with preparations for the eventuality of a strike while he attempts to warp off one with his plans of compromise. The simplest incident becomes the potential seed of disaster.

A clothing manufacturer had been given permission to do a fashion layout in front of Rosecliff. Before starting it, one of the men from the agency wanders in back of Rosecliff and with his 8-millimeter camera begins making a home movie. Men from other craft unions see this and start to raise hell. Frantic phone calls go to Gordon Weaver in New York. He is Paramount's Executive Director of Publicity, a reliable voice of reason, and his voice is more calm than the situation warrants. After going over the options with his boss, Charles Glenn, Vice-President in charge of Advertising, Publicity and Promotion, Weaver recommends patience. The unit publicist is for throwing the fashion people off the set. Weaver wisely persists. Explanations are made to the union's officials on the set. Apologies are offered. Nobody believes anybody. Everything is still up for grabs. But the fashion people manage to finish the layout.

Chapter IV

Getting Ready for the Party

The advertisement in the local newspaper invited people between the ages of twenty-one and thirty-five who might be able to do the dances of the 1920s—or were capable of learning them—to come after supper on a Saturday night to the production office. Only fifteen show up at Sherwood, the white mansion across from Rosecliff.

Less regal than most of the homes along Bellevue Avenue, Sherwood has the look of a building that harbors past social triumphs. Its interior has been subdivided into summer apartments, the movie company having taken over four large rooms on the ground floor to the left of the stark marble hallway in the center of the building.

One room, cluttered with desks at odd angles to each other, is for general purposes. In it are Stan Bogest, auditor; his wife, Marie, the payroll secretary; Herb Mulligan, set decorator; and Gene Rudolf, American art director, who when he is not on the lawn of Rosecliff supervising the raising of party tents, is bent over a drawing board amid photographs and sketches designing the intricate party sequences to be shot over nine consecutive nights.

There is really no privacy in this room. Telephone conversations can be heard across the expanse. Temporary partitions have been put up. They are panels on which are tacked reminders, pictures of the sets, newspaper clippings and telephone numbers.

The suite of two rooms in the front of the building is really the nerve center of the production. In the outer office are Norman Cohen, production manager, Julia Lisberger, production office coordinator and Doreen Kranz, her assistant. In the adjoining room, which he has pretty much to himself, is Hank Moonjean. There is another desk in this office that is used by David Merrick when he needs one, and it is here the production staff gathers after a day's shooting for a round of drinks before going into the fourth room, where the dancers have now gathered, to look at rushes in the cutting room.

It is a large, rather empty room. In one corner, the teamster drivers wait for calls. Across from them against French windows that open on a wide lawn is the coffee machine and a table filled day and night with buns and pastries.

The turnout is disappointing. More women than men have showed up, and they bunch at the side entrance where the cutting room is located. One young girl has on a 1920s outfit, complete with headband and feathers, looking as if she has raided her grandmother's attic, but it is not quite right; the dress is much too long and the thickly applied rouge on her cheeks makes her look like a patient trying to fool a doctor to get out of the hospital earlier.

Tony Stevens, the choreographer, welcomes them graciously, as if each has the talent to be in the chorus line of a Broadway musical. He shows them how to do the Charleston. It is very stylized, with severe dips, leg thrusts back, hands open and forward in front of the chest, as if fending off a closing door. They perform it with the grace of those who come to dancing as a form of physical therapy suggested by a psychiatrist. Arms and legs do combat to the dance step worked out by Tony, and he grimaces when he turns his back on them to put the needle to a recording of the hit tunes of 1925.

"O.K., kids, let's try it again," Tony says, a charitable noun for some of the people in his chorus.

One elderly man remains stationary, placing right leg in front of left, swinging it back, out of time to the music. He seems delighted to have mastered the dance, or his version of it.

"Once again," Tony says, standing in front of the pack. Behind him the fifteen frantically try to keep up, eyeing each other to see how it should go, as if they were children cheating on an exam.

One woman tries harder than the rest, and the more she tries the more impossible it gets. She resorts to a high kick with her leg locked at the knee. When Tony calls a break, she goes to the corner behind the soft-drink cooler and stomps out the dance pattern, her leg always held crooked in its awkward flight.

Stevens was the assistant choreographer on *Irene*, and was with it on its horrendous tryout in Toronto. He is familiar with what it takes to put a show in shape, and he understands the odds working against him with amateur dancers. There will be no production numbers in the film; most of the dancing will be seen briefly as background action in the parties. One consolation is that when the shooting starts Tony will have six professionals from New York to flush out his line of amateurs.

The audition has become an attraction. The production staff from the other rooms are crowding the doorway. They do not laugh, at least overtly.

"Again, kids."

"Do you think this movie will bring back the Charleston?"

"God, I hope not."

"Back and down," Tony chants, "That's it . . . dip. . . ."

The woman's locked knee does not unbend in her dip.

A young man with a red farm bandana around his neck does his variation of the Charleston. He has the studied aloofness of one who has spent several summers in Newport. It is a reasonable approximation of what Tony has asked for.

The workers drift off. The lights blink on the telephone panels. Moonjean has watched the dancers for a few moments and returned to his office. In the day-to-day operation of the company, the myriad problems over which conferences are held, decisions made and tempers lost—someone must be sent to the airport to meet a company executive, a star wants a special favor, drivers have to be paid, bills must be accounted for—find their way into Moonjean's office because, in most routine matters, he is the man who can say yes or no. On details of production which have no reason to go to the director, the buck stops at Moonjean's desk.

Moonjean is a man of early middle years, short and stocky, going to paunch at the waist, with thick black hair and a round face. He has been with the production of *The Great Gatsby* for two and a half years, and was Merrick's associate producer on *Child's Play*. As Moonjean likes to describe himself kiddingly, he is a "veteran associate producer." Before settling in Newport, he had been one of the production's chief wanderers, scouring New Hampshire to Virginia for a residence suitable for *Gatsby*. His virtue is an efficacy for smoothing things out when he is hemmed in by conflicting voices and unreasonable demands. He also has the knack of putting people off from lingering in his office; he makes one aware his time is limited even before the next ring of the telephone.

He is very much aware of the stratification in a movie company by position and privilege and will do nothing to disturb the ranking, even to being polite to personnel he does not like. He is the man to see before a request can go any higher. He is never unreasonable, or offensive, but he can be abrupt with a turn of his head.

"This picture was originally planned to be shot entirely in the United States," he says, "but the production was shifted in May, 1972. We were supposed to shoot it last summer, but we couldn't get the costumes quick enough; and then Ali MacGraw left so it was decided to do it this year."

Julie buzzes from outside signaling the incoming call is important enough to disrupt the conversation. He says "yes" into the receiver with a sprightliness that fails to conceal the weariness of the besieged.

In the other room the stomping and thumping goes on. Tony has not lost his enthusiasm for the Charleston. "Dip . . . slide . . . three, four. Dip . . . slide . . . three, four."

It is time to choose those to be in the movie. "We'll

have to have some twenty-five dancers in the picture," Tony says, surveying the few. "At this point we're in no position to turn anyone down."

The selection is made. Among the chosen are the man in the red bandana, the young girl in the 1920s dress, a very pretty matron who acted from the start as if she knew she would be given the nod and another attractive woman whose straight carriage adds several inches to her height.

The woman with the locked leg is not selected, and she wanders among the rejected looking for someone to talk with, a sad woman in search of a friendly face in a crowded room.

One Britisher taking up temporary residence in the production offices is John Box, the brilliant set designer, winner of four Academy Awards in five nominations. He arrived the previous day from London with two suitcases of empty liquor bottles bearing labels from the 1920s, which startled customs officials.

A tank commander during the invasion of Normandy, a student of architecture before and after World War II, Box is now in his early fifties. Full-bodied rather than overweight, his face is florid and his short cropped hair and moustache touched with gray. He is extremely cordial with his associates and lauds profusely Gene Rudolf, the American art director who has been with the production daily in Newport while Box has been supervising the construction of sets at Pinewood Studios in England. There are rumors, however, that he has been involved in fierce struggles with Clayton, which he acknowledges in a casually understated way.

"One of my faults is that I get too domineering on a set and try to impose my own way. (Box has directed some second unit work, as well as the brilliant scene of the Russian Army in front of the Tsar's palace in *Nicholas and Alexandra*.) Eventually you have to fall in line with the director or there is anarchy. I think Jack and I now talk the same language." This is his concession that Clayton is in control of the picture.

Box was hired in February, 1973. He had learned of

the project from Douglas Slocombe, with whom he had worked on *Travels with My Aunt*. Slocombe suggested he get in touch with Clayton.

"I had read *Gatsby* back in the 1940s when I was a young man, and I've kept the book in my house. When I was in Kenya over Christmas I reread it. The writing has such a relaxed, marvelous quality.

"Of the characters in the book, I particularly like Jordan. She is the kind of beautiful, quietly complex woman who appeals to a staid Englishman. The script has brought out her quality very well. Jordan is a catalyst. She makes things happen. And Nick wouldn't have liked Gatsby as much if Jordan hadn't been around."

One does not have to be an American to appreciate *The Great Gatsby*, Box insists. "There is a strong Anglo-Saxon quality to the book. It's about people with weaknesses who make good. They're the sort who put up fronts to cover a certain sensibility. Jordan wears hers to hide the fact she cheats. Gatsby uses his to disguise his past and his hurt. The setting is America, but the strata of wealth to which Tom and Daisy Buchanan belong is not just Long Island; it's the kind that moves from country to country.

"The difficult thing is to get the style of the book to the screen. Call it the quality of a butterfly or a bird. The book has a rather precious feeling about it."

In designing the sets, Box said the basic visual color he has tried for is white. "Everything has to be airy and infused with light. Gatsby's house is light colored, and the kinship between his place and Nick's cottage is white. By getting this color in the film, and keeping everything fragile in appearance, I help Jack achieve a unity among the characters."

The Valley of Ashes, Fitzgerald's symbolic dividing line between the wealth of Long Island and exotic, exciting New York City, described surrealistically in the book, is a stretch of road between West Egg and the City where it parallels railroad tracks and a bed of ash that takes the shape of ominous, gray buildings. George Wilson's garage and apartment are in the Valley of Ashes. This set was built at Pinewood. "We had to do it in the studio," Box said, "because the only place that had the iron, hard look of New York is a suburb of Madrid."

The Valley of Ashes was a tremendous problem for Box, but it was the party sequence that gave him the most trouble. "I didn't know how to lay it out. One does get preconceived ideas about a scene. They may not be practical, but one holds on to them. I sat at my board doodling. Then came the idea of putting a dance floor around the pool at Rosecliff, and having tents around it and to give each of the three parties a distinctive look by changing the colors of the tents for each party. The film can not be static. It has to be visually very fluid."

As for the decorations inside Rosecliff, "Everything was awful," he says, "filled with the kind of furniture which prevented light and air from getting into the room. We stripped it down and put in glass mirrors to reflect the lights of the party. At one time I thought of having an aviary in the ballroom, but I decided it would compete with the mirrors and windows.

"Rosecliff and Nick's cottage had to be a particular place on Long Island at a particular time. The only thing that shouldn't be there is the cliff at the end of Rosecliff. It was tough getting the juxtaposition of the two houses, but I remembered two principles from my days as a student of architecture: nothing must be arbitrary; nothing must be self-conscious."

Before designing Nick's cottage, Box spent two weeks on Long Island studying the architecture of the older, more modest beach houses. He went through many books and photographs to find the precise style and then returned home to build the model. On his return, carrying the model in a case, Box was stopped by customs, who were not satisfied when he opened it. He could not pass until he had lifted the roof of the model.

It was left to American carpenters and painters to build the actual house, and Box has only praise for them. "When we first came together on this picture, the British and Americans stood around looking at each other. Once we started working together, everything went along splendidly. They're first-rate."

Box did not stay for Gatsby's party. He had to return to London for final work on the Valley of Ashes. He left behind detailed instructions for the packing and shipping of the articles found by his two researchers, Jozefa Stuart and Virginia Burke, outside New York to fill Wilson's garage and other interior sets in Pinewood.

For Wilson's garage there are gas pumps, rubber tires, wood-spoked wheels with metal rims, car jacks, gas cans, a wire rack for oil bottles, headlights, car horns, crankshaft for a 1919 Chandler, brake linings, copper gaskets, eight license plates dated 1916 to 1925, a 1915 Oliver typewriter, a painted tin wall rack advertising Whiz polish repair, a cash box and two American flags with poles.

For Myrtle's apartment on Riverside Drive: two flower prints in art deco frames, three electric fans, a white marble clock, a silver-plate filigree flower basket, two tin tobacco jars, an electric toaster, a kitchen scale, a small 1920 Windsor chair, dinner gongs, a pair of sterling candle sticks, a Kodak camera and a pair of lace pillow shams.

For Myrtle's apartment over the garage: a meat grinder, a tin wall clock, an electric toaster, a Red National Biscuit cake holder, an enamel dishpan, a blue spatter roaster, a hanging tin match holder and a ten-piece French Ivory dresser set with the monogram *M*.

June 18-21

The set is closed to press and public, but the demand builds. Everyone wants to get on: Press, photographers, local newspapers, foreign publications, would-be extras, friends of would-be extras. There is a file of more than fifty requests, principally from the press, and each has to be turned down politely. They may be needed when the film is released.

Weaver and his boss at Paramount, Charles Glenn, are following a script they wrote with Yablans about publicity for *The Godfather*. The idea is to control the output to build up suspense and create the aura that the film is truly big, something special. They have set a release date for publicity of February, 1974, and now must work with national and international outlets to get them to go along with an arbitrary date that they know will be adjusted.

There are good reasons for the set to be closed at this time. There has already been an inordinate amount of publicity about *Gatsby*, particularly generated by the fashion industry which has succeeded in putting many young men in ugly baggy pants with wide cuffs. There is a conviction at Paramount that the public will have tired of the film before it has been shot. This concern is justified. One man in the company told a friend he was going to Newport to work on *The Great Gatsby*, and the friend said he thought the picture had already been made.

Also, the scenes shot in the first week were some of the most intimate in the film; and a rapport had to be established between the director and his actors, which would have been impossible with journalists and photographers hounding them.

And the new breed of journalists are hardly literary. Almost all who requested to get on the set were at best unfamiliar with the book. Gone are the days when reporters had a Great American Novel in their top desk drawer and wanted to be the new Hemingway, Faulkner or Fitzgerald. One reporter asked where the scene between Fitzgerald and Zelda in Alabama would be filmed; another inquired who Nick was, but the best was an intelligent woman who asked blithely, "Does the film have a happy ending?"

"Have you read the book?" a company employee asked incredulously.

"Of course. Several times."

"Then you know Gatsby is killed?"

"Certainly. But it's a Hollywood movie. Don't they always change things to make a happy ending?"

A more incredible exchange took place with a representative of a women's magazine. She requested stills of Scott and Zelda. She was told Paramount did not have these pictures, but that she might try Putnam's, which had just published a photographic biography of Fitzgerald.

"I don't want old ones," she said knowingly. "I want pictures of them on the set."

Some reporters refused to be turned off by the ban. A pretty coed from the University of Rhode Island wandered off the street into Rosecliff, past unattentive guards, and was adopted by the grips who never leave pretty, unattached girls alone for very long on the set. Her visit went unnoticed until she began snapping pictures of the actors. She was escorted to the production office and was already in a sweat when asked how she had succeeded in getting on the set. She stammered that she was a stringer for a variety of publications from the student newspaper to the *Mexico City Times*, but she refused to divulge the name of the grips who had allowed her on the set, steeling herself for an inquisition. Her terror at the unknown, the hard-breathing Hollywood types in front of her, was enough punishment. She left properly chastised.

The shooting on the second Monday of the production began at the water's edge, on the styrofoam steps leading up from the real rocks to the artificial arch. In the film it is dusk, but it is really morning; a mist is there before dawn, changing now into a steady rain. Nick has found a dead seagull by the water. When that shot is done, a scaffolding on which the camera is placed is rolled into position on the landing to the sea side of the arch, and in the drizzle Gatsby appears in a green velvet smoking jacket and shiny black pumps with bows to greet Nick. They turn and begin walking up the lawn towards Rosecliff.

The scene starts with Nick coming up the stairs to the landing. Behind him, men have woven branches from trees into the metal framework that holds up the lights. At the bottom of the steps Sam goes through limbering exercises, shaking his arms loosely, locking his fingers and snapping them. Further along the cliff walk, a dozen sightseers, their eyes covered by small cameras, have been stopped by the guard. The rain is no impediment to their enjoyment of seeing their first movie.

"God knows why they stand there in the rain," a guard says. "We've got one woman who sits over there in the bushes watching everything that goes on. She's no bother, just sits there and stares, so we don't chase her away."

After each rehearsal, while Slocombe studies the sky before making adjustments to the camera lighting, the actors sit in their canvas chairs that are protected by striped umbrellas. A football sails over the camera and bounces harmlessly on the soggy lawn. Two grips have been passing it, and now they look sheepishly toward the director.

"Would you mind keeping the football under control," says Tringham, with the familiarity of one who has never seen an American football.

Redford comes back to the arch. A dye brush is applied to the front of his hair by Liddiard.

A Navy helicopter circles overhead. Steve Felder, the young production assistant who gave up a chance at playing pro baseball to work in movies, grabs his walkie-talkie from the holster on his hip. "They've been told not to fly over here when we're working," he says, nonplussed at the idea the Navy would divert its aircraft for Hollywood. He calls the production office to relay a request to the Navy to order the copter away.

"Every day is a new day with them," Felder says. "Once you tell them not to come, they've immediately got to."

Watching the copter circle a few times before changing course in a jerking sideways motion towards the sea, someone absentmindedly raps the false section of the wall. It gives off a soggy thud. "The magic of Hollywood," he says.

Overhearing the remark, a British grip says grandly, "Hollywood has nothing to do with it. It's the magic of London and New York."

Mia also has a scene in the rain. It is another time in

the story. She and Gatsby have resumed their affair, and she is regularly visiting his mansion. On this day it is raining, and holding an umbrella she hurries up the stairs from the dock—nonexistent but there in the mind of the audience—pauses under the arch, stares at Rosecliff and then starts running towards it, a watery presence made indistinct by the drizzle and slight fog.

She has a stunning outfit for the scene, a beige raincoat with matching hat; and she runs well, though veering too much to the left, and is called back on course by Clayton. It is the stockings that give her trouble, wrinkling into bunches in her run for the mansion, and after each take she dutifully tugs them up, much like a young child hurrying home late from school who knows she must look presentable when inspected by her mother.

The crew starts discussing the romance inherent in the film. One of its most appealing aspects is the bittersweet quality of a romance that dies with youth.

"If the rain keeps up, they can call it *The Umbrellas of Newport.*"

"Alas," the friend says, "they don't make romantic comedies anymore."

Bruce Dern overhears the conversation. "That's right," he says. "The last romantic comedy was *Portnoy's Complaint.*"

For the next two days scenes are shot of food being delivered to Gatsby's mansion for his parties. Extras dressed as tradesmen and servants carry the food down the cement stairs to an open basement. There are boxes of apples, lemons, vegetables, fresh fish, sides of beef, pheasants and lobsters. The food is refrozen at the end of the day and kept in a refrigerated truck parked in the circular driveway in front of Rosecliff. There are a hundred lobsters live in the barrels crawling through the ice. There could have been more if the barrels were filled from the bottom rather than only at the top.

Redford is on standby the first afternoon, and he leaves the set to play tennis at the exclusive beach club on the ocean where he has been given a visitor's membership. He is a superb athlete and has already beaten the club's pro. A middle-aged man is now waiting for Redford to arrive and has been there for an hour. Redford casually had said he would play with him some-day. The man took it as a definite commitment and arrived with his whole family to see the star in action.

Redford rallies with the man and realizes he does not play his fast game. He devises a variation on the rules to eliminate serving. He plays for an hour, toying with the man.

The club's pro, sitting on the grass outside the court, asks if he can get on the set to see some shooting.

"A lot of people around here are going to be extras in the picture," he says. "For many it will be the first time they've spoken to each other in years."

The opponent is gallant, volleying reasonably well, perhaps too quick to approve Redford's trickier shots.

There is the sound of gears being ground with determination on the road outside the club. A 1925 convertible chugs past. At the wheel is Lois Chiles, a blue denim hat pulled over her ears, a lock of brown hair whipped by the wind over her forehead. She is learning to drive a shift car for the picture, and she holds the wheel with both hands. The man next to her tries to remain nonchalant, but his eyes are transfixed on her hands. She does not take her eyes off the road.

Her loveliness is an asset. She is friendly without being overly familiar and is sometimes coquettishly shy, fixing the glance of her eyes away from the person to whom she is talking. The crew accepts her femininity and distance; they have been in the business long enough to know familiarity can destroy illusion, and they want to remain happy in their jobs. To most who surround her on the set—prop man, grip, hairdresser and makeup man—she is an unknown person, still very new in the business.

She passes without noticing Redford finishing an hour on the court without a break. He is sweating, and the sun has brought out his freckles. He can not leave the club without going down the reception line provided by his opponent, and Redford goes through it pleasantly, giving no more of himself than a smile and a courteous "how are you."

"Are you going to give the extras booze to keep them convivial?" the tennis pro says to his departing players.

The fog is always around Newport, even on the clearest of days, and this time it comes off the sea to blanket one side of the peninsula. The green light by the arch is a disconnected lump in the thick mist surrounding Rosecliff, and though it is not on the schedule, Clayton calls for another shot of it.

That night the Rotary Club meets at a second-rate fish house on the waterfront, and a very successful attorney talks about Newport and the social divisions into the Navy, rich and peasants. With the military about to pull out, Newport will be left with a more rigid social stratification; the rich and the middle-class shaped by their degrees of indebtedness. The movie company, eagerly anticipated by those who make a way of life out of giving parties, is really of no moment to those who run the town's commerce and serve the rich; the movie people are adornments for the season. The interest is in how many extra jobs are there for local people and whether Mia and Lois are pretty and nice.

The next morning, in a third-floor corner room of Rosecliff, Lois resumes her dance lessons with Tony Stevens. She has been working with him an hour a day for the past week. The rug is pushed back, and with Tony's assistant, Maryjane Houdina at her side, Lois goes through her routine in front of a full-length mirror. She keeps herself erect; the impression she gives is of a regal beauty whose stance sets up barriers against unwanted intimacies.

She practices to a recording of the Charleston, and when she gently slaps her backside while side-kicking in a circle, Tony says, "You're too gentle on the buns!"

Lois smiles through half-closed eyelids.

"Lois is not a dancer, and not real quick with her steps," Tony says, "but she is good, and because she has been a model, she understands the lines of a dancer and knows how to hold her body."

That night Tony resumes his search for amateur dancers and holds another open audition at the production office. It is a mob scene. Close to 100 hopefuls show up, still more women than men and quite a few in bizarre costumes. Some of those who have been rejected are back; a few young men are excellent dancers but too obviously faggy.

Clayton sits with Moonjean in back of the room watching bemusedly while Tony and Maryjane patiently organize the throng into groups of five. Maryjane is the instructor tonight. She is in front of each group, her trim figure in tight slacks moving to a rhythm of the phonograph music few behind her hear or refuse to listen to, and she has amazing stamina, outlasting each clumsy group. Clayton goes over to her and gives her a reassuring tap on the shoulder.

"The women are easier to teach," Tony says. "You have to get the men through the psychological barrier of thinking the only use they have for their bodies is to hit someone."

Tony will have three days to work with the women extras and only one with the men. "The difficult thing for these people," he says, "is their lack of stamina. Professional dancers can go all day and never get tired."

Out of this group Tony selects most of his dancers. He again warns them the party sequences will require working all night. Their eagerness to be in a movie in any capacity prevents them from hearing the words of what he says.

The surprise of the audition is the success of the woman with the locked knees. She returns in a costume of the 1920s—not the red shorts which had showed her figure off to a disadvantage—and has learned a passable imitation of the Charleston.

"But . . ." someone says who has recognized her.

"I know," Tony says, "but she must have worked hard to learn this much."

Preparations for the Ben Hur of movie parties goes on daily at Salve Regina College where five persons tend to the two thousand costumes that hang neatly on racks in two classrooms. About 20 percent of the men's and women's clothes have been made; the rest have been rented in New York and London, mostly from theatrical costume houses.

The dresses come in all sizes and designs, but most have the distinctive flapper look, cut to hang loosely over bosomless chests, many stitched with beads. Costume jewelry to be matched with the dresses are in boxes on a long table against the blackboard, and across the room are shelves of shoe boxes.

The men's clothes are presumably less of a problem since most of the male extras will be wearing tuxedos at the parties. But many of the formal clothes are from England, and when American men come in for fittings, they find the clothes do not fit. Made or rented in England because they would have to be shipped back there for further use in the British end of the production, the suits are generally found to be too small, most waist sizes 30 to 32. A feature of the affluent American male frame now is the incipient pot belly and chests going to fat.

"For me and most adult American men to have a 32 waist size," Bernie Styles says, "we'd have to be in the morgue for two months."

Work goes on. Seams are ripped open, hems raised and dropped. Waists are widened. The alterations proceed through the day. When the parties are over, much of the clothing will be shipped to England.

The next day, Thursday, the company takes over the pantry of the Breakers for one day's shooting in the most extravagant mansion in Newport. The kitchen is structured into tiers of pantry shelves that are higher than the size of most modest middle-class homes. It will serve in the film as the kitchen in Gatsby's mansion, and in the scene Daisy stands at one side of a long table, touching the copper molds spread the length of it, walking slowly towards the end where she meets Gatsby and they look into each other's eyes.

It is very crowded around the table. The bright arc lights make it almost unbearably hot. Outside the kitchen windows, the tourists who are allowed in the other rooms of the mansion are lined up in shorts and straw hats, cameras at the ready.

Redford is chewing bubble gum. "Is this a take?" he asks Clayton as the camera is rolled into position in the cramped quarters. When he is told no, he snaps off a bubble.

Mia wears yet another lovely design by Theoni Aldredge, a white suit with blue pleats in the skirt and a mandarin collar. She also has on a dazzling diamond necklace and bracelet valued at $25,000. A guard stands near her, a pistol jammed into his belt under a loose fitting polo shirt.

"It's very difficult to do an intimate moment on film when you have twenty-five people hanging over your shoulder," a grip says.

But there is a painfully sensual intimacy to the scene in the way Mia caresses the copper molds, touching them as if they were the surfaces of exquisite paintings. She looks up from them only when she gets to the end of the table, and then into Redford's blue eyes.

"God, it's sexy," says a female visitor to the set.

At the lunch break, Mia improvises a picnic on the lawn outside the Breakers with her twin boys who play in a stretch of high grass and wild flowers. Sasha brings to his Vietnamese baby sister a garland he has woven and puts it on her head.

Mia is entranced by her children, and those who knew her in the *Peyton Place* days say she has changed greatly —all for the better—and they attribute it mainly to her motherhood.

It is over without any formal announcement, and it is detected on the set with the arrival of a tranquility unknown during the first days of shooting. Clayton is less tense and smiles more easily. There are no new reports of his outbursts at the production meetings, of throwing chairs against the wall in a rage against the problem over which he has very little control.

The word is passed that the union problem has been settled. The threat of a strike has been lifted.

The specifics of the dispute were never completely clear to the crew. The workers had been infiltrated with and infected by rumors and secondhand reports, as well as the edginess of the director and his assistants. The latest report is that the union went to court to force Paramount to hire Americans as the operator and first assistant cameraman, and the court said it had no jurisdiction, that only a jury trial could decide the issue.

If the class struggle still has any validity, the unionized crew should have sided with the cameramen against the management. From all statements, they took what amounted to a neutralist position in favor of Clayton and getting on with the picture.

From the start the Americans on the film were vocal about Clayton's professionalism and his fairness. They liked him, though they did not know him as a private man off the set. To them, he was considerate and clear in what he wanted, and they were appreciative of it. The rapport was so solid that the Americans and British both felt they were part of one of the best crews assembled for any recent film, and much of the credit for this has to go to Clayton who orchestrated them so well.

At the same time the cameramen's dispute is resolved, the writer's strike ends in Hollywood. Coppola is now free to do rewrites, but by now Clayton has already done them.

June 22, 23

Actors are notoriously disinterested, or at best uninformed, about the outside world, often signing up for causes of which they have never heard only because their agents tell them to do it. Watergate has been the exception, and Redford is the principal conduit, relaying to those on the set concerned about the implications of the domestic espionage emanating from the executive branch of the federal government his observations on the hearings after watching them on the television set in his Rosecliff dressing room. Redford is a superb story teller, getting down precisely the inflections of the person he is dramatizing, and he does justice to the cast of characters in the Senate hearing room.

But the U.S. Supreme Court's decision yesterday on pornography is eliciting comments from almost everyone. The legal terms, the arid prose style of Chief Justice Burger, the suffocating moralizing behind it, may have muddled what he was trying to say, but most on the set believe it is bad and will encourage local censors who still think Hemingway and Faulkner are unfit for eyes under fifty.

Redford shakes his head and says the decision shows how close America came to Fascism. The only good words for the decision come from Waterston and Annabel.

"I think it's pretty good," Sam says. "A town should have the right to determine its own standards." He says it with the innocence of one whose bias is usually in favor of the locally constituted authority.

Annabel is just against pornography and thinks it should be eliminated, though she is aware the constitutional guarantee of free speech is at issue in every censorship case.

Annabel sits in her script chair in the corridor beside the back terrace of Marble House where filming will be for the next two days. She is the one person who constantly knows where to go to be out of the way.

It is not a pleasant day. The fog over the sea is impenetrably dense. Beyond the lawn it seems like the end of the world, and there is the smell of rotting fish in the fog.

"This place is more American than European," Annabel says, "whereas Rosecliff is more imitation French."

Marble House was built in 1892 for William K. Vanderbilt, and it has a majestic gaudiness. Marble is everywhere, in varying colors to enhance the sense of massiveness, and a person can not escape his image as he passes one of the many full-length mirrors. In the ballroom there is a ceiling mural of overripe pink ladies embracing, and over the biggest mirror are gilt figures. At its worse, in some of the corridors, the mansion looks like the basement lounge of Radio City Music Hall.

At the right of the main entrance is a full-size painting of the revolutionary mob attacking the door of a mansion, the way barred by a loyal servant. It is a message the former owners, before the building was turned over to the Preservation Society, would have enjoyed.

Upstairs the rooms are quite intimate, meaning they are somewhat smaller than a train station. Robert Grimaldi, the standby American hairdresser, touring the upper reaches, says, "An Italian would appreciate these rooms."

Downstairs, Clayton is working on probably the trickiest single shot of the picture, and he frequently goes to an ice-water bucket, dips an elastic tape in it and wraps the soggy material around his wrist. He has been suffering from a cold, and the compress is to keep down his pulse rate and fever.

It is a tracking shot of Gatsby, Nick and Daisy walking down the corridor of Gatsby's mansion on her first visit to it. (Through the magic of movies, Gatsby's mansion in the film will consist of rooms from three Newport mansions.) They enter a room with a huge fireplace where Gatsby's boarder Klipspringer is doing exercises in his pajamas. Gatsby tells Daisy he was left over from a party several months earlier, and it was weeks before he discovered the guest had moved in. He tells Klipspringer to play the piano, and while the trio continues the inspection of the downstairs room, he plays "Ain't We Got Fun."

In this sequence the camera follows the trio down one corridor, into Klipspringer's room, turns the corner into the ballroom and goes back parallel to the corridor it has just come up. This has to be done without showing the many arc lights along the way or catching reflections of the camera and crew in the many mirrors.

"The way Dougie Slocombe has lit this scene separates the men from the boys," says Jack Stager, the still photographer.

There are many rehearsals before Clayton calls for a take. One proceeds after another with only Clayton really seeing what goes into the scene, the rest of the crew following his eyes, seeking from his direction the correct interpretation.

After one take, Redford breaks up laughing. "Don't listen to what I say, watch what I do," he says, flubbing a line, replacing it with "The Indians are coming." After another take, Redford goes behind the camera slapping his own left hand in mock anger. He has touched Mia in the take, and he is not supposed to.

There are more takes of the long march down the corridor and around the bend to Klipspringer at the piano. He is played by a fine young New York actor, Ed Herrmann, who in this scene displays a comic talent appreciated by Clayton. He laughs at the actor's work and goes over to compliment him with a slap on the back.

The takes are resumed. Nine, ten, eleven.

"Ah, shit," someone says, his anonymity protected by the wall of lights extended behind the camera.

"How many times do they do this?" a woman visitor exclaims loud enough for her to be shushed by a production assistant.

Between takes Mia is surrounded by hands to maintain her look of fragile exquisitiveness, touching in place a curl of her wig, patting more makeup on her face. When she is off by herself, in concentration, she has the habit of tapping her thumb to her teeth, and she does this walking alone down the corridor.

It is the fourteenth take.

"He's a terrific director," Stager says. "He's not like the old-timers who work from a master shot and the more traditional cover shots. He keeps the camera moving constantly, getting right into the scene. He's really thought out this picture before he started to shoot."

Someone in the crew makes a noise and ruins the take. Clayton walks to the water bucket and resoaks the compress.

Stager's comments are perceptive. Clayton does eliminate many conventional ways of directing in this scene with a two-shot, which is photographing one person talking to the other and then reversing it, having the second person respond or taking a long establishing shot before going in for the close-ups. In the corridor tracking sequence he begins it immediately with the trio in action.

On the sixteenth take, Clayton calls an end to the scene and slowly unwraps the compress.

The next day is the first the extras of Newport have to do what they are famous for in the summer—going to a party—and fifty natives, dressed in the finery of the 1920s, are waiting in the basement of Marble House to perform.

The scene takes place in a crowded corridor where Gatsby's party, the first to which Nick has been invited, is in full swing; and Nick, escorted by Gatsby's bodyguard, makes his way around waiters with trays of food and drink and couples chatting, to an elevator.

Led by the production assistants, the extras in single file come up from the basement through a narrow stairway. The young assistants are called "sperm" by the crew since most are related to someone in the movie business. This is said affectionately. They are generally good workers; if they are bothersome, it is because they are the last voices spoken in a chain of command, and sometimes they overreact to what the original order was.

The gossip between takes is about the confusion the previous night at the Viking Inn where the annual state Veterans of Foreign Wars Convention convened in turmoil at the reception desk where patrons found the hotel in bureaucratic confusion. There were more patrons than available rooms, and angry veterans were steered to other possible lodgings. The youngsters behind the desk bravely took the abuse for mistakes they did not make.

"And did you know what went on later in a motel room?" says Ramon, the hairdresser, the source of the best show-business stories on the set. Before giving any details, he makes it sound very lascivious.

"What were they doing, Ramon?"

"Fucking," he says with feigned horror.

"Civilians or veterans?"

Ramon raises his blond eyebrows, indicating any identification without clothes is impossible.

"Boy and girl, or boy and boy?"

Ramon remains noncommittal.

"A bit of everything?"

Ramon wears a Mona Lisa smile.

His favorite story of the week is about Marlene Dietrich, with whom he has worked in recent years, when she has been doing her one-woman concerts.

He and Marlene went into a London restaurant where they spotted the veteran British stage actor Emlyn Williams. It had been a bad siege for Marlene. Several friends had died, and she was attending a rash of funerals. It was not necessarily a depressing experience for her, Ramon says, since she loves these events. Her fans, however, kept clawing at her, and she was concerned how they would act when she slipped into the next world. Williams put down his fork and asked why didn't she die at sea.

Ramon makes the story slightly bitchy but basically very jolly, and it is retold around the set.

At lunch break the crew and cast are fed in the mist under a huge tree. The American grips go off on the soggy lawn to have a touch football game, and it is fairly vigorous with bodies slapped heavily by hands.

Bruce Dern, who comes to the set every day though he still has not worked in a scene, notices most of the extras in the morning shot were discharged before the break.

"Is that the British system?" he calls to Clayton. "You get rid of the extras before you have to feed them!"

In the afternoon twenty couples are arranged in the gilt and mirrored ballroom to the right of the entrance. They wait for the taped music of a sprightly two-step. By the piano at one end near the camera are Tony Stevens and Maryjane. There has been an extraordinary transformation in his appearance. His hair was never long; rather shaggy and tapered at the neck. It now has been cut, slicked back and parted in the middle. He could pass for George Raft in a twenties gangster film.

A transformation of more importance has taken place in his amateur dancers. Granting the two-step, a variation on a natural walk speeded up, is one of the easier dances to learn; Tony, with only twenty minutes, has the

74

dancers going through a glossily professional routine in the basement. He beams over them like a proud father.

Near Tony and Maryjane is Ed Herrmann and his partner, an older woman several feet shorter than he. Her feather, stuck in a silver band around her head, almost reaches his chin. The musicians, framed by the side mirror, hold instruments not to be played. The music will be dubbed in later.

In the first rehearsal the dancers are splendid, but they are not too close to the camera. They constrict themselves into smaller circles each turn on the floor.

"You're a bit camera shy," David Tringham says. "Come closer to the camera when you dance by it." The assistant director has replaced his megaphone with a whistle. "When I blow my whistle will you please start."

Ramon comes from an adjoining room and goes around the line of male dancers brushing stray hairs off the shoulders of the tuxedos.

The music comes on, and the dancers whirl off. "That's very good," Tringham says, and then, as if questioned what he said, "Actually it is very good!"

This time the dancers bunch around the camera. Eyes of women rise like moons over the shoulders of their partners in search of the lens.

"Nice and lively," Tringham says. "Enjoy it."

The feather in the hairband of his partner strikes Herrmann in the chin, and the impact knocks the band crooked on her forehead.

"That's very good. We'll sign you all up," continues Tringham, functioning as a coach on the sideline of a grueling contest.

Clayton, holding a steaming cup of coffee—he consumes gallons of it on the set—walks over to Herrmann and winks encouragement. Behind him the prop men fan out through the dancers, filling those holding glasses with a soft drink.

"Now don't look at the camera. Forget it," Tringham says. "Have a good time. It's a party."

The scene is done in seven takes, and Clayton orders four of them printed.

There is more gossip to enliven the set. There has been a fist fight in the wardrobe room at Salve Regina between two production men over what sounds to be a misunderstanding, easily blown out of proportion by the residue of tension from the labor unrest. One of the men carries a bruise and slight laceration over the right eye, confirming his participation.

Mia arrives holding the hand of her husband. Andre Previn, who is visiting for a week. She is a Southern belle, circa 1917, in an empire-cut dress with pink rosebuds and white lace. She is not a beauty in the conventional Hollywood sense. Her slim figure in a bathing suit would not have graced the barrack lockers of servicemen in World War II, and her face is dominated by her overlarge, dark haunting eyes isolated in her alabaster skin.

But she has what so few actresses have now in Hollywood, the look of a star.

Mrs. Janet Auchincloss is visiting the set, and as the mother of a woman familiar on the pages of every fan magazine, she is aware of what makes a star, and she stares almost reverently at Mia who is also given cordial treatment by Merrick, who is reputed to be not overly fond of actors, though he has created more stars than any other producer. But he walks over to Mia and says with an old-fashioned courtliness how nice she looks.

The scene Redford and Mia will do is not in the book. Daisy and Gatsby, alone in his mansion, are in the clothes they have worn as lovers eight years earlier. The present becomes the past, and to the music of Irving Berlin's "What'll I Do" they dance around a candle stuck in a wine bottle on the floor in the empty ballroom. It is a scene for romantics who remember lost loves and the pain they can still cause when recalled by the strain of a shared song or a brief reunion.

While the scene is rehearsed, guests are allowed in the room. Merrick is by himself. There is an observable hostility between him and Clayton; they move as if enemies on opposite sides of a truce line, giving only the slightest recognition in passing. Most often it is a cursory glance, as if trying to determine what each other is up to. Clayton works closely with his actors. He has taken the role as protector of them from Merrick.

"Being a producer is like being a fireman in the firehouse waiting for the gong to go off," Merrick says.

Someone adds, "If Redford dances Mia any closer to the candle, he'll have her dress on fire."

"That's when the gong goes off," Merrick quips.

Redford and Mia have been rehearsed for the waltz they will do in the scene, but they are not comfortable with the large space available in the ballroom, having practiced in the cramped quarters of a Rosecliff dressing room. Tony and Maryjane take them off to a room across the hall where they work on a more elegant, sweeping step.

The room is cleared of guests when the couple returns and stands by the candle. They have two of the most famous faces now in Hollywood, and their eyes make contact the way only those do who know how to use the camera to their advantage. When the music begins, they start the waltz, Redford at first slightly stiff, Mia shyly looking away from him as he holds her at arm's length. They move slowly, formally, around the flame of the candle; and as they circle, the camera follows them, each going in the same direction, the actors and the instrument that gives them life on the screen.

Clayton loses his temper only once when the music tape gets stuck and the soundman is unable to fix it quickly.

"It's snarled," he yells to Clayton from the other room.

"Unsnarl it and get it to work now!" Clayton says, enunciating every letter, his voice rising gradually until all the force is in the "now."

By the end of the takes, which is several hours later, Clayton has the wet compress wrapped around his neck.

Back at the Viking Inn that night, the veterans—most of them from two wars back—and their wives attend a banquet in the drab, unfinished basement ballroom. How aged they now look, heavy in body and face, gray and tired. They reveal how far many have come from the days of youth when the country was held by a simple faith in a great destiny and the correct way in doing things.

Their wives stand in front of high-school musicians who play mostly off key. They imitate the dance from "Zorba the Greek," and when it is over, some of them go with their husbands upstairs to a discotheque where the young of Newport go on the weekends. Many from the movie company are there, and some of the gay males dance with each other. The veterans are confused by it. They do not react angrily in defense of their masculinity or taunt them as "fags." They stand there stunned by how far they, too, have come.

The next day, Sunday, in the ballroom the ladies auxiliary spends hours giving out awards and installing new officers. The women walk to the dais as if in step to military music heard long ago, and they are at attention by the American flag when they get their awards.

In a barren cement area next to the room is the pool, and at the edge, drunk, asleep in a chair, his mouth open, is the youngest veteran, from America's latest war. The children in the water pay no attention to him.

June 25, 26

This is the way the rich still live in Newport—in mansions on rises back up from the water, with stables and cottages surrounding the main house, and around a bend in the road. The tombstones are partially concealed by weeds, and there's a cemetery for pets with their names fading into the stone.

It is Hammersmith Farm, owned by Mr. and Mrs. Hugh Auchincloss, and for two days the movie company will do scenes along the water and on the dock where a few years earlier the *Honey Fitz*, carrying the President of the United States on a visit to his inlaws, docked. He represented power as does the encampment on the water's edge represents another kind of power now, which in its own way is as pervasive and commanding as the political power of a politician. It is a movie company involved in one of the biggest productions done on the East Coast in years, and behind every person there on the Farm are those who are powerful and those who want to be—investors and agents, executives and actors —and behind each of them are even more people who have or want power.

But power is for nothing when the weather is bad and beyond human control. There is now a sickly mist and haze, and from under the new Newport Bridge swiftly comes the indistinct outline of a ship. When it gets closer to the dock, it becomes a U.S. Navy destroyer heading towards the Atlantic, probably one of the last times it will take to these waters. The morning newspaper reports that some of the ships have already been reassigned from Newport to Norfolk and are in the process of moving out.

The sailors on the deck are watching a young man in a white summer suit steer his rowboat, propelled by an outboard motor, to the pebbled shoreline about a half mile away from the massive, brown shingled house standing there with a singular grandeur like a mansion lost in the English moors. He steps ashore and is greeted by a line of movie technicians. The bad weather has not prevented Clayton from rehearsing the scene, hoping the weather will clear by noon so the whole day will not be wasted.

On the other side of the dock, Robin Vidgeon, the first assistant cameraman, in a black rubber wet suit, wades into the chilly water to a platform where the camera rises several feet out of the water.

The scene is of Nick arriving for his first visit to the Buchanans. In the book he comes in mundane fashion, by car, and is greeted on the porch of the Georgian Colonial mansion by Tom. In the film Tom is introduced in a somewhat more spectacular fashion. The camera pans to a knoll to the right of the dock. The mowed field is empty, and then over the crest appears Tom on horseback with a group of riders who are playing polo.

Bruce Dern is no stranger to a horse. "I was the guy

who killed John Wayne in *Cowboys* and rode away like the fucking wind," he says, pausing for the effect of this cinematic crime to take hold. Then he proceeds to minimize it, and says with an impish smile, "the Japs got him once, too, I think in *The Sands of Iwo Jima*."

With some consternation, Dern gingerly mounts the horse. He has never ridden an English saddle before, and he looks for the horn up front.

The haze begins to lift at 11 A.M., revealing across the channel an outcrop of rocks that makes it look like the coast of Maine. On the hillside to Hammersmith Farm, where it has been freshly mowed in a wide swath for the movie trucks, the wealthy friends of the Auchinclosses have gathered to watch actors impersonate the rich; they are very attentive to the smallest details of film production, even moving back when they are told, as if they were professional actors responding to a cue.

Visiting the set is Mrs. Auchincloss's son. A personable bachelor, twenty-six-years-old James makes his home in Washington, D.C. when he is not pursuing photographic assignments across the country. Though he is very much interested in politics, his mother says she worries because he has not settled on a vocation. Today he is a photographer, a camera around his neck, and he snaps off pictures when there is any activity around the dock.

He sees the men in the water around the camera struggling with it, as if it had suddenly been given buoyancy and was about to float off. "The tides come in rather quickly around here," he notes.

For forty-five minutes Waterston has been in the boat circling the shore then steering towards it. Someone comments that Sam is getting more inscrutable as the film progresses. He is always formally correct, striving to be friendly and to be one of the boys; yet he remains rather aloof with the reticence that comes of insecure boys who are forced to go away to private school when they would rather spend their teenage years at home.

"He hasn't learned what role to play off the set," Dern says. "He has a 1950s attitude about being a Broadway actor, that it really makes any difference today. But look at Broadway today!"

"This picture has a cast of loners," Dern is told.

"Yeah, everyone in this picture goes his own way," Dern replies.

James calls attention to the flagpole next to the boat house. Because of the lack of any breeze, the flag is wrapped closely around it. "They're such sticklers on this picture! We had to find a flag with forty-eight stars, and now look at it. Who'll see it in the picture."

Dern mounts his horse, this time assertively without his hand automatically going for the saddle horn, and he gallops off with the other riders who are members of a polo club from Fairfield, Connecticut. They had played a match at a polo club outside Boston on Sunday and were induced to stay with their ponies a day in Newport to appear in this scene.

Mia and Andre arrive after lunch, and Clayton greets her with a kiss. She is very affectionate in public with her husband, holding his hand or impetuously kissing him on the cheek. Her actions are too spontaneous to have been entirely thought out in advance, and she gives them a youthful enthusiasm that is appealing.

She chats with her brother, John, who has changed jobs. He has left Bernie Styles as an assistant casting director, a victim of a personality clash with his boss, and has been put on as a production assistant, bringing the total to five.

The last scene of the afternoon is a long shot of Wilson, Myrtle's husband, walking along the beach carrying a brown paper bag. His wife has just been killed, struck by a car which he thinks was driven by Buchanan. When he sees the mansion in the distance, he leaves the beach and starts across the field toward it. Wilson will be played by Scott Wilson in England. Here an extra is used because his face will not be in the scene.

Nor is it Hammersmith Farm that will be seen in the movie as the Buchanan mansion; it is a huge false front, a piece of wood painted blue and white, propped up with supports behind it in the woods to the right of the Auchincloss house. In daylight it looks like a false front, but at dusk, in front of a grove of trees, it looks real.

As Wilson walks toward the mansion, the green light on the end of the dock behind the director and his crew, Daisy's light that Gatsby has seen for so long, blinks on and off.

The next morning the rain continues, causing momentary havoc with the schedule. When the weather breaks about noon, and some blue disrupts the oppressive gloom of the cloud covering, Mia and Lois, as Daisy and Jordan, get into a motorboat and are driven out into the channel where scenes of the two women will be shot with Jordan piloting the boat among other craft in the harbor.

It is a painful experience for Lois. She has learned to steer the boat at a relatively fast speed. In the scene at sea, however, she has to drive it in low speed, and she has difficulty keeping control of the wheel.

Back on land Lois rubs her backside. "I've blisters there from riding a horse yesterday."

For another scene, a long shot of people getting off boats and walking the length of the dock to cars waiting on the side of the boathouse, Clayton and his camera crew have gone to the balcony around the windmill house where he is living during his stay at Newport. It is a popular residence. It has a television set, and Haya Harareet, Clayton's companion of many years, has it tuned throughout the day to the Watergate hearings. Each revelation by John Dean as to President Nixon's alleged improprieties that border on the criminal is reported back to the set and is well received.

From the dock area Clayton and camera crew are miniature blurs. The director communicates with his extras at the end of the dock by walkie-talkie.

Bruce Dern has changed from riding habit to white flannels, blue blazer and striped tie. He squints towards the windmill house and says with mock outrage, "Someone want to tell me what the hell is going on in this

82

shot?" Nobody thinks he is very angry. After weeks of waiting he is pleased to be working at last.

"With that outfit, Bruce, you could play *Sabrina* in summer stock," someone says.

"If I don't get laid in this outfit, I never will," he snaps back, the quick smile making it all sound innocent.

"But your yachting hat is too big for you."

"You should see the hat I wore in *Silent Running*," he quips. (It was a space helmet.)

There is a discussion about the daily rushes being shown nightly in the production office on movieolas in the partitioned room where Tom Priestley and his two assistant editors work during the day. The film is developed in New York, taken there each night by a driver and returned the next day so that Clayton and his assistants can see what they have shot the previous day.

Actors respond to rushes with the bravado of children confronting the town bully, not sure whether to make friends or fight. On some films actors are automatically barred from the rushes. There are even actors who do not want to see them, afraid their conception of what they are doing will be destroyed by seeing their work in isolated bits and pieces.

Annabel, the script supervisor who sees rushes continuously, says Redford, particularly in the footage shot in Marble House, is "dazzling."

Someone asks Waterston, in an attempt to be friendly in a casual manner, how he thinks he is doing in the film.

Defensively, rather than with any intentional rudeness, he says, "I don't look at rushes," and then adds, "They say I'm doing well. That's what's important."

"They" are never identified, remaining anonymous, clutched for reassurance, a positive ally in moments of self-doubt.

June 27

"Get your ice cream here and see the stars!"

The barker is a young man in sleeveless undershirt and jeans, well-built, tough, sitting on a chair in the doorway of the food store, close enough to the entrance to see the filming across the street and just back enough from the overhang to be protected from the dense mist that gives everything in the light a watery sparkle. He is an employee of the business. It is late in the evening, and he would rather be elsewhere. But at his age all is fair in the general pursuit of girls, and he is in an envious position, inside the barricade that blocks off both ends of the street to visitors. He has a clear view of the movie-making and knows what he will tell the girls standing at either end of the street behind the policemen and the wooden horses—how close he was to the stars, how they really look off camera and what they say to each other.

The night is chilly, the weather unsuitable for ice cream. The caterers have set up food tables on the sidewalk next door, and hot meals will be served at midnight. He has nothing else to sell, and when there is human traffic in front of his store—prop men going to their vans, wardrobe people taking clothes from the dressing trailers—he says again, "Get your ice cream here and see the stars."

The only stars working this night in the rain are Mia and Redford. It is a flashback to Louisville, Kentucky. The year is 1917. Gatsby is stationed there. He has met and fallen in love with Daisy. Wearing his army uniform and hatless, Gatsby is walking her home from a dance. They stop on the sidewalk in front of a brilliantly lit house, kiss and begin to waltz. They wear the same clothes they had on in Marble House, the Army uniform and the white dress with pink flowers—here, where they first spoke of their fresh love, and in Marble House, where they try to reclaim the love years later. What remains the same for them are the clothes and the sentimental music of "What'll I Do" coming eerily from a tape machine as the two dance in the mist.

This flashback to Louisville is in the book. The reference to this earlier love affair cames from Jordan when she tells Nick about her friendship with Daisy in the South and the romance she had during the war with the young lieutenant, Jay Gatsby. The scene will certainly enhance the feeling in the film of doomed romanticism.

The movie company did not have to go far to locate a street to resemble Louisville in World War I. The town is Bristol, Rhode Island, an attractive seaport twenty minutes up the peninsula from Newport. The house looks as if it could have been used in *Meet Me in St. Louis,* that superb musical re-creation of another America.

It is an enormous three-story house shaped into a block with a columned front porch, oasis of gardens in the front yard and a black grill fence along the front of the sidewalk. The crew has lit it spectacularly; the house glows in light, an enormous birthday cake. It is owned by Jack Colt, son of actress Ethel Barrymore, and it is authentically American in design, an architectural spin-off of the colonial plantation, with the rooms off a center hallway that is dominated by a circular stairway and a grandfather clock. The furnishings in the rooms are austere in the fashion of an English manor house. There is an original Gilbert Stuart on the wall in the living room —the artist was born not too far from Bristol—of a nineteenth-century Colt ancestor. In a side porch there are three Rodin statues and a pool table. During a break in the shooting, Mia and Redford play pool—she with the eager finesse of the novice, he with the sureness of one familiar with pool halls in his youth.

In the street there is anxiety because of the weather. Clayton is particularly nervous. The mist alternates with a persistent drizzle, and there are unexpected visitors— friends of friends, each carrying a small camera—jockeying for position closer to the stars on the sidewalk. Others are hanging over fences, having bypassed the street blockades and made their way through the back lots of the stores. Clayton's hand brushes frequently at his long fringe of hair, and the smile is crooked, as if he is trying to bite his lip. He occasionally calls to a prop man and nods; that being instruction enough, the man returns to the director with cognac mixed with black coffee. Clayton's work clothes remain the same: faded blue jeans frayed at the bottom, a V-necked blue sweater over a white T-shirt and, when it rains, a blue nylon windbreaker.

A British journalist and her photographer are guests on the set, and they wish to be introduced to Clayton. It is obviously not a good time for such amenities, and this is proven a few minutes later when Clayton confronts Merrick by a trailer in front of the crew and shouts him down with threats of violence. The dispute is allegedly over something Merrick had said earlier in the cutting room.

The outburst is picked up by a pretty reporter from *Women's Wear Daily* who also notices the Bedouin knife Clayton wears tucked into his shoe top. She prints both in her paper—the dispute and the knife wearing.

Merrick said Clayton's outburst was a delayed reaction to a comment he had made earlier in the day at rushes. There had been concern that the bad weather at Hammersmith Farm might have ruined the footage shot there, and Merrick, a perfectionist when it comes to a production under his name, said if Clayton thought it was necessary he could reshoot the day even though it was a $50,000 shooting day. Clayton misunderstood and thought it was a criticism of the day's work.

As for the knife, Clayton later tells the *Women's Wear Daily* reporter, with what degree of tongue in cheek is not known, "I might have used it sometime, and I'm quite good at it. During the war I had to kill three people with my bare hands. I can be very fiery, very dangerous and cut people in pieces. I'm very tough."

This might be too dramatic, too self-consciously tough-guy to be totally plausible, but Clayton, who insists he dislikes publicity for himself, and will give interviews only when it is to benefit his performers or workers, knows how to give a good one when he has to.

Still, there is a violence within Clayton that is real. It is there in the nervous agitation that overcomes him even when he seems to be most relaxed: the flicking of his hair, the chain smoking and black coffee, the constant rearranging of his lips into a twisted smile. It is there in the broken windows and chairs. Often it is closely checked; usually he is kind, generous and courteous. But the threat of something darker, hidden, is always there, and it makes those who know him wary of this clash within him of the hostility and the generosity.

"I don't know why people think he's always so calm and collected," says an intimate after his outburst with Merrick. "Don't they see what's within him?"

It becomes impossible to delay the shooting. The company has permission to be in Bristol only that night, and when the drizzle becomes a fine mist Clayton calls for a take.

By the time Mia and Redford come out of the Colt house where they have dressing rooms the mist is more a steady drizzle.

"God, there goes my wig," Mia says.

The amateur photographers get closer. The off-duty police find teenage girls prowling the grounds of the Colt house. The roadblock check become's lackluster after midnight. Anyone can get on the set, but the rain has driven most of the spectators home. The banquet for the crew spread over three tables becomes soggier as the rain falls into the pans of chicken bubbling in a thin gravy.

Under a striped umbrella attached to her chair, Mia sits talking with the British woman journalist. She does not like to give interviews, believing she has been the victim of many when she was younger and very much a product of Hollywood's star-building process, coming off in them as an inarticulate flower child or a social-climbing actress. As she once said on the set rather haughtily about a Hollywood gossip columnist, "I don't need her anymore."

Mia is a contradiction. In this period of her life, the courtly manners she has adopted during her life in England are very pleasing. She seems agreeable to the demands of publicity as long as they are in the indefinite future. She balks only when the dates become specific, and this gives her the appearance of having an inner toughness. She says she has nothing to say, and this may come from a natural shyness and insecurity. Hollywood children are not known as sensational conversationalists. Yet when she engages in a private conversation, she may still be an actress giving a performance—few actors are ever really off—but she is extremely intelligent and witty, often with a refreshing earthiness.

She was at her best in her brief conversation with the British journalist. Having first said she is a bad interview, that she really doesn't like talking about Daisy, she proceeds to be quite articulate about her character, omitting only the professional details of how she goes about playing her part. In the driving rain, she astounds everyone by reciting the four lines of verse which Fitzgerald wrote for the title page of his novel and signed it Thomas Parke D'Invilliers, a character from his first novel, *This Side of Paradise.*

"Lover, gold-hatted, high-bouncing lover, I must have you!"

She finishes the poem with those words, smiles and expands her big blue eyes until they seem to encompass the world. Whatever has been said about her, and much has been unpleasant, she is what others have said and not quite believed—a star.

Chapter V

The Parties

David Merrick once told visitors on the set of his picture that *The Great Gatsby* had never really been done on film. He rendered this judgment while standing on the lawn of Rosecliff, the mansion beyond the dazzlingly lit fountain. On the steps of the terrace are hundreds of extras in fabulous clothes, many of them made for the film; actresses in jewels that elevate them for one night into being some of the richest women in Newport; and men in finely pressed tuxedos, posturing as if on diplomatic missions to exotic potentates. Over the throng on the wooden dance platform around the fountain comes the taped sound of the music of the 1920s. On cue some of the extras start a frantic Charleston.

In this panorama on the terrace, steps and lawn of Rosecliff, a detailed re-creation of a moment in history that helps explain how America arrived at the moral turmoil of the 1970s, Merrick is correct. *The Great Gatsby* has never been filmed before; the two other versions were done in cramped quarters of a studio and were not given the room to become bigger than life and history. It is not false modesty for Merrick to take pride in what has been assembled in Newport.

For those who read Fitzgerald casually, if at all, sentimentalists who see the book as nothing more than an account of the social activities of the rich in Eastern America for one summer in the early 1920s, the parties do have a significance greater than an evening's divertissement. They epitomize the age, showing the values people had of themselves and what their money could buy.

The parties were very important to Fitzgerald, in fiction and life. In a letter to Van Wyck Brooks, he wrote, "Well, don't you think, though, that the American millionaires must have had a certain amount of fun out of their money? . . . Think of being able to give a stupendous house party that would go on for days and days, with everything that anybody could want to drink and a medical staff in attendance and the biggest jazz orchestras in the city alternating night and day. I must confess that I get a big kick out of all the glittering expensive things."

The parties had to be lavish, each bigger than the previous one, the size rather than any individual component of them determining the worth. But the parties are different. The Buchanans's are anachronisms, gatherings of the old, established wealth, with faces long familiar at the right Wall Street law firms and Long Island yacht clubs. They are people with pasts. The Gatsby guests are the New People from obscure backgrounds, holding on to money made sometimes deviously in rum-running and stock-market manipulations, acquiring it without the moral restraints inhibiting the older rich, who had to live up to images made for them by the past. Gatsby's people had no guidelines other than those established by ambition and greed. Tom Buchanan and Jay Gatsby are American materialists. But Buchanan inherited his wealth and Gatsby had to make it on his own, and the parties they give reflect this difference.

Gatsby has no ground rules for his invitations. He has to improvise from his own limited background. He mixes up his guests. There are shady people and rich people and show people and commoners, and they all are under a compulsion to act a little bit crazier than had their parents, to enjoy the loosening of the Puritan moral bondage the country had been chained to up through World War I. They drink a bit more and have sex more casually, and they try to do these without being affected by guilt, a built-in condition in the American experience. They want desperately to proclaim their new freedom, and their parties are the vehicles for a moral catharsis. Parties. Every night. The dancing never stops. The music continues to dawn, when the guests stumble into the half-light, another night having passed without an accounting of what they are doing to their lives.

Gatsby's parties are more than visual spectacles; they are at the heart of the story told by Nick, who is the last of the Puritans. He is the one to make the judgment on what happens around him and to Jay Gatsby in one summer of the 1920s on Long Island.

June 28

It is the first party mentioned in the book, the one Nick, who has just moved out from the city, sees while sitting on the porch. He is watching the commotion of servants bringing food into the mansion, the musicians setting up their stands and the guests arriving. The camera on the lawn is Nick's viewpoint, and it sees the striped tents past the line of trees and the shadows of the guests inside them moving around tables of food. On the lawn, down from the platform where the band is, the guests are doing a Charleston, their feet kicking forward and backward to the fast beat of the music, strings of pearls flying away from the bare necks of the women, sweat forming on the brows of the men.

There are five hundred extras ready to be used each night in the party sequences, most of them residents within fifty miles of Newport. It is well not all are called tonight. The mist off the sea borders on a riveting drizzle, and the activities on the lawn of Rosecliff look as if painted in a hazy liquid light. The grass gets wet quickly, and the dancers have trouble keeping their balance. A few stumble, slipping to their stocking knees; others—the professional dancers brought in from New York—are more surefooted, and they do the Charleston as if they have learned it under the most adverse conditions.

There is a woman writer from a national magazine doing a feature story on Redford. She sits in the darkened living room of Nick's cottage talking to Bruce Dern. The time of work for him gets closer, and his daily visits to the set when he is not working are accepted as normal occurrences.

"It's the first time he's used a director outside his own circle of friends. It's also the first time he's had to play

91

someone other than Bob Redford. It's an important film in his career," Dern says.

The interviewer comments about Redford's competitiveness in sports. Dern replies, "The director George Roy Hill says Redford has a tremendous ego when it comes to sport. He doesn't like to lose."

Someone makes a reference to having seen Dern and Redford running together in what could have been a race on the roadway by the sea. "Did he beat you?" Dern is asked. "No," he smiles, shaking his head. "That's my sport."

Dern is the runner in the company, doing up to five miles daily and using any space available: roads, highschool athletic fields, parks. An injury forced him to give it up several years ago, but he has returned to it with a vengeance. His dedication would be punishment to almost anyone but a professional runner. But the process of aging does war with the best intentions to stay in shape, and the flesh is thick and loose around Dern's waist.

Soon the interview gets away from Redford and back to Dern, who is a fascinating subject. He brightens the conversation with funny one-liners, devastating gossipy insights into his co-workers and an eclectic—at times indiscriminate—mind that rummages over facts, distorting some, reporting others slightly unreliably, but always entertainingly. He can also be charmingly confused towards politics. His father was a law partner of Adlai Stevenson, whom Dern seems to admire; but he confesses the last presidential candidate he voted for was Goldwater and in the same sentence says he would have voted for Thomas Bradley, a black liberal, against Sam Yorty, a white conservative, for mayor of Los Angeles.

The fog continues to roll in and the 150 extras are probably having second thoughts about accepting an invitation to this party.

On the lawn of Nick's cottage behind the camera Lois Chiles sits, her beautiful face half-concealed under her floppy denim hat. She works tomorrow, really for the first time, the boat scene just a shot with no dialogue.

She talks conversantly about the many levels of her character in the film and says she hopes to do justice to Jordan.

Ramon Gow passes. His silver-blonde hair in the mist is curling at the ends in huge waves. "Any resemblance between Ramon and Marlene is purely contrived," he says. The laughter is programmed. By now everyone has heard his Marlene story about dying at sea.

The Dern interview continues. He has told her his great-uncle is Archibald MacLeish, the poet-writer, one of the last alive of those who made Paris their creative capital in the 1920s for varying lengths of time—MacLeish much shorter than Fitzgerald, who was there less than Hemingway.

(Later in the week another female reporter asking about Dern is told that MacLeish is either his grandfather or great-uncle. The person asked about Dern says he will speak with the actor to find out the relationship with MacLeish. "It's not important!" says the reporter, taking notes furiously.)

Dern tells the woman he comes from Winnetka, Illinois, a town of twelve thousand people famous for the number of actors born there, and he starts to rattle off the names: Charlton Heston, Richard Widmark, Hugh O'Brien, Ann-Margret, Ralph Bellamy, Rock Hudson. . . .

Then he says he has made twenty-eight films and can name them all. Someone dares him to do it. He begins before the darer finishes his sentence.

Hush, Hush Sweet Charlotte—I have my head and hands cut off in that one—and *Marnie*,—Tippi Hedren beats me to death with a poker—and *Wild Angels, The Trip, Will Penny, War Wagon, Waterhole No. 3, St. Valentine's Day Massacre*,—I have a club foot and glasses, and two pictures with Jack Nicholson,—*Rebel Rousers* and *Psyche Out*,—and *Castle Keep*,—I get blown up— and *They Shoot Horses, Don't They?* and *Number One*, —I'm Heston's buddy who tells him he should retire as quarterback. . . .

"And *Thumb Tripping, The Incredible Two-Headed*

Transplant, The King of Marvin Gardens, also with Nicholson, *Support Your Local Sheriff, Hang 'em High, Bloody Mama, Silent Running, Cowboys.* I even did one with Sam Waterston for a week. It was an adaptation of the novel, *The Moviegoer.* We were down in New Orleans in pre-production, and I'd rented a basement apartment when the project fell through. . . . And *Drive, He Said.*"

This picture won him the award as best supporting actor by the National Film Society for his performance as the basketball coach.

"That award pleased my mother," Dern says. "She thought the President of the United States and the Vice President had voted for me."

At 1:15 A.M., the party is over and the last dancer has slipped on the wet grass. The camera is turned on Sam Waterston for a close-up of Nick watching the party.

In another part of town, through the fog obliterating the Newport Bridge, comes a chartered bus from New York bringing some fifteen actors, so-called speaking extras for the party sequences. Among them is Apollonia Van Ravestein, the current publicity queen of fashion models, and Regina Baff, an off-beat young actress with a mass of red hair and a face that in repose seems always about to disintegrate into a cascade of tears.

She has a cold, her nose is red and her body aches. The ride has been uncomfortable and the bus was several hours late in picking up the extras at the Gulf and Western building in New York. On arrival in Newport, she thought she would be staying at the Viking Inn with the rest of the crew, but the bus took a left turn off the Newport Bridge and went up the fog-shrouded road to the Ramada Inn, a good half hour's drive from Newport. There are a number of roads surrounding the inn and a tying-up of traffic loops; getting through them is like descending a sterile maze of concrete. Once inside the lobby, wandering around the luggage, she asks herself why she is there and then remembers it is one of the most important films of the year, as she has been told repeatedly.

June 29

The nerve center of the film remains the production office across the street from Rosecliff and the human lightning rods attracting the innumerable, moment-to-moment crises. In the outer office are Norman Cohen, production manager; Mrs. Julia Lisberger, production office coordinator; and Mrs. Doreen Kranz. In the inner office, usually alone and on the telephone, is Hank Moonjean.

It is a particularly busy afternoon, the last hours before the first really big party sequence. As the calls come through, the row of buttons on the telephone board is an unbroken line of lights, and the voices spoken into receivers are a jumble of garbled sentences, disrupted thoughts, fragments of decisions. It goes on, the unbroken clatter of voices, a gauge of the lunacy snapping at attempts to give order to the production as the clock hand moves to the time when 450 extras descend on Rosecliff.

DOREEN: (Serenely) She can't catch the monkey. But the animal is definitely needed in tonight's shooting. (Voice rising) Mrs. D———. Is that you? What is the address? (Louder) Where are you now? (Desperately) The monkey's where? Loose in the basement! You want someone to help try to catch it!

NORMAN: (Picking up phone) O.K., Julia. Get me TVE. (She dials)

DOREEN: (To woman with monkey) Somebody will go down to meet you in wardrobe. You can be assured of it.

JULIA: (To Doreen, holding hand over receiver) Does she know she's to go to wardrobe first and then get her monkey? (Removes hand from receiver) O.K. I'm holding.

HANK: (Enters and crosses to his office) (Ruefully) What are you making so much noise for?

NORMAN: (Into phone) Now you come on the night shift. The day shift is nearly over.

(Across the road, behind Rosecliff, the grips, working from three in the morning, have changed the tents from yellow to red stripes. The fake flowers around the fountain have also been changed from red to yellow. It was a simple process. Red colored paper had been wrapped around the yellow plastic petals.)

DOREEN: That's right, 846-83 . . .

HANK: (Enters office) . . . the noise!

NORMAN: . . . the night shift!

JULIA: Bobby. Hold on a moment. (Holds receiver with hand over mouthpiece) Norman. (Nods)

NORMAN: Bobby, can you talk up? We have a bad connection.

(A person from wardrobe wanders through muttering to himself, "Pants torn, too tight, wrong size. . . .")

JULIA: (Hand again over receiver, to Norman) Mrs. —— is on the line.

NORMAN: Why didn't he send up the mechanic? (He swings in his chair and faces the open window.) Call him! See what the hell it was. (Pretty girl passes window. Norman stares.)

JULIA: I'll tell . . .

DOREEN: I'll tell . . .

NORMAN: Shit! Don't let that happen again. (Slams down phone)

DOREEN: (To Norman) He's on another line.

NORMAN: (Again on phone) . . . otherwise call Robin . . .

JULIA: I told him what our problem was . . .

NORMAN: That's not working out. We'll be up the creek.

JULIA: . . . I'm sorry. . . .

DOREEN: Please . . .

NORMAN: I don't know if it is going to rain.

(An extra wanders into the office.)

EXTRA: Where is my per diem?

NORMAN:	(Snarling) Room four!
	(Extra starts to walk into Hank's office)
NORMAN:	(Shouting) No! Not there! (Points to outer offices) Out there!
DOREEN:	The horses should have gone to Connecticut. I think they came from a club in Fairfield.
JULIA:	(To Norman) It's Dick on one.
DOREEN:	The monkey.
JULIA:	Huh. The monkey!
DOREEN:	(Meekly) It's still the monkey!
NORMAN:	Where is it?
DOREEN:	It crawled into a pipe in the basement.
NORMAN:	Can we get it?
	(Doreen shrugs)
JULIA:	(Disbelieving, repeating) The monkey . . .
NORMAN:	What's the weather report?
JULIA:	Rain probable . . .
NORMAN:	What else is new?
DOREEN:	(On phone) Now, Mrs. D———, about the monkey!

In a rare moment of serenity, Cohen talks about the production with which he has been involved since April. He is a man in his early thirties, tough and bright, somewhat taciturn on first meeting, which is the kind of abrasivenesss associated with New Yorkers on the defensive. It is a practical front only. Underneath he is a very entertaining person, capable of a humorous detachment from the madness about him. He is also capable with a dollar and came to the attention of the production as having made impressive financial savings on his last picture.

He was among the first of the small band to arrive in Newport with the job of assembling the production within six weeks. The first problem was logistical, how to house the large crew within a reasonable distance of their work. For a town which wants to become a major resort, Newport has inadequate housing for tourists. A deal was made with the Viking, originally for some 83 crew members. The number was soon expanded to 150, rising at one point close to 200. The company eventually had to take over the whole motor lodge, including the new wing of the hotel, for the working crew. The people associated with the fringe of the production, transients from publicity and the press, were given rooms in the non-airconditioned old hotel.

For the first month, the production offices were in the Viking, and then in May they were moved to Sherwood, which was rented for $800 a month, a considerable saving from the $5000-a-month asked-for space in the building next to Sherwood.

Next came the construction work: building Nick's cottage, renovating the dock at Hammersmith Farm, changing some of the ballroom at Rosecliff, putting up the facade along the sea wall and the dance floor around the fountain at the mansion. Then the old cars had to be lined up. Ads had been running in New England newspapers since January. The company had available more than 100 cars, most of them kept in a seventy-five-mile radius of Newport and rentable to the company for $1, the prestige of having these antiques in the film being more than enough payment for the car owners.

"By the end of the film these cars will triple in value," Cohen says.

Extras had to be found. "Early on we had contacted the War College at Newport about getting us some men for the picture, and possibly their wives. They forgot to tell us the War College was out in June, and then we found the Navy wives would only work for one night. They weren't interested in any long runs."

Some decisions had to be made on the spot without consultation with Clayton who was in New York casting the leads. An important one was the precise location of Nick's cottage in relation to Rosecliff.

Money continued to be spent. Tents were rented for $15,000. Party tables had to be decorated. Some things were bought—dishes and glasses, which extras started to make off with the first night—and other things, notably the silver, was rented. The tables required flowers. Some were artificial; others would be fresh daily. There was also the food. At first it was going to be flown in from California. But a deal was made with a local caterer who would provide food for both the crew and the party tables. "It was a package deal," Cohen says. "We only paid for the crew's food. The stuff on the party tables is free."

In the actual filming, the biggest job, Cohen says, is the lighting. "We're using twelve arc lights on this film when you'd normally use four. We need the lights for both inside and outside Rosecliff because there's so much area being covered by the camera in the party sequences."

But always, it comes back to the unions. "If the unions didn't consider us a runaway production, it would have been a lot cheaper. Look, on every film deals are made with the unions. This is the first picture I've seen played by the book."

The company was involved with thirteen unions: electricians, grips, props, makeup, wardrobe, musicians, teamsters, art designers, director, script girl and cameramen. Not only was a strike a real possibility in the dispute with Local 644 over the British camera crew, but there was also a threat by the Boston teamsters to take over the production. It was resolved in favor of the New York and Providence teamster unions.

And when the crew works through the time set for a meal, there are penalties, and the budget provides $50,000 for meal penalties, according to Cohen.

Any labor problems that could shut down the production would be a financial disaster. The estimated daily cost for a day's shooting in Newport is $53,000 and $100,000 for a night's shooting.

"I was hired to make the production run smoothly here," Cohen says, "but we've had no concessions from the unions. They were laying for a runaway production."

At dusk, Salve Regina resembles the orchestra pit of a big Broadway musical before the overture. Everyone has his assignment and knows what to do when the conductor taps his baton. But now it is all commotion with people aimlessly shuffling about trying to cope with the jitters that come before the actual performance.

The female extras are in varying stages of dress and are going from makeup and hairdresser to wardrobe—half of a bosom is bared here, smooth skinned legs are showing below a short silk slip there—shuttled by assistant directors and production assistants. They have been met at the main door by Bernie Styles and his assistant, Joan Walker, who sit at the side door holding back the hordes until the dressing area in the second floor is cleared and another group can be sent up to be processed. When the women are de-bra'd and girdled, and covered with feathers, junk jewelry, hair bands, beaded dresses and pointed shoes, they are joined with the formally dressed men and sent to an auditorium where they sit patiently facing a blank blackboard, waiting to be told what to do.

Communications are maintained with the production office a half mile away by walkie-talkie, and the looks on the faces of the production assistants show how commands are getting lost in the static.

"Take them out of here," says an enraged assistant director when he finds some of the nonprofessional extras have wandered into a room assigned to the speaking extras from New York.

But everyone pitches in to prepare for the party. The work force of wardrobe and makeup personnel has been doubled for the party sequences. Redford's wardrobe man, Bernie Pollack, pitches in as does the star's makeup man, Gary Liddiard. Eyes are darkened, curls are rewound around the handles of combs, powder is applied to the valleys of flesh running into the low-cut fronts of dresses. The men have their hair clipped on the back of their necks so the skin shows; the women roll up seamed stockings. At a table by herself, Apollonia Van Ravestein applies makeup to a skin darkened and with the quality of rubber. She wears a panel dressing gown, and when it falls away from her spread legs it is obvious she will not have on underwear for the party.

100

Down the corridor in a dazed condition, her eyes watery and with a glazed look, her nose powdered but still showing the redness of her cold, comes Regina Baff, the most incongruous of the party-goers. Her pale green beaded dress is ill-fitting, her tiara lopsided on top of her dark red hair which is wound in bunches on both sides of her head and projecting like the corners of a Tyrolean hat. Her stockings, knotted above her knees, hang in loose bunches down to her ankles. The women were supposed to have their hair cut short, but Regina, who is scheduled to go into rehearsal for a Broadway play next month, and must have long hair, has talked the hairdressers into giving her this bizarre styling which gives the illusion of her hair being short without having it cut.

"I feel like a beaded bag," she says as her tiara tips further.

As she descends the stairs to the auditorium, more extras in civilian clothes come up. The process of dressing the 450 extras goes on from 4:30 to 9:30 P.M., when it will be dark enough to start shooting. Now, an hour away from the moment when the clapboard is raised for the start of a take, something begins to happen to the extras. They have been transformed by the 1920s clothes. They no longer are the awkward men and women who were uncomfortable at their first audition, intimidated by the possibility of being in a movie. They are now people from an identifiable period in history. They have significance and they begin to handle their new status well, moving in a stately fashion, treating each other with noblesse oblige.

The person most responsible for this sartorial magic is Theoni Aldredge, a Greek-born costume designer who is best known as the woman who has dressed Joseph Papp's shows for the past fourteen years.

The search for a costume designer was almost as frantic as finding a Daisy after Ali MacGraw departed. After several had been announced, one even getting into print as the costume designer in hopes of making the selection inevitable, Theoni, who had a brief meeting with Clayton in New York, was chosen in March, 1973. She was given ten days to design the clothes for the leads.

She read the book and script, and talked with the stars. "The book inspired me in my designs, but more importantly, it was how the director saw his people clothed. Jack has such a feeling for his characters it made my job much easier. It was love at first sight with Jack."

First came the clothes for Gatsby. "Who is he? In the book there are so many stories about how he makes his money. He is a mystery man. I met Redford and saw in him a moody, brooding quality. He is so good for Gatsby, who I see as basically an unhappy man, trying desperately to fall into the category of what he thinks is society at that time. That's why he has a pink suit. But it's not quite right. Some say Gatsby is defying society, that he's a rebel. But even if he were, he wouldn't go out in a pink suit.

"I would have liked to have the men's clothes made by a custom shop, but I couldn't afford it with our budget. Instead, I went to a manufacturer." These clothes were executed by Ralph Lauren under the Polo trademark.

She disagreed on one point about Redford's appearance. She was against having his hair dyed. "It makes Gatsby look too hard, I thought."

Of the other male characters, she saw Nick Carraway as an intellectual. "He doesn't have all that much money, so he has fewer clothes and they are a bit more casual. He was the easiest of the men to do. Tom Buchanan is the most meticulous dresser. I have Bruce wear an elasticized modified corset to keep him erect. The clothes he wears don't look good if he slouches."

As for Daisy, she said, "Before I met Mia I didn't think she was right for the part. Then I saw her. The star quality was there, what with those big beautiful eyes. I knew she was right. I asked her one question, her favorite color, and she answered quickly, rainbow. I made her clothes delicate, very pastel and light. I saw her with lots of fabric, and fluttery in it. Her clothes should breathe as if shaken by a wind machine.

"When I was able I followed the descriptions in the book. When she meets Gatsby for the first time in many years it says she wore a pale lavender dress. It's my favorite color and probably my favorite dress in the film. She also wears a blue and white suit, the colors of the Greek flag, and being Greek I'm very partial to blue and white. So is Jack.

"Her ball gown is silk chiffon, all hand-embroidered. It's so light you can hold it in your hand.

"I also gave her big enormous hats of transparent material so the camera could shoot down through it to get to her eyes.

"Jordan is more sophisticated, a strong-willed woman. If there had been a Women's Liberation Movement then, she'd have been in it. Her clothes are more geometric than Daisy's, with stronger colors.

"Myrtle is someone very pathetic and sad. I never saw her as a tart, and she didn't dress as one. Her clothes are more showy, louder than the others, and she does have bad taste. Tom gives her money, and she goes out and buys the wrong things. She is no whore, though. She doesn't sleep with every man. She really loves Tom. He's the only man she's been with besides her husband."

Theoni's invaluable guides during this intense period of designing the clothes for the entire production, a total of six weeks, were the twenty volumes of old magazines and books on period clothes from the public library. "I was locked up in a room with my two assistants, and for three days we did nothing but turn pages.

"The clothes had to be very free. It was a time when everyone thought they were free and they went crazy. It was a time of insanity, and the clothes had to reflect this state of mind.

"Will these clothes come back? Who knows? I doubt it, though. The real good ones are hard to reproduce. The beads are very expensive."

When she was finished with the leads, she set out on a frantic commutation schedule from London to New York to Los Angeles to round up existing twenties clothes in costume shops. Some had to be made, and she gave this job to a New York friend, Barbara Matera, who had done a number of shows for Hal Prince. Many other dresses were rented, then fitted, trimmed and dyed.

Shoes had to be bought, 2,500 pairs of them, and there had to be silk stockings with seams, which she found by the boxes at Paramount in Los Angeles. Junk jewelry had to be bought to make the female extras look properly bedazzled.

Once the clothes and jewelry were assembled in Newport, and the extras chosen, they had to be fitted and alterations done on the clothes. This monumental task went to Marilyn Putnam, a veteran of many East Coast movies; George Newman; and the two Britishers, Ray Beck and Erica Eames. All totaled, Theoni had four women and three men to dress the extras for the party sequences.

"For what will show on the screen we didn't spend that much in wardrobe, about a quarter of a million dollars."

It was all for this moment at Rosecliff, the beginning of Gatsby's fabled parties. The buses arrive from Salve Regina, the extras begin filling up the steps and lawn behind Rosecliff, the lights come up and the fountain begins erupting a steady stream skyward.

"This is what a six-million-dollar picture looks like," says Bruce Dern, standing on the terrace now crowded with tables covered with linen, silver and wine glasses.

From inside the ballroom, stepping over light cables, comes a mystified Reggie Baff, looking very much like a slightly tipsy housewife trying to make it back to Scarsdale after a lunch in town with the girls.

"So I'm mingling at a party," she says in her best Bronx accent, her tiara more crooked than ever.

Around the spraying fountain, the dancers get into position. Gone is the gangly awkwardness of the amateurs; they blend in well now with the professional dancers from New York.

The orchestra is in white at the furthest end of the dance floor. On closer inspection one notices the piano

104

has a fake keyboard and some of the instruments are missing functioning parts. The music for the dancers will come from a tape, with the soundtrack dubbed in later.

At 10:25 P.M., David Tringham positions himself on top of the steps next to Clayton and the camera, and calls into a megaphone, "Welcome and have a nice party. Glad to see you all could make it. We're not usually quite so hurried, but we are expecting bad weather. Film-making is like ordinary life. It's very easy. We want you to have the maximum of relaxation. You know most of the people here, so say hello to each other with a lot of enthusiasm."

It's not quite a correct observation. Not only has distance made many of these people strangers to each other —they do come from a wide radius—but so has money. A few of the extras, many less than the publicity made it seem, are from Newport's wealthy summer colony, doing it for amusement to enliven cocktail-party conversation, and they would hardly be in the position to know the tradesmen and shop girls. The commoners remain anonymous. The rich are swiftly spotted and identified.

"There's Wiley Buchanan, chief of protocol for President Eisenhower, and his wife. She's a Dow of Dow Chemical."

(Buchanan was later quoted in the press: "They asked me my Social Security number, and I've never known it. I guess I'll get a paycheck if they find out what my number is.")

"There's Oatsie (Mrs. Robert) Charles!"

(She worked only one night as an extra and later said: "We were paid $1.65 an hour, and I'll probably have to pay a surgeon God-knows-what to repair my legs. We worked until 5:45 A.M., and I'd do it again if I could stand up.")

"There's Mrs. T. Oakley Rhinelander."

(She lasted two nights as an extra. "No more, thank you," she said. "I don't know whether it's the feet or the back that gets you, but it's one of them.")

On the dance floor Tony Stevens does limbering exercises, stretching and knee bends.

The young woman has found her monkey. It is perched on her shoulder as she is led to her partner near the orchestra.

At 10:40 P.M., Clayton, in a mild display of annoyance, says, "O.K. Come on," and claps his hands. Nothing happens. More time passes between Clayton saying "let's go" and the take beginning.

"What are they doing?" someone asks.

"Going into overtime," a cynic answers.

Clayton decides not to have a rehearsal of the dancers around the fountain. The forecast is for more bad weather.

"Shoot it," he says.

The taped music begins, but the dancers don't move. They have no idea what is going on. Tringham now has a whistle and he blows it. The mob comes to attention.

"Start the tape," Clayton says.

Nothing happens.

"Put it on playback so I can hear the music," Clayton says, seething.

"That's known as controlled emotion," the cynic observes.

"What is happening?" Tringham says, trying to approximate with the sound of his voice the anger of his boss.

"I'm testing it," says someone from the soundboard. "I'm checking it out."

Finally the music starts and the dancers begin moving in circles, doing a two-step. The monkey remains motionless as the woman sways with her partner. He eyes the animal with dread. The monkey does not blink.

Redford arrives with his family. "Do you like my party?" he smiles to the grips.

David Merrick stands quietly by himself, wearing a suit and tie which immediately separates him from all the others behind the camera, who are in beat-up jeans and sweatshirts.

11:10 P.M. Another take. "Young man, you there," Tringham says, pointing to the dancers, "you were not listening. And that take was not good."

106

A chilly breeze comes off the sea, and the extras not in the scene huddle under blankets.

"The dancers are tending to bunch up too much at this end," Tringham says.

On the next take the dancers come unstrung and scatter around the fountain like pearls rolling away from a broken necklace.

Tony Stevens and his partner, Maryjane, are really attacking the two-step with boundless energy.

"Do you think this picture will bring back the old dances like the Charleston?" someone asks.

"It'll bring back Medicare," Bernie Styles answers.

When the dance sequence ends, Clayton goes right into a scene where Nick makes his way through the crowd by the food tent and goes up the steps to Jordan who is standing with friends on the edge of the terrace. It is Nick's first party at Gatsby's, and he does not know exactly why he has been invited, nor has he met the party-giver.

Lois is beautiful in a blue dress, languishing against the stone railing, holding a cigarette holder. She is wearing a sapphire bracelet, a diamond and sapphire ring, and pearls worth about $100,000. The guard stands just behind the camera; the outline of his pistol is visible under his sport shirt.

When the camera rolls, the extras respond with very stylized, fluttery body exaggerations: arms are locked and rigidly held; fingers clutch a cigarette holder or a glass with colored water or a soft drink; heads are unnaturally erect, as if suffering from sore necks; feet progress gingerly over unfamiliar terrain. It is as if they had been studying old magazines and are approximating what they think are riotous flappers.

The taped music is turned off and the two-step is pantomimed by the dancers while the camera continues to photograph them.

There is a stirring among the dancers near the woman with the monkey on her shoulder. A wardrobe girl dashes in that direction.

"Oh, my God!"

"What!"

"The monkey's shit on her shoulder!"

"Do we have another dress for her?"

"No."

"Oh, Christ."

"Get a wet towel."

"He couldn't. He wouldn't."

The monkey remains motionless, impassive on the shoulder while the dress is mopped by wardrobe.

The word gets around quickly.

"Shit on her!"

On the terrace, William Talbort of the Preservation Society surveys the spectacle on the lawn: the tents and lights, the dancers and the piles of food from lobster tree to trays of unplucked pheasants.

"Do you think this place will ever be the same?" he sighs.

"The day after we leave," he is told by a production worker who knows how ephemeral are the illusions of film.

June 30

The rain now is unrelenting, coming from the blue-gray darkness beyond the false arch with a fierce intensity. There is also a thickening fog, and lights played against it are held back and diffused into rainbow patterns. There are several dozen sightseers from town along the sea wall, some training cameras and binoculars on the backs of the tents and the empty bandstand where the torrential rain makes huge craters in the surface of the puddles. The guards at the false arch do not have to restrain the small crowd. Indifferent to the rain, they wait patiently for even the smallest glimpse of the stars, wherever they might be in the throng around the bandstand.

But now it is empty; the dancers and extras are seeking a haven in the food tents. The camera is covered with big pieces of plastic, and the crew stands inside the Rosecliff ballroom waiting for the rain to stop, anxiously looking to the sky for any signs of clearing much as do boys held inside by bad weather on a Saturday afternoon.

"We've got one little old lady who comes here every night and she sneaks off into those trees over there," a guard says. "She doesn't do any harm, so we let her sit there staring up at Rosecliff."

The rain lets up, and Clayton calls for the extras who are in the food tents. They are led to the set by production assistants over a grassless lane worn into the lawn. Any movement on it raises chunks of mud which are splattered against pants cuffs and silk stockings.

No one wants to cancel a night's shooting. The cost, estimated anywhere from $53,000 to $100,000, makes it almost prohibitive; besides, everyone is there, the extras are dressed and the banquet tables are set.

Clayton quickly places the extras around the pool. His crew follows his instructions. It is obvious the American crew idolizes this polite, withdrawn Britisher who gives them the sense he is concerned about their welfare and genuinely appreciates everything they do for him to help bring off a film everyone believes in. The crew does more than he asks of them, even to the point of some danger to their lives. The night scenes require a great deal of light—almost more than the generators can provide—and when more light is needed for a scene, though the downpour makes working with electrical outlets dangerous, the men go right on working with the wet lines and sockets. This loyalty to the director is striking since they don't really know him. He is a distant man, and it is not just from a reticence supposedly indigenous to the British. As are all well-mannered people, whether by instinct or training, Clayton knows the correct thing to do, and does it instinctively to make one believe a personal relationship does exist there. It is something else—something in his personality—that prevents him from giving more than he does, perhaps a natural shyness or an insecurity. With him, moments of intimacy have a habit of drifting off in half-finished sentences, with a haunted blankness coming to his eyes when his attention is diverted. In the energy he gives to his total involvement in the process, filmmaking seems to be his whole life, and the people who make them and those on the fringes of it are subordinate to it.

In an interview with *Women's Wear Daily*, Clayton said, "I'm only interested in my films. I don't talk to anyone about my films." Asked if this included Haya-Harareet, who received a co-writing credit on his last film, *Our Mother's House*, he said, "I am sure she may have some very constructive things to say, but when you get someone else involved, it's no longer yours. You see, I'm very selfish in my work and very unselfish outside of it. Right or wrong, you have to do what you want. It's much better to be wrong in one direction—your own.

"I don't make pictures very often because I get bored very often, and I can't make any film exactly like the last one. I've made four and one-fourth films and I'm not ashamed of any of them.

"I am only interested in the characters of people and in romance of some kind. Money margins don't make any difference. The actual filmmaking is exactly the same whether there are two people or five thousand people on the set.

"I had the good fortune to be brought up by women, and most of my total early contacts were with women. I have no sexual complexes, and I find women totally equal, both socially and intellectually. I generally prefer their company for just those reasons.

"Gatsby's greatest mistake was that he was a romantic, which is actually the totally correct thing to be in life."

Commenting that his hobby is raising racing pigeons, he said, "They're very interesting, especially if you imagine yourself as a pigeon who can fly five hundred miles away and yet always return home and nobody can explain it. Now that is ultimate romance."

Someone who says they know him quite well confesses that Clayton is a true loner with very few close friends. The only time his reserve seemed shattered was when his mother died several years ago, and for days he was distraught, almost inconsolable.

"She was an amazingly alive woman," the friend said. "She loved to bet on the horses. Jack loves the horses, too."

Clayton was now being overwhelmed by the problems posed by the rain. His nervous habit of twisting his lips became more pronounced, and he kept in his hand the paper cup of cognac from which he sipped infrequently.

Erica Eames, the wardrobe mistress, wanders through the extras inspecting the wet shoes. "I don't have any more shoes when these are gone," she says forlornly.

The extras are extremely indulgent of the time consumed in setting up a scene, even if it means getting wet. "I didn't realize how considerate and polite the British are," says a woman whose soggy feathers are sticking together in her hairband.

The rain prevents the scene around the fountain from being shot. Clayton has many of the extras returned by bus to Salve Regina to be fed and entertained by Mike Haley, the American second assistant director who takes them into the auditorium. When seated, he gives them a detailed, knowledgeable lesson on filmmaking. At the conclusion he asks for questions. The only ones are when they can see Robert Redford and Mia Farrow.

There are three food tents behind Nick's cottage, two for the extras and one for the crew and stars. The extras, including the rich, get box lunches of sandwiches and fruit; the crew and stars get hot meals with several choices of meat and vegetables. The discriminatory system works well until one night when they run out of box lunches and a portly gentleman makes his way to the crew's tent and refuses to budge from a narrow lane between the tables. Finally, Steve Felder, a production assistant, blocking the man's way from the food table, convinces him a truck is on the way with more box lunches.

The food tents are near the tank trap-shaped outdoor latrines. The humidity and closeness prevents the odors from rising. They remain close to the ground and tents, polluting the air through which the extras and crew make their way to their food.

Inside the crew tent, sections of boards have been laid

111

down in the two aisles among the tables, but there is no protection from the mud in front of the food tables. Someone has put down plastic garbage can lids for a foot path, but these soon sink into the mud, as do the chairs on the wet ground near the sides of the tent when someone sits on them.

Everyone is fairly depressed by the weather except Apollonia who becomes more frantic when she sees signs of anyone's spirit flagging. She hops from table to table, bending over someone's food, striking a flapper pose. Her feigned hilarity is bizarre under the circumstance. No one is about to revive the madcap twenties in the mud with thunder and lightning outside.

After one frightening clap, the lights go out in the food tents and along Bellevue Avenue. They gradually come back on over the next half hour.

It is after 1 A.M. and a decision has to be made whether to scrap the evening's shooting. But as it has done so often over the past few days, the rain slackens, and in the sky over the sea someone claims to have seen a star.

The extras are regrouped around the fountain, and then when everything is ready the rain comes back, harder than ever. Clayton will not give in to the elements. There is a madness in every creative person, according to some psychologists. The director will use the bad weather; he will not let it defeat him. There will be a party sequence disrupted by rain, and the extras can then race up the steps into the ballroom of Rosecliff to seek shelter. He works out the scene quickly with his assistants, Douglas Slocombe, Chic Waterson and David Tringham. It is agreed that Apollonia, who will have a dog on the end of a leash, will lead the charge into the ballroom.

The rain is heavier now than it has been all evening. The beads on many of the dresses are made of plastic substance, and when they get wet they expand—like spaghetti.

"My God, they look like snakes," Theoni says. She also notices the feathers on the fans are sticking. "They

112

look like tail feathers on a wet turkey." And the shoes split when wet, as do the dresses clinging to bodies when they are forced to yield.

Later, Theoni says, "Looking around that lawn and seeing it filled with beads and feathers and knowing I didn't have doubles on most of the dresses, and the shoes would have to be reordered, I knew I would have to learn how to live with it, this bad weather, or leave and never return."

Clayton takes Apollonia aside and carefully goes over with her the improvised scene. When he calls "Apollonia," she will come running into the ballroom, which will be the cue for the hundreds of extras to follow. The extras hope she learns the scene quickly. They are getting drenched.

"Now you understand," Clayton says.

She nods.

"The cue is when I call 'Apollonia,' " he says again.

She understands.

Clayton goes behind the camera which is inside the ballroom facing the downpour.

"O.K.," Clayton says, "Apollonia."

She sticks her head around the door and says, "Yes."

There is a collective groan from cast and extras.

There develops a rate of attrition among the extras. It becomes less glamorous being in a movie which requires standing in the rain all night. People discover relatives are coming into town, or they have to leave for the Fourth of July holiday. Sudden illnesses and car breakdowns occur. Before the party sequences are finished, more than seven thousand will have been seen for jobs as extras. About fifteen hundred will have been approved by Bernie Styles, and of these Clayton will take about six hundred.

After the first few nights of filming, the dropout rate was approximately fifty each of men and women. Especially hard hit were the men since it had been more difficult getting and fitting male extras.

Styles held periodic casting sessions at Salve Regina

throughout the shooting of the party sequences, which drank up extras like a man coming upon water after a month in the Sahara. These sessions lasted all day and went according to established procedure devised by Styles, who was an exotic endangered species to the Newporters—a fast-talking, funny character out of Damon Runyon.

Those hoping to be extras would line up outside Styles's laboratory-casting office, and every half hour he would call them in and give his standard speech, something of Gatsby and his penchant for throwing huge parties.

"There is such a thing as the Gatsby look. It's chic, swank, glamorous and elegant," he says.

Into his office have come rich and middle-class, servicemen and executives, housewives and debutantes, hoping to have the Gatsby look.

"Don't be discouraged if you get turned down. We may return and do the *Son of Gatsby*."

The laughs are made titters by nervousness.

"Now when I bring you in my office I'll have what I call a sight audition. That's all it takes. Remember there's nothing personal in being rejected."

In his office Styles has a bulletin board with the names of people seeking to be extras who should be hired because they are friends of friends. He had incurred the wrath of Redford for turning down a friend of his who had come down from Boston.

"How was I supposed to know who he was? He said Redford sent him, but no one told me he was coming. If any of the brass want friends in the picture they send me a note and I put it right up here."

One of the celebrities sent in for an extra's job was the daughter of U.S. Senator Claiborne Pell. Told she would have to get her hair cut, she turned down the job.

At this casting call, the first one through the door is a young black woman. Styles smiles at her and consults the application form she has handed him. He could tell her that blacks are not being used in the party sequences, but, after so many refusals because of race, it is doubtful a black would believe Jay Gatsby did not have blacks at his parties.

"I have to say no, darling," Styles says, the smile not leaving his face.

A young white girl enters. She starts to sit in the chair next to his desk. He says it is not necessary.

"I have to say no, sweetheart."

"I'm waiting for the *Son of Godfather*," she says. "That's my type."

A plump lady enters.

"Sorry, sweetheart."

She looks about to cry.

"Please."

"Sorry, sweetheart." The smile does not vanish.

Two women are selected, neither of them have particularly distinguished features of the so-called Gatsby look.

"It's something in the way they walk and look," Styles says after they leave. "Clayton basically goes for the plastic look."

One of the few male applicants is an officer from the naval base.

"Your waist size," Styles asks.

"Thirty-two."

Styles looks at the protrusion over the belt, and the soft flesh under the jaw.

"O.K. Go in the next room and have your picture taken." After he departs, Styles says incredulously, "Thirty-two!"

The last to enter is a young pregnant lady.

"I know, she says forlornly, already damning the man who put her in this condition and prevented her from becoming an extra.

"I'm sorry, sweetheart," Styles says, looking toward her swollen stomach. "If I take you, they'll say it happened at the party."

MEMO

To: Assistant Directors, Production Assistants, Casting
Read and weep—but it's necessary for two reasons:
1. Some of the food will not be edible because it will

be thawed each day and then refrozen each night. If people eat any of this food they will get sick.

2. If people start eating this food we will not have enough for the parties.

Norman Cohen

July 2

The extras do not have to be told. The food is already beginning to smell, the tons of it spread across long tables under four tents. Turkeys, hams, pyramids of roast beef and lamb, trays of unplucked pheasants, lobster trees, chickens, varieties of cold cuts, different cheeses and fruit, trays of cookies. To keep the food looking fresh on camera, it is coated by the prop department and then sprayed with Lysol to keep bugs away from the decomposing food. A woman extra stationed next to the tables complains of feeling sick.

Some 450 extras have been called (fewer than Friday night) to dress the party scene as indistinct but valuable figures on the dance floor, on the lawn and in the food tents. Rosecliff in mid-evening resembles an army encampment, with buses transporting the extras rumbling up to the mansion through the mist and extras disembarking in protective gear, led by the production assistants in single files through a passageway in the hedges to the tents where they wait to be called.

There is a whole different party going on in these tents, a cross-fertilization of moral and social lines which amuses the movie company to whom almost all games humans have devised in pursuit of pleasure through the body are familiar. The conversations have the brittle sophistication, the slightly false timing, of a drawing-room comedy being rewritten on the road prior to opening on Broadway.

Inside, the women in groups of twos and threes talk as they would at a party of intimates or in the powder rooms of their country clubs.

"There goes my first husband," says a woman as if she were speaking at a distance the length of a nose. "I would always find him upstairs with the maid."

116

Another woman gets slightly hysterical. She has discovered that her much younger lover, who she thought was home, is an extra and is across the lawn with his new young girl friend.

Other liaisons are forming among the extras with people from the company—mostly of the opposite sex, but a few with their own. Sex is almost as great a leveler to them as money, and when a company arrives to make a film about the rich in Newport it is catastrophic to some, creating confusion about which is more important. Sex and money are both visible on the grounds of Rosecliff now in this parade of well-turned-out men and women, if not beautiful and handsome at least interesting.

At the sea wall twenty-five people have placed themselves in an orderly row to watch the filming. One young man tries to make light of why he has come out on a bad, wet evening to watch a movie being made. "Why aren't they doing a blue movie?" he sneers, trying to sound indifferent, but around his neck is a camera hanging in anticipation of the moment a celebrity will come close to the wall so he can take the photograph that will make his miserable wait worthwhile.

The scene to be shot is of Nick and Jordan sitting at a table with the twin girls, Klipspringer and Miss Baedecker—who attends all of Gatsby's parties, usually drunk, and inevitably has someone dump water over her head. Nick has not yet met Gatsby, and the conversation at the table is about their host: who he is and what he might have done. Some say he is a spy. An impression is that he has killed somebody

Lois Chiles is at the end of the table next to Sam Waterston. She is cooly elegant, her smile obvious, somewhat aloof, her attitude almost condescending towards the people around the table. In the middle of the table is Regina Baff, who plays Miss Baedecker. She is already into character, half falling out of her chair, swaying, her tiara ajar on the pile of twisted, uncombed red hair. Her line is that she thinks Gatsby has killed a man. A few chairs away is Ed Herrmann, as Klipspringer, and around the table are Janet and Louise Arters, the twins. Watching them is like looking into two mirrors giving off one image. One of the twins brushes her sister's nose with powder and the other does the same to her. It is a hypnotizing performance.

No scene can be blocked out completely before it is actually set up in front of the camera, especially one in which the director has given the actors some leeway for improvising their lines. Clayton has put the camera on an L-shaped track at a right angle to the table, and as the guests talk, the camera tracks them on two sides of the table.

In the rehearsals Clayton keeps rearranging the guests at the table. He places Regina to the right of Herrmann so that when she half falls into his arms she will be seen in close-up. Clayton obviously sees something in her bit performance that he thinks deserves a better camera angle, and when she runs through her line about Gatsby killing a man, it is less what she says then how she looks and says it that makes Clayton laugh.

It takes Clayton a long time (almost forty-five minutes) to set up the scene, and while he works with his actors David Tringham lines up the extras on the steps and dance floor at the bottom, telling them how and where to move. There is a great deal of confusion about where to go, and extras still seek out the camera or gape when they pass Nick's table.

"If you can't get to the group to which you have been assigned," Tringham says, "take evasive action. We should have no jam-ups on the stairs."

When Clayton thinks everything is ready for a rehearsal, that he has everyone's attention, he hears the twins talking to each other.

"We haven't started the scene yet, darlings," Clayton says patiently. "Wait for me to say 'action.' "

While the scene takes place at the table, the dancers below must pantomime their dance without music. They quickly become sluggish in their movements.

"Don't let the dancers lose their vigor," Tringham calls down to them.

"And keep it quiet," he adds.

The feet of the dancers on the wooden boards sound like the heavy tread of those rushing up the aisle of a theater at intermission.

There is some urgency in getting the scene underway. The fog coming off the sea has formed a white wall across the end of the lawn.

"We'll be fog-bound in fifteen minutes," someone says to Bernie Styles.

"What do you mean fifteen minutes?" he answers. "I can't see the extras' feet now."

The extras on the steps are getting restless under the repeated directions. No one will say they are bored. It is a Hollywood movie!

Jay isn't going to be here tonight," one extra says, referring to Redford by his character's name.

"Who cares," her young friend replies.

Clayton calls for many takes, each one clicking off smoothly, a slight variation made in each to give him options in cutting and assembling the film.

"It takes about two and a half hours to get a scene that will last a half minute on the screen," someone says.

Clayton gets the scene completed before the midnight food break, and he says to the lopsided, departing figure of Regina Baff, "She's going to be a big star."

Regina walks through the glittering ballroom to the front driveway of Rosecliff, and only when she is there, away from the cast and the range of the camera, does she begin to sob, the mascara cutting black lines into her cheeks, the red curls falling in soggy twists. She really has had to act that night, getting into character the method way as soon as she arrived on the set, lurching instead of walking, setting her head at a crazy tilt, letting her pale green stockings sag towards her ankles to cover a terrifying hurt she has experienced that day.

Broadway may be finished, but what actress does not want to become a star there, to receive glowing notices and have them read to her at Sardi's, to see lines outside the theater's box office the next morning? Her chance was so close, she cries, a lead in a Broadway-bound play, *Veronica's Room*, by Ira Levin. But something has jeopardized this. She signed contracts to go into a midwest repertory company for a season. Her personal representative had assured her she could get out of the contract, and now it doesn't look as if she can, she says. There might be a union suit. They might force her to go to the repertory company. But why, she asks? They've already hired a replacement. It's not fair. She blames her personal representative for not having read the contract closely. What can she do? The sobs are heartfelt. No matter how self-centered the scene, how dramatized out of proportion, it is about something real, a career that is on the line and a young woman fighting to save it.

A friend assures her no one will force her to work where she doesn't want to. It's not the eighteenth century. Nothing reassures her, and it is difficult to see what is rain and what are tears on her cheeks.

She reminds one of how vulnerable those who make their living by playing roles are, by being children forever. They are what they are because of a need to act, to be someone other than themselves, often someone with whom they feel more comfortable. This makes them so open to hurt, to shattering experiences, to repeated crisis, always leading to the totally narcissistic moments of forcing people and events to focus on them.

She is more fragile than most. She is alone in Newport, stranded in a motel way outside of town. She is a young girl not pretty by conventional standards. Her nose is too prominent. Yet she has the power to transform herself believably through acting into another person; in *The Paper Chase*, it was into a wealthy, attractive gentile Boston heiress, and this ability to act is more important then her physical appearance. It takes her away from the Bronx, where she had gone to school to become a laboratory technician.

As an actress, Lois Chiles is also being subjected to an identity crisis. But she is a star in this film, and when she is upset, agents and a special friend come to Newport to reassure her she can act. What brought on this self-doubt is rumors. One of her co-stars supposedly said something to upset her. She is also having difficulty with one of the assistant directors, who has complained about her being curt and snobbish.

Blame is not easily apportioned on a set where egos crash and separate with the speed of comets passing in the sky. Lines of defense must be established and people assembled to protect and to flatter. For a while she lets herself become the domain of the homosexuals. They surround her and tell her things she wants to hear. One remembers a night when she is dressed up for a party sequence, radiantly beautiful, sitting on a sofa on the top floor of Rosecliff encircled by her gay friends, a terribly sad countenance on her face; and as they talked, (though not to her) saying clever, funny things, she appeared more alone than ever.

The problem is her lack of experience as an actress. This is only her third film and the first in which she has a substantial role. Though she protests her modeling career has coincided with her acting one, she is still better known as a fashion model.

Later on in the filming, when it became certain she would stay, she said, "It bothers me I'm the most inexperienced in the cast. It would be ideal if everyone pulled together in a scene. But with certain people in this picture you feel everyone is for himself. I guess it's one of the facts about moviemaking."

When she got the part, Lois says she "thought out, analyzed the character. But I didn't feel right about it. Suddenly I realized I was cluttering up my mind with a lot of unnecessary things. I understood I was dressed up to look like a twenties girl, but all this stuff of figuring out what they did in those days was not necessary. I knew I had to be myself in front of the camera. I watched the different actors in the picture and saw they were themselves. Acting was learning how to project certain sides of yourself before the camera.

"All of us are like the characters we play in the film.

121

The only difference between me and Jordan, though, is that I don't cheat like her. But I understand why she does it. She has the American drive to win. She wants to win the game. And she has this pressure to win not only in golf, but in life. All Americans have a bit of that in them."

Does Jordan love Nick?

"She is intrigued by Nick. She doesn't love him. He is more sensitive than most men she has known. He sees through the games they are playing. Jordan wishes she had a man look at her the way Gatsby does Daisy."

Asked if she saw any difference between the young and beautiful in the 1920s and the 1970s, she says, "It was a more structured society then. They couldn't experience the different types of people like we can today. But within their own social group the flappers were very free.

"I like the naiveté of the 1920s. It's very appealing today when the world's become so big. The 1920s were when America began having its own sense of style, the first time it broke away from Europe. We suddenly had our own writers, and when they lived in Paris, the Hemingways and Fitzgeralds, they had their own friendships. I would have liked the experience then of having a close-knit artistic community.

"After World War II, life became different. Before, people were more concerned about their fellow men. They were more courteous and kind to each other.

"But I guess Jordan is the kind of girl who would go right along with the world's changes."

From the perspective of being a lovely, sought-after model and actress, Lois is curiously detached about her natural endowments. "When I was growing up in Texas I never thought of myself as being beautiful. People started saying that about me the last few years. It just never occurred to me in Texas. Sure I had a lot of dates, and I was always more comfortable around men. But when I looked into the mirror I didn't say to myself: 'You're beautiful.' When they started saying it I was not comfortable having my exterior self separated from my interior self. But I learned feeling good about yourself can make you beautiful."

Having her face on national magazine covers and being associated for a time in New York with the jet set has not upset her, she claims. "Those men just wanted a pretty girl on their arms. They couldn't care if I were deaf and dumb.

"Now," she adds, "I have a very quiet life-style. I enjoy dining at friends' homes and having friends to mine. I see a lot of different people. I'm an insatiably curious girl who is intrigued by people. As did the young women of the 1920s, I also want to be free. I don't want to get stuck with any one group."

As for marriage, she says, "I'll eventually get married, but not in the near future. I don't think you become yourself, if ever, until you're thirty. I'll appreciate marriage then for what it is. I won't expect my husband to be a knight in shining armor.

"I prefer sensitive men, intelligent ones who are older. But it's hard to find older men who are free. They are a product of their generation, and there're not that many men who are free."

But now in the scene she is unhappy and frightened, as is Regina Baff; they are made sisters by being actresses, sharing the common hazards and anxieties of their craft. Sadly, they are also strangers to each other, on other sides of the table.

July 3

Clayton stages a fight in front of a food tent from which an overwhelming smell comes: not strong, but subtle, persistent, finally sickening. The food is really rotting. No amount of oil and Lysol can keep away the fact of its decomposition.

In this scene a heavy, bald-headed bully boy, drunk and angered by a hired comic who is telling stale jokes, goes over to his table and throws champagne in his face. The heavy-set man with the pink shaved crown is Arthur Haggarty, and the comic is Sammy Smith, who is properly impressed by the size of the production. "I haven't seen these many extras since de Mille," he says.

The scene ends with Gatsby's bodyguard, played by John Devlin, making his way through the crowd, taking the drunk by the shoulder and, though he is twice as big, turning him around and hitting him in the face. The guests at the surrounding tables flinch and duck in surprise.

Clayton carefully explains the scene, crouching in a fighter's stance, his arm bent, shielding his face. He shows Devlin how to fake the punch. The camera is behind Haggarty's head and when Clayton's fist speeds toward him, Haggarty's head snaps back from the impact of the faked contact.

The director is lean and in good physical shape. He could convincingly play the bodyguard. It is obvious he knew how to punch before this picture. There is too much expertise in its execution. Somewhere in his past, probably during the war, Clayton had to learn how to use his hands in self-defense, and it comes back to him now, much as driving does to one who has been away from the wheel of a car for years. Clayton's past, which is inaccessible to most, comes through in these suggestions, rather than in anything specific he says about his past. To his self-amusement, expressed with an inner laugh that his eye cannot conceal, Clayton often varies the facts of his past from interview to interview. It puts the questioner off-guard, less apt to ask things that might get closer to the truth. There is also the suspicion, however, that his past might not be quite as exciting as he would have it, and this may be his best laugh against those who would seek the truth.

After what Clayton has shown Devlin to do, he promptly smacks Haggarty in the face and knocks out a capped tooth. But troupers all, the scene continues with Haggarty occasionally turning his head and spitting blood.

Near morning, Clayton decides to have some of the extras jump into the pool and continue dancing in the water. It was not originally in the shooting script but is something improvised and inspired by the continued bad weather. Besides, what would a party be in the fiction of Fitzgerald without someone jumping into a fountain? Didn't the antics of Scott and Zelda at the Plaza Hotel lead them to jump into the fountain outside the front entrance? That act summed up the liberation of the 1920s, the fun to be free to do crazy things on the spur of the moment and let personal life-styles be the pop art of the time.

The mist and fog is ever-present, cutting to the bone swifter than a sudden downpour does because it is there seemingly without an end, coming off the sea, a deathly gray-white expanse beyond the false arch.

The nine couples who will go into the pool are excited by the prospects. This is what Fitzgerald is about, especially to those who have never read him—the freedom to throw off personal restraints imposed by an oppressive Puritanical culture.

The scene begins with a long-shot of the pool and the dancers doing the Charleston with Apollonia off by herself revealing yet another talent—juggling oranges. On cue from Clayton, those who will go into the pool run down the stairs and plunge into the water, and after the initial immersion to their knees, resume dancing.

Tony Stevens leads the charge. After working with his amateur dancers for several weeks he has discovered the best of them keep coming back each night while the bad ones have dropped out.

"The local kids are so eager to do good," Stevens says.

And now their big test. "Get in there and go crazy," he says to them.

Braced for frigid water, they are surprised that it is rather tepid.

The clothes stick to the body, and for a few seconds raising one's leg is like pulling a finger from sticky taffy. But motion makes it easier to do, and the more frantically they move, the more sense it makes. Soon the pool is a scene of churning bodies and water.

Another take is called. The dancers charge down the stairs. The impact of bodies entering the water sends geysers up to compete with the fountain's towering spray. The dancers are freer, used now to wet clothes clinging to their bodies.

This is the end of my work, Theoni Aldredge worries off camera, seeing her creations come apart in the pool: beads sinking quickly, feathers drifting off on the turbulent water. "I didn't design a wet look," she says, knowing she has no doubles in costumes except for those to be used near the end of the shooting in the Plaza Hotel sequence.

It will not be fun for her the next day. The dresses will have to be re-embroidered, the beads replaced and the shoes patched.

For the dancers it will be a day off because their clothes will never be dried out and repaired in time. And it is the Fourth of July, so now they stomp and shout, their inhibitions dissolving in the water, their feigned madness looking real.

July 4

At 11:30 P.M. the fog has made it impossible to see beyond the false arch, but the celebration begins with the playing of "God Save the Queen," followed by "the Star Spangled Banner," both recorded on tape. From the roof of Rosecliff the American flag is lowered.

"Three cheers for the British," an American yells. Most of the crew responds, though someone good-naturedly boos.

Redford has said he heard there is friction between the American and British crews. If anything, this interlude in the night's shooting shows how well they are getting on when it could have been so bad, what with the British camera crew doing the actual shooting of the film on American soil, and the American union constantly threatening to strike. There is no genuine cameraderie between the nationals. For the sake of the production there is something much better, a mutual respect of each other's skill. Though most go their own way on the one day off each week, they join as craftmen for their long hours together on the other six.

When the music goes into historical American rebel-rousing songs, fireworks begin exploding over the sea wall, almost indistinctly, losing the glowing sparkling colors in their ascent into the fog. The Americans have each chipped in five dollars to buy them, and the men have their wives and children on the set.

A startled, slightly bemused Britisher says, "Pray tell what are the Americans celebrating?"

Connie Brink, the American property master, says, "This is really a tribute to Jack Clayton. We think he's fantastic."

The wives stay on for a few hours to watch the post-midnight shooting. It is the scene which many think is the funniest in the film. It takes place at the end of the first party Nick has attended at Gatsby's and in dialogue and situation is quite similar to the scene in the book.

A car leaving the party crashes into a wall. The impact shears off a front wheel. Out of the car from the passenger side emerges Owl-Eyes, played by the distinguished actor, Tom Ewell, in what amounts to a bit part. Someone asks what has happened; he claims not to know.

The front door swings open, a hand crawls over the edge of the open window and from the driver's seat comes a man in a wet bathing suit wearing dancing shoes. He asks what's the matter. Did he run out of gas?

Ewell, who played with Marilyn Monroe in the film version of his 1950s comedy hit, *The Seven Year Itch*, has put on a great deal of weight but has not lost his comic timing. His scene goes well and professionally.

Vincent Schiavelli, who is the driver, is a striking visual comparison to Ewell: his body is very thin and his face is the same, stretched out and defined by its angles. Between takes he gets out of the car and does limbering exercises, touching his toes with his fingers. "It's cramped in the front seat," he says to the extras watching him.

Outside of Rosecliff, twenty-two old cars are lined up on the curved driveway behind the wrecked car. Their headlights, turned on, expose the mist as a blanket of fine drops floating slowly to the ground.

The drivers of these antique cars are the owners, and some of them, on cue, get out and go over to the wreck as do the extras leaving through the front door of Rosecliff. In the first few rehearsals they run over too quickly to the accident. David Tringham tells them to slow down.

The visual punch-line is Schiavelli pointing to the dashboard and saying the wheel came off. Each time he says it he gets a suppressed laugh from Clayton and the crew.

In the hour before the fireworks display, Karen Black, who plays Myrtle in the film, arrives at Providence airport. Though she is not scheduled to shoot any scenes until New York, she has come to Newport for wardrobe fittings and to rehearse with Bruce Dern.

In the daytime, Providence airport could be out of a 1940s war movies: sailors with duffle bags stand forlornly waiting for transportation to a new port, wives and sweethearts say goodbye, hasty beers are drunk at the bar, and there are cheers and farewells all around.

At night it is different. The coffee shop and newsstand are closed. The lights have been dimmed, and a janitor brushes a broom across the stone floor.

It is not an auspicious entrance for the movie star. Her luggage has been lost somewhere between Los Angeles and Newport, and while her driver, John Cramer, checks out the situation with the one ticket agent at the long line of empty booths, she stands in the center of the small terminal, humming a tune from an unrecognizable era.

Her reputation has preceded her to Newport. She is supposed to be a genuine kook, and her most recent publicity has enhanced this reputation. In a recent interview with a gossip columnist, she talked about her recent remarriage to actor Skip Burton. For the second ceremony (never making it clear why a second was necessary), she said they wore sheets with nothing underneath. It somehow didn't come off in print as either imaginative or cute.

The woman here in a khaki-colored safari suit, if not

SHOOTING GATSBY

Robert Redford as Gatsby, epitomizing the Jazz age as he stands before the symbol of his wealth, the yellow Rolls-Royce

Upper — Looking innocently beautiful, Mia Farrow portrays Daisy Buchanan, Gatsby's lost love

Upper right—Director Jack Clayton and Redford conferring on the interpretation of the Gatsby role
Lower right — Robert Redford as F. Scott Fitzgerald's tragic hero, "The Great Gatsby"

Upper left—Their rekindled romance now in full swing, Gatsby presents Daisy with a ring as a token of his love

Lower left—Scott Wilson, left, seen here with Lois Chiles, as Jordan Baker and Sam Waterston, as Nick Carraway

Upper—During a break in the shooting, Redford keeps track of the unfolding Watergate scandal

Upper—Extras wade out of Gatsby's fountain to prepare for the retake of a wild scene in which they end up dancing the Charleston in the water

Upper right—Redford and the crew take a break in the shooting to mark the actor's birthday. Helping him blow out the candles is Matthew Previn, one of Mia Farrow's twins.

Lower right—Daisy's husband, Tom Buchanan, and his mistress, Myrtle Wilson, are portrayed by Bruce Dern and Karen Black

Daisy and Tom Buchanan stand on the dock marked by the famous green light that is a major symbol in the book. The location is actually Hammersmith Farm in Newport where President John Kennedy's boat "The Honey Fitz" was often docked

exactly reticent, is somewhat more reserved than her publicity (almost shy) and better-looking than her photographs. Her eyes do tend to approach each other at the bridge of her nose, and her legs are perhaps too thick with muscles from her dance lessons as a child. It is her vitality that takes one's mind off these individual physical characteristics, making them unimportant against the overall appearance of a very handsome young woman.

In the car to Newport, she talks about the literature of John O'Hara, showing an erudition not usually revealed by her publicity. She also says she has not seen the 1949 version of *The Great Gatsby*.

"But I know I won't play Myrtle the way Shelley Winters did," she says.

She is overcome with a craving for food. Newport after 11 P.M. is hardly the place to find it. "I'm hungry for a hamburger," she says, being a waif in a foundling home asking for a second portion of dessert.

Don't you have to diet? she is asked.

"I'm always on a diet," she says.

Her pleading has its effect. Cramer says he knows where there is a hamburger stand that stays open to midnight. He finds it, and before anyone can help her out of the car she is inside the garishly lit stand, the floor decorated with grease-stained paper plates that overflow the trash can. She orders a hamburger and French fries. In the car she discards one half of the hamburger roll in a concession to her diet.

"I have to wash my hair," she says next.

But she doesn't have shampoo, and this is impossible to find since no store is open. She resigns herself to a good night's sleep instead of washing her hair.

Back at Rosecliff, Bruce Dern discusses a news item he has heard on radio about a pro football player reporting a bribe. It seems natural to be talking about corruption at a Gatsby party, where the pursuit of money is the sanctified quest of those who attend. If the pursuit is not for money, then it's what it can buy: these mansions, a place for a mistress in the city, the latest car, the best clothes. They are the revelers of their age, but how familiar they would be in contemporary America in different clothes and cars! Their drives would still be the same, the acquisition of wealth being an ultimate goal, but the means of getting it would be less important—if one can avoid jail. The football player and the man who allegedly offered him the bribe should read *The Great Gatsby* to understand each other and the society that has made them.

July 5

The Newport rich have adopted *The Great Gatsby*, making it this season's symbol of distinction, the place to visit—like the Mona Lisa on one's first trip to Paris.

They come nightly in their gowns and tuxedos from other parties, stopping off on the set on their way home. They seem enthralled by the panorama of lights and cables, sound equipment and extras being herded about. "They're incredible," someone exclaims. "They get excited watching a lightbulb being changed." At first they obey orders, staying behind the camera, nodding to each other, observing who has the position closer to the working stars. Then they creep forward, oblivious to the commands of the lowly production assistants. Only a few seem really interested in moviemaking. Among this small minority is Mrs. Janet Auchincloss. One night while the company was working at Hammersmith Farm she left the set early to see a bad old Redford movie on television, which even he would not have watched.

To the rich, the actors and top brass in the company became the sought-after guests at the first parties of the new social season. Status was immediately awarded a hostess who could come up with Mia Farrow or Robert Redford. The actors were reduced to objects moved across the social board, pretty vacant pawns talked *at* but not *to* at these parties; for few, if any, knew who the stars were before the company arrived in Newport or had seen any of their films.

One wealthy woman, spotting Mia doing a scene in a stunning gown of crystal and turquoise beads, commented that the woman in the hat was very attractive. Told it was Mia Farrow who plays Daisy, the woman could only nod incomprehensibly. Had the name of Mia Farrow ever turned up on a guest list before?

The rich of Newport responded to the actors differently than had New Englanders early in the twentieth century.

In a Providence newspaper interview, local ex-silent film actress Martha Nelson said, "After I finally left Providence in 1919 and remarried in Boston, my husband never allowed me to return to Providence. I wasn't to be associated with the time when I was a moving-picture actress, when people from surrounding towns used to drive out to watch us shoot every Saturday, curious to see what immoral actors were like . . . a time when we were freaks."

Not so now, and, incongruously, the hit of the social season is Bernie Styles. The more he used "sweetheart" and fired off his Broadway-tainted quips, the more he was loved. To everyone's amazement he received an invitation to Wiley Buchanan's party, which officially opened the social season. Bernie rose to the occasion. On meeting Doris Duke, he said, "Sweetheart, you're a pretty lady. If you'll cut your hair we might have a part for you in the picture."

There is really so little for the rich to do in their few months of summer in Newport but give and go to parties: a charity ball in one of the mansions to raise money for the Preservation Society to save other mansions; the parties before the month of classical music which replaced the much better-known and attended Jazz Festival, which moved out of town when drugs, riots and open, interracial sex took over.

Then there is Bailey's Beach, the socially authorized place to swim. Very unassuming from the road, with no more physical distinction than any other bath house along the East Coast, it contains more real wealth than almost any other place in America at this time of year.

"The thing you don't realize," Sam Waterston once

131

said, "is how much real money is left in Newport. Not Texas money, but real money."

The rich of Newport could read in their spare time, but they do not seem to, at least not Fitzgerald. Few of the visitors to the set know anything about the book, and repeatedly ask who the characters are and what happens to them.

Sam, who seems more at home with the wealthy than do the other actors, goes over to talk to a few before Clayton shoots a very difficult tracking shot of Daisy, Tom, Nick and Jordan getting out of their cars and walking through the ballroom of Rosecliff to the terrace.

"Who is that?"

"Sam Waterston."

"Who does he play?"

"Nick."

"Who's Nick?"

"Have your read the book?"

"No, but I should. Everyone is, you know."

It is dubious reportage.

There are many rehearsals before Clayton calls a take. The rich on the terrace are told to stay clear of the platform over which the camera tracks the actors walking through Rosecliff. Everyone seems to understand. Clayton nods. The camera is pulled parallel to Daisy and Tom.

On the terrace, one of the guests decides it is time to go home and she gets on the board and walks toward the camera. A tormented production assistant pulls her back.

On the steps where the extras wait for the camera another rich woman hands out American flag pins to be worn on collars.

There is another camera crew there to do a featurette of the movie to be shown on television just before the picture's release. Mia is reluctant to do it. She insists she is a bad interview although manages to be very intelligent in them. A list of questions is submitted to her. She agrees to answer some of them. When the camera rolls she responds flawlessly, but there is no real rapport between her and the interviewer, and she is aware of this. The next day she asks that it be killed and promises to do it over in London.

Redford refuses to be interviewed face-on for the featurette but agrees to be photographed in candid shots during the filming and will do a voice-over later. He is submitted a list of questions, none of which fits him exactly. Only when he puts them aside and talks on his own does it become apparent how definite are his views of Gatsby.

He suggests to the camera crew that he be photographed alone, in tuxedo, on the wide marble stairway of Rosecliff.

"I see him as a loner," Redford says. "All the people in the book think of Gatsby as being in the past, except possibly for Nick."

July 6

It is the third party in the book, the one which Daisy and Tom attend at Gatsby's. The filming goes on from dusk to dawn, through rain squalls and clearings when the stars are brighter for having been concealed so long behind the fog off the sea.

There is the music from another time and the hysterical chatter. The clothes, almost garish now, were made for people who desperately wanted to be different from those who went before them—as if clothes could change things, give one a different personality and social connection. There is a pattern to these parties now, as there must have been for Gatsby—a compulsiveness to lose oneself in the music and dancing through the night.

There are also the endless preparations—the extras by the hundreds to be transported from the girl's college to the tents, then the intricate lighting to be supervised by Slocombe. Before that, in the afternoon, the prop crew directed by Rudolf set up the parties on the lawn of Rosecliff—dressing the tables; putting out the coated, rotting food; and making sure the colors of the flowers around the pool correctly match the color of the tents.

Next there are the rehearsals: Clayton, soft-voiced, placing his actors around tables or in the crowds as if he were arranging beautifully clothed figures in a doll house. The director is a god in film. He is the last authority, the final arbiter, and the actors know this. They may try to show their independence by suggesting alternate ways of doing a scene, but eventually, before Clayton's impassively strong, almost laconic stare, there is the surrender and the scene goes on.

There are so many small details. Extras have to be told not to wear their eyeglasses because the contemporary frames were not around in the 1920s. Men must be reminded to take off their watches, that they are not right for the era of the film.

The dancers are positioned around the fountain; the couples stand erect, motionless, figures on Swiss clocks ready to move when turned on.

"The most difficult dance for these kids," Tony Stevens says, "is the fox-trot. It's foreign to our way of moving."

By saying this he establishes himself with his generation, and one is forced to remember he is not the gigolo dancer of the 1920s, moving through the crowd with the finesse of one who has had to pay for his lessons. On film, appearing in another time, he is ageless, belonging neither to then or now. But on the dance floor before the cameras roll he is young, twenty-five years old, from a small Missouri town on the Mississippi River thirty-two miles south of St. Louis. He is already a veteran of Broadway, arriving in New York when he was eighteen, working in the chorus of more flops than hits, dancing regularly on the Ed Sullivan show, getting his break as assistant to Peter Gennaro on the hit musical *Irene* and, after *The Great Gatsby*, his own musical on Broadway, *Rachel Lilly Rosenbloom and Don't You Ever Forget It.*

Life is one continuous prospect for him now, and he infects his dancers, amateur and professional, with his warm enthusiasm. When the music begins, he sets them in motion in front of the camera. "Get in there and go crazy, kids!" he says.

Many of the faces in the crowd are no longer unfamiliar. There is the rich lady from the mansion down the road with only the roof showing through the foliage and the high brick wall, and the elderly man who had a job in Washington, D.C., and the pretty middle-aged woman who lost her young lover to a girl more his own age.

There are also the ever-present twins, Janet and Louise Arters, their hair, except for a fringe of curls, covered by close-fitting yellow hats. Dark shawls cover their shoulders, and they move as one double image, disconcertingly, their motions synchronized—eyes blinking in unison, shoulders slumping together.

"I'm taller and one minute older," says Janet, the distinction not apparent as they lean against each other, weary travelers in a strange land.

This is their first feature film after having studied acting four years in New York, surviving on commercials and modeling. They know they are novices in movies.

The next scene is worked out. Daisy, gorgeously gowned, moves past the dancers, accompanied by Tom, Nick and Jordan. In the middle of the guests on the terrace is Gatsby, in tuxedo, his dark hair flattened and parted. He stands out from the other guests, isolated by the intensity of his concentration on the woman on the bottom of the steps, and when he moves toward her it is as if there are no others at the party. Attention is on the two lovers; she is not yet aware he is moving towards her. Is it because his face is familiar (Robert Redford, the superstar) or is it because he is Gatsby—and we know something of the shadowy past that has brought him to this mansion—that we follow with fascination and sympathy his progress toward disaster?

How much this man is like the heroes Fitzgerald needed and worshipped in his youth at Princeton, even carrying on this need beyond youth in his attachment to Ernest Hemingway, based in part on his belief that Hemingway had more manly virtues and was in better control of his personal life. How much also is this man like Gatsby, someone who with time's passage has a past becoming less defined, without the substantive events

135

that give depth to a man's life, leaving present drives and ambitions to tell what is not known of his past.

Redford has reached his present position in the movie industry as a superstar in spite of himself and a series of movies over the past decade which did not do sensational business at the box office. But when an actor is in demand, it makes no difference what the box-office grosses of his past films were or what his abilities as an actor are. It is the demand for his service that counts, and producers now believe it is essential to have Redford in their films.

If Redford's career can be said to have two distinct parts, the first is when he began working as an actor, almost by accident—and resisted—even taking off for Europe after several important films he had the lead in. The second part, the one to which he has now committed himself, is being a superstar and accepting this status (however grudgingly), doing things expected of him, surrounding himself with a carefully selected group of people to protect him from the public and to make key decisions for him—while rebelling constantly against what he considers unnecessary invasions of his privacy. Where once he was reticent about making films, he does them now one after the other as if he knows the life span of a superstar can be the run of one picture, the position under the assault from the fickleness of public and producers. In this turnover from reluctant actor to superstar, his ease with casual friendships is gone. "I react strongly to people trying to get too close to me," he said. More wary and suspicious of people's motives, overcritical when people do not live up to his expectations, he more often now seeks shelter within the circle of his entourage, his independence that was so resolutely maintained in the first part of his career less easy to sustain now. But he has retained his quick, nonintellectual intelligence and a sense of humor that comes out not so much in what he says—he is no master of the quick one-liner—but in how he says it. Redford is a superb story-teller and, when relaxed and not on guard, a wholly charming companion.

Redford is very much a man of a specific time in contemporary American history: Southern California in the 1950s. He is from the end of the James Dean era, when the inner-directed, troubled young men believed weak parents and not society or themselves were the cause of their troubles—a time just before the social activism of the young in the early 1960s.

He was born on August 18, 1937, in Santa Monica. His family was comfortable, if not particularly well off, his father, an accountant who moved frequently through the sprawl of the Los Angeles suburbs, finally settling in Van Nuys. He was an only child. When he was ten-years-old, his mother had twin girls who died at birth, and when Redford was about to enter college, she died suddenly of a brain hemorrhage.

"I was not a terrific son," he said in an old interview. "I shut them out. I had private feelings I'd never discuss with them."

In his adolescence he was very much the robust handsome teenager, excelling in sports and girls, stifling an interest in art because it was not expected of one in the new affluence of Southern California. Still in that time and place skill in surfing was more important than an ability to paint. There was also a rebelliousness, a running with a gang and engaging in acts of minor vandalism, a reaction to the boredom of growing up in the 1950s. There was a conventionality to his partial disengagement from his milieu: the young Werther at war with the philistines.

"I'd take a girl on a date to the beach and discuss the meaning of life, and the mist from the sea forming on her hair was more interesting than the boredom of my life," he said. "I was in rebellion against the boredom. I was more artistic than I knew, and it was not the time or the place to be an artist. I had an eye for what was going on around me. I was always sketching, and people remarked how well I'd draw likenesses. The things I did best were sketches of people with problems, whose faces showed character."

As did Fitzgerald, Redford had difficulty reconciling

the academic demands with a romantic artistic temperament. Fitzgerald, who discovered the escape value of liquor at college, always seemed to be flunking out of Princeton because of bad grades he could have raised if he bothered to do the work. Fitzgerald went to college to learn to be a writer; Redford went to college in Colorado to be an athlete.

"I boozed and partied and blew my baseball scholarship because I didn't show up for practice. The academic subjects which were supposed to help me to survive as a person fell by the wayside. The only subjects I was interested in were anthropology, geology and English literature."

Fitzgerald dropped out of college to enlist in the U.S. Army during World War I. Redford left to study art in Paris, a city Fitzgerald had made his own thirty years earlier.

"I felt I was drowning," Redford said. "I knew that anything I would learn from life had to come from the road."

Redford stayed abroad long enough to get some painting done and to have his own art show in Florence. He returned to New York in 1958 to continue studying art at the Pratt Institute. A teacher suggested he take acting lessons to help his visual eye in painting.

"I'd never been in a play in my life," he said. "Acting seemed ludicrous to me, but people kept telling me I could do it. I hated the Academy until one day in movement class, when we had to put choreography to a poem. I was damned if I was going to do it. But the teacher kept calling on me, and I finally got up without even thinking and went right into "The Raven," the only poem I knew by heart, and I just went wild. I used the entire room. I was all over it, doing flips and twists, running out into the hall, grabbing people out of their chairs. I got to the end and the teacher said, 'Fine, now do it again,' and I did it again! I was suddenly so free I could do anything."

His first Broadway role was a walk-on as a basketball

player in *Tall Story,* and then he did *Little Moon of Alban* and *Sunday in New York,* produced by David Merrick. He also married a girl from Utah, Lola Jean Van Wagenen, whom he claims was most instrumental in saving him as a person when he returned from Europe.

After four pictures in a row, *Situation Hopeless—But Not Serious, The Chase, This Property Is Comdemned* and *Inside Daisy Clover,* he became fed up with acting and took his wife and two children to Europe for six months, living most of the time in a stone house on the side of a mountain in Mijas on Spain's Costa Del Sol. On his return he went into Neil Simon's *Barefoot in the Park,* an enormous smash on Broadway, and then to Hollywood and another series of movies, among them the movie version of *Barefoot* and *Downhill Racer* before doing *Butch Cassidy and the Sundance Kid,* the one film more than any other that propelled him into being a superstar. Then came *The Candidate, Hot Rock, Jeremiah Johnson, The Way We Were* and *The Sting.*

This and the fact that he now makes his home in Utah where he has a ski resort are what is known about him publically. How much has his interpretation of these events been given color, perspective and significance by time? How many motivations added to give a life a definite point of view? When it is retold there is left an essential mystery at the core of the man, as there is in Gatsby, of walls going up to conceal; of images being created of him by others, as happens when the guests talk about Gatsby at his parties. It is the process of myth-making so necessary for heroes.

Ultimately, the mystery should be his, as should be his private life. Conversely, the image of him created by expensive publicists should be rejected or ignored as being wholly irrelevant. What matters is his performance on the screen, and what he does with his natural, superb talent. He has done more with his than most of his contemporaries. He is one of the few actors to systematically put together a body of performances to help reveal the variety of American experiences, both modern and historical: the self-centered jock in *Downhill Racer;* the rebellious Southern youth in *The Chase*; the alienated, idealistically soft politician in *The Candidate*; the anachronistic bank robber riding out the string in Bolivia in *Butch Cassidy and the Sundance Kid.* Redford is still relatively young. Bogart's great work came after he was forty. There will be more American males to play. He plans to do a film about businessmen, and after *The Great Gatsby* he will play a barnstorming pilot in a script by William Goldman, who wrote *Butch Cassidy.*

Some critics claim a certain monotony is now tainting his performances, that he is repeating the same safe role by transforming every one into the standard cool antihero. Basically, his screen performances remain more interesting than the body of criticism about them. One can understand a great deal more about American men in his work than in what his critics say about him.

In his search for heroes, Fitzgerald wrote in his notes for *The Last Tycoon*: "At certain moments one man appropriates to himself the total significance of a time and place." As he gets offered almost every major script around, and continues to define different types of American men in his screen performances, Redford is today's ultimate in screen heroes, and if he were alive today in Hollywood, Fitzgerald would probably be writing a script for him.

July 7

It is the end of another week of night shooting, and the crew is on edge, testy, taking out their bone tiredness on the invited guests who move in elegant dresses and tuxedos across the lawn, getting in the way of prop men and electricians. "These rich people are getting to be pains in the ass," someone says. It is of no moment to these people, many of whom come back night after night, as if the picture was their own blue-chip stock. "It's a real Hollywood picture," one exclaims. The starry-eyed are not only outside Schwab's Drug Store on Sunset Boulevard.

The tents are lit, the rotting food is put out, and the

mist is fine and penetrating off the sea. The camera will only take in a small section of the panorama of this scene: a tiny portion of the dance floor and below, at a table on the ground, some of Gatsby's guests, including Tom Buchanan, Jordan Baker and a very drunk Miss Baedecker.

It is Regina Baff's big scene, and she arrives at the table already into character. She looks as if she has been drinking all afternoon. Her stockings are knotted just above her knees, which would be a sign of promiscuity on any other flapper, but with her it is the slovenliness of a drunk. Her tiara sinks irregularly into her red curls, and her dress fits at peculiar angles, flopping over natural curves, giving her body a sexless shape.

Regina has survived the latest career crisis. The contract negotiations have been resolved. She can go into her Broadway play after *The Great Gatsby*. Her distraught emotional condition of only a few nights earlier is not even a painful memory; it is a routine condition brought on by the conflicts and traumas normal in the life of a rising young actress.

How easy it comes to those who act to make a performance of their own life.

The guests at the table, in their drunkenness and general dishevelment, make an incongruous tableau. Annabel says, "It's the Mad Hatter's tea party."

Miss Baedeker tries to slump against Tom's shoulder. He looks bemused in a bored manner. He has been to too many of these parties, and suffered the abuses of social inferiors. When the water is dumped over her head, she half stumbles, dripping, from her chair and lunges across the table for a bottle of liquor.

There are many rehearsals of the scene before the first take. One often reads in the fiction of moviemaking about the moment when someone's performance is so intriguing that people not in the scene stand by to watch. It happens during her performance. Crew and cast drift by and stay to watch her play a drunk. She pops her eyes and sways; she is practically asleep one moment and then is wildly alert to a bottle passing away from her. It is a

141

minute of sheer driving force, and her accolade is the gathering of professionals around the camera to watch her work.

Clayton does little to stem her performance. Once, he asks her to lunge more forceably against Bruce Dern. When the ice water is dumped on her the first time she screams and shudders. Clayton makes sure blankets and towels are wrapped around her between takes. He is extremely indulgent with her, waiting for her to grind into the part, like a corkscrew into a bottle of wine.

"What's the wait?" someone asks.

"We're waiting for Regina," he is answered. The actress, her eyes closed, beatific, is in deep thought before slumping against Dern.

"For what," says the disbeliever of her method school acting.

Extras pass the table during the scene. They are directed by David Tringham, and he notices they are not moving with animation. "We're getting a bit mechanical," he says to them without making it sound like a warning.

There is a bank of lights at the edge of the dance platform where the band usually sits, and one of these lights falls. A grip working under it looks up in time to catch the heavy light, but not before his forearm gets pinched. People around him think it is more serious and someone calls for the nurse. Clayton stops directing and goes to him immediately, pushing through the crowd to get to the injured man. He asks about his welfare and, seeing he is not seriously hurt, that the arm is not broken, has one of the prop men bring a shot of liquor to him.

It is this intuitive consideration that has made Clayton such a favorite with the crew.

July 9

MEMO

To: All Department Heads
From: Norman Cohen

For the remainder of this job you will assign one of your men to be responsible for locking up your equipment. Unfortunately, it seems that we have some people who have decided to disgrace this job by making off with other people's personal equipment.

Fellas, the job has been beautiful so far and I am trying to stop any of the petty thievery that has started. If you know of anybody who is ripping-off other guys' stuff—get to them. It is a shame that this kind of nonsense has to go on now.

Let's be careful the last week so that you don't lose all the things that are valuable to you and are valuable to the production.

Asked later what the biggest problem was for him in the last week of the Newport shooting, Cohen said, "Making sure Rosecliff was still standing when we left, stopping some guys from taking out anything that wasn't nailed down."

July 10

It is the last party for the extras, the hard-core numbering several hundred who faithfully showed up each night to be rained on and get fed box lunches of cold sandwiches at midnight. It has been an opportunity for some to start new relationships, for others to break off tiring ones. It has given many a chance to be away from home during the dangerous hours of night.

It is also the last big night for spectators. Bernie Styles, who has become the Pied Piper of Newport's rich, arrives with two dozen of them and sits them in several rows of chairs by the camera as if he were a tour director. A socialite says, "Mr. Styles has become very dear to us all." They wait now to be amused by him and the filming.

Among those at ringside are Doris Duke and escort; Mrs. Oatsie Charles and Mrs. William C. Langley, the former Jane Pickens of stage and television, who on the previous Sunday had invited the cast and crew to her mansion for a picnic of homemade Chinese food and a game of croquet on her spacious grounds. After his hotel room was robbed, Sam Waterston accepted her invitation to move into her place for the remaining week of

143

shooting, and he was the unofficial host and the ranking star at her party.

"Sam is such a darling, fine young person and, of course, you know he is well born." It has already been noted by some that Sam, like the character he plays in the film, was educated at Yale, and that his background helps him move with such ease through the social activities of Newport. His stylized graciousness was in evidence at Mrs. Langley's party.

Acknowledging his Groton-Yale background as an influence in his young life, Waterston says, "I was never in the heart of the social thing. But you can't walk around the places I grew up without absorbing some of it."

In the local newspaper, Mrs. Langley denied Newport socialites were out to corral and see the stars. "These people don't care if they're in a movie. Newporters were interested not so much in the individuals making the movie, but the fact that the movie is being made in Newport . . . in surroundings that are so familiar." She continually referred to Robert Redford as "what's-his-name" and made it sound patronizing.

The rich that night were being upstaged by pigeons, which had been kept in cages under a tree near Nick's cottage since the company arrived a month earlier, for what purpose no one quite knew. Tonight they are moved to the lawn near the dance floor and a grip takes some out and puts them on top of the cage. They are beautiful, with white fan tails, but they don't fly. They walk majestically to the edge of the cage's roof and fall off, landing on their feet. Some have had their wings clipped; others have rubber bands on them to prevent them from flying. In the scene they will parade with the guests on the terrace.

"In the month you've had them in the cage have there been any babies?" the keeper is asked.

"It would be a miracle," he says. "They're all males." He pauses. "I'm not sure about one."

"But there's no reference to pigeons at Gatsby's parties in the book."

"There's none in the script, either," he says.

A bold pigeon with his chest puffed out waddles away from the cage, his talons making tiny marks in the mud. "If this pigeon was in New York on Eighth Avenue he'd be king of the roost," his keeper says, letting Mr. Bird have a few more strides of freedom before he is picked up and put back in the cage.

Upstairs in Rosecliff, Redford is being interviewed by a national magazine which is interested in putting him on the cover when *The Great Gatsby* is released. Redford worries constantly about interviews, rejecting most requests, fretting about those he has accepted, at times seemingly afraid a clever interviewer might go into areas of his life which he wants kept unknown. Invariably, he makes a good interview, coming up often with quotable remarks. More than one person has said after meeting him for the first time how intelligent he is, as if actors were naturally stupid.

This initial interview with the magazine reporter takes place in a study that Redford uses for his office. The walls are covered with bookshelves and filled with dated titles showing this study has not been kept current for many years.

The first few minutes are taken up with an inquisitive sizing up of each other; the talk is small and uninteresting because each is more concerned with appearance than substance.

Redford brings the conversation around to the film. He says Gatsby is vague but a "great character," and he tells the reporter that Clayton is the only person on the film as far as he is concerned. A discussion begins on the society portrayed in the novel, and Redford says, "This place has the sense of death about it," making it an ambiguous remark so that he could have been talking about the room with its dusty books, or Newport, or that which is considered high society. It is a remark open to interpretation, which, on the level actors and writers work, is often the best because it gives imagination a chance. It could mean nothing; it could mean a great deal.

145

The social world of the bizarre parties that Fitzgerald knew is gone. Parties still exist (some are quite sumptuous and elegant), but the need to show off freedom at frantic parties is absent from current social behavior. The other features of the Gatsby parties, the wild clothes and the fast music, have been taken over by the masses. The young of the rich, middle and lower classes, in their standardized, extravagant plummage, can all afford to see Alice Cooper in concert, and attendance is enough to identify one as being among the liberated. Rock concerts, not parties, are the showcases of the free life-style. The rich are left with their money. It is vulgar to display wealth the way Gatsby did. There has to be a purpose: a favorite charity, a new cause to justify an elaborate party. What is left to do?

So they come and stare, and outside in the mist and dampness the rich get in the way. They must go. The order is sent down through the chain of command. The party is over. They go quietly, taking with them the sense of something parting from the American scene, a life-style with which the rich were once comfortable. Inheriting wealth is not enough any longer. There has to be more of a purpose than accumulating wealth for wealth's sake.

When they have gone, the path of torches to the false arch down the empty lawn burns away the mist.

July 11

There is one more scene at Nick's cottage. It takes place at the entrance on the side of the house away from the ocean. Nick returns by car from the station where he commutes by train to his bond office in Wall Street. He has met earlier with Jordan Baker in Trinity churchyard and was asked to arrange a meeting between Daisy and Gatsby. It is raining now. Nick stops the car in the driveway, tucks a newspaper under his arm and gets out. At the porch he is met by Gatsby, in formal dress, coming across the lawn from his mansion, which is lit up. Nick comments that it looks like the World's Fair. Gatsby says he has been glancing through some rooms. There is an embarrassed shyness between the men, as they are aware of a certain intimacy that has grown between them. Nick tells Gatsby he has talked with Jordan and that he plans to telephone Daisy tomorrow and ask her to tea. What day would suit you, he asks; and Gatsby, quick to establish the right priorities when it comes to manners, replies, "What day would suit you?"

It is a small, important scene because it re-establishes that the central relationship in the book and movie is really between Nick Carraway and Jay Gatsby. As he often is about the characters he plays in films, Redford is right. Everyone talks of Gatsby as being in the past. His love affair with Daisy took place years ago; only his drive to revive the affair is in the present, and when they finally meet it is to try to reclaim something from the past, not to start something fresh in the present. The only new relationship Gatsby has of any significance is with Nick Carraway. In the book and film, it is through Nick that we come to understand Gatsby and his romantic dream. It is Nick who provides the moral point of view to Fitzgerald's fable; it is he who gives the benediction to Gatsby's tragic chase after a lost dream.

While the film was in production in Newport, a lawyer from Boston read *The Great Gatsby* for the first time and asked a friend who was working on the film if Nick was a homosexual. This point has often been raised.

It would be difficult to imagine Gatsby crawling into bed with Nick. There is, however, undeniably an attraction between them, if not physical—and nowhere is that suggested in the book—at least social. A man like Gatsby, self-made, nouveau riche, is foreign to Nick's world. Fitzgerald spends the first few pages of his novel explaining Nick's background, establishing that he comes from a well-to-do, if not particularly wealthy, Midwest family whose money has come from three generations in a hardware-store business. He has gone to one of the best eastern universities and will take his place in the business community after a suitable apprenticeship in Wall Street. It is a secure world to which Nick is attached, devoid of the financial traumas and the emotional highs of Gatsby's. Cool and detached, Nick is used to being the sympathetic listener, attracting the unsolicited tales of woe from strangers. His involvement with Gatsby—allowing himself to set in motion the meeting between Daisy and Gatsby—is almost an emotional luxury for him. It is Gatsby who gets him to do it. It is the unknown factors of Gatsby's life, his mysterious background and how he made his money, that intrigues Nick, as does Gatsby's ability, however trapped he is by a charming social naiveté, to rise above the hordes at his parties and be an authentic person in the world of spiritual and moral bankrupts.

"I don't remember Nick from the first time I read the book one summer when I was going to college," Sam says, which places that experience in the early 1960s. "All I can remember from that reading is this vivid image I have of the old cars going from Long Island to New York.

"I've reread the book several times now, and Nick is a terrific character. I like the humor and irony of his point of view, and also his objectivity. He stands apart from the crowd. He gets more and more removed until he knows he has no relationship of consequence to what is going on around him.

"Everything is completely unreal that summer except his feeling for Gatsby. Everything of Gatsby is real, especially his lies. His lies are as naive as his impulse to tell them. The impulse is so pure. Gatsby's manipulation of Nick is so obvious as to be very straightforward. Nick believes in the absolute virtue of straightforwardness, which he can't practice with the Buchanans.

"I think Nick is kind of crazy about Jordan. But they eventually relate more to the heart of the story, which is Daisy and Gatsby's romance, than they do to each other. Besides, Nick is basically a Puritan. He's fascinated by their life-style, but he knows he can't live it.

"Sure I have some of Nick's qualities. I can relate to the problem Nick has of being deceived by his detachment. He ends up getting trapped by it.

"I'm like Nick. Sure. You name it," he smiles. "I'm like Nick. And Redford in a way is like Gatsby. Redford believes you can live the dream. Hasn't he gone off and built his home in Utah to get away from everything?"

They stand there now in the rain, two actors as dissimilar in backgrounds and temperament as Nick and Gatsby, and behind them in a small clearing behind the cameras are the last diehards of the rich. Mrs. Langley has brought several friends with her, among them Mrs. John Nicholas Brown, of the Brown University money, and they are seated on logs in the rain and mud patiently waiting for the scene to be shot. Mrs. Langley felt obligated to watch her houseguest act in one scene with "what's-his-name."

Because the rain comes and goes in torrents, Clayton decides to shoot the scene both in and out of the rain. When it comes time to do it again in the rain, it doesn't, so a rain-making machine, a hose with a wide nozzle, is hooked to the roof and played down on the actors.

During one of the breaks in the shooting, Sam wanders through the cottage to the front porch. Some of the prop people feel the interior of the cottage has not been properly used, that the camera never took in Nick's bedroom or his desk in the corner of the living room with the ancient typewriter and the small objects on the desk so dear to the prop department that visually establish the film's historical period.

The cottage has been closed for several weeks, and there is a musty stench inside. The sealed-in dampness permeates everything. On the porch Sam stands alone until an old woman, struggling over the muddy grass in a downpour, mounts the steps. She is also rich, and is considered an eccentric by Newport society. Before she is asked anything, she tells Sam she is from the south and knew Zelda.

"I read the book so long ago I don't know anything about it," she says more to herself than to Sam. "Who are you?"

"I'm . . ."

"Who?"

"I'm . . ."

"Who's that over there?" she points to Redford.

"Robert Redford," Sam replies.

"Is he directing the picture?"

"No."

"Who is?"

"Jack Clayton."

"And who are you?"

"I'm . . ."

"Everyone's coming out here to see the shooting. I guess I had to. Whose place is that over there?" In the direction where she is looking, a point of land jutting into the black water, there is the shape of a massive building.

"It's the . . ."

"It can't be," she says without listening to Sam's answer. "It's in the other direction."

"No, it's not."

"Don't tell me, young man. I've been coming to Newport before you were born." She is confused about the place. "The Breakers is on the other side."

"No, it's over there."

"Who do you play?"

"Nick."

"Who's Nick?"

"He's . . ."

"Who are you?"

"I'm . . ."

"It's crazy to stand out here in the rain. What a bunch of fools they are. I'm going home."

She makes her way across the lawn towards Rosecliff, oblivious of the lights, camera and rain, like a pigeon finding its way home after a long flight into hostile territory.

July 12

Rosecliff still stands. The thefts have been minimal. It will take at least two weeks for it to be emptied of paints and costumes, cables and tools. Most of the American crew will stay behind, after several days of locations in New York, to do the cleaning up while the cast and British crew return to London to resume shooting in Pinewood Studio.

Everything has been stripped from the lawn: the tents, tables and dance floor; it looks desolate with big sections of the lawn trampled bare. The production hopes to bargain with the Preservation Society. The offer is Nick's cottage as a tourist attraction for next season if the Society takes on the cost of reseeding.

At the end of the lawn by the false arch, the green light rests on top of a pole. It is turned off, and beyond it the white mist has lifted and the land is clear in the sun.

Chapter VI

New York Interlude

July 15

There might have been at one time serious thought given to shooting more of *The Great Gatsby* in New York, but because of union costs, the rental of the Plaza Hotel for a few vital scenes, and vehicle and pedestrian traffic-control on exterior locations, it was unrealistic. Of the few scenes to be shot in New York, the most important was the entrance by car of Gatsby, Daisy, Tom, Jordan and Nick to the city from Long Island. There would be other scenes shot: Nick and Jordan talking in the cemetery courtyard of Trinity Church when she tells him Daisy wants to see Gatsby—in the book it takes place as they ride together in a victoria through Central Park—and exteriors of antique cars and extras outside the main entrance to the Plaza Hotel near the fountain. But the most difficult scene in New York was the tracking shot of the old cars across the Queensborough Bridge.

In a way it is sad more of the film, if for no more than sentimental reasons, could not have been done in New York, the city so associated with Fitzgerald's youth when he was starting out as a writer. Upon his graduation from Princeton and after having finished the many re-writes on *This Side of Paradise,* and having had it accepted by Scribner's, he wanted to be in New York for its publication, and there to marry the beautiful Zelda Sayre of Montgomery, Alabama. There was no other city in the world of the 1920s in which to experience success at such an early age (Fitzgerald was twenty-three). All of his Princeton friends were in the city making a literary name for themselves, most notably Edmund Wilson, who would remain his intellectual mentor for the rest of his life. Before exiling himself to France for the summer that was to give fame to a whole literary generation, Fitzgerald and his wife made several places their home in the first years of their marriage. They stayed in St. Paul, Minnesota, for a winter, quickly returning to New York, a dingy apartment on Claremont Avenue near Columbia University and a job with a downtown advertising agency. There was one brief foray to Europe. They quickly came home, disappointed with London and Paris. Again, New York was theirs and the parties never stopped.

By then, the Fitzgeralds had shifted their social world to Great Neck, Long Island, and the parties were brought there while the author worked on his third novel, *The Great Gatsby*. There were good times and fabulous stories, but also nights of insomnia, mind-stifling drunks, and worse, a piling up of debts. Being a Puritan about both sex and money, Fitzgerald responded to this with a sense of guilt that troubled him, but not enough for him to change his way of life.

Zelda Fitzgerald wrote it was a period when: " 'We're having some people,' everybody said to everybody else, 'and we want you to join us,' and they said, 'We'll telephone.' All over New York people telephoned. They telephoned from one hotel to another to people on other parties that they couldn't get there—that they were engaged. It was always tea-time or late at night."

Now it was 4:30 A.M., and under threatening dawn skies, the movie crew walked as somnambulists under the elevated subway tracks at the entrance to the Queensborough Bridge.

The Valley of Ashes could not be found in New York and would be re-created on the back lot of Pinewood Studio. But in the dimness, the uncertain early light robbing the men of specific forms, they could have been the ash-gray men Fitzgerald described.

It is a different New York now, the skyline so altered as to be useless for the movie. Few, if any, of the buildings now on the skyline were built in the 1920s. The bridge was there, however, and by having the caravan of cars move along the lower level, the camera would not photograph the new buildings.

The antique cars that had already been used in the

153

film, Gatsby's yellow Rolls Royce among them, had been driven down from Newport. The other twenty-five cars in the motorcade were located in the metropolitan area.

An arrangement had been made with the city that the bridge's lower level could be used until noon. Any later, and those returning from Long Island on a Sunday afternoon would make an incredible traffic jam on the bridge.

Again the weather was the production's worse enemy. Through the night the weather reports had not been optimistic. Now the eye could see what those men on radio were hesitant to say, that it was going to rain, and it came in a tremendous downpour. The crew, covering their equipment, abandon some of it in the street and run for the shelter of doorways.

In a matter of minutes the streets are flooded, the gutters unable to take the volume of water running in them to drains clogged with debris left by a careless public. One recalls that Queens always seems to be the victim of crippling snows, power failures or rains that halt traffic.

The worst part of the storm is accompanied by thunder and lightning. Soon it is over. Someone had forgotten to cover the food on the coffee table; bagels and doughnuts have disintegrated in water-filled boxes.

It is now early morning. A few drunks have not gone home and stand in the doorway looking through the rain to a new day as seen through a mind-obliterating alcoholic haze. The Sanitation Department never seems to be where it is needed, and workers from the movie company must clean out the gutters to permit the flood waters to recede.

It is 9 A.M., and the actors arrive in their chauffeur-driven limousines. Owners of the antique cars will drive them in the scene; they wait patiently at the wheel.

"It's a perfect Los Angeles December day," Dern says, watching a man poke a stick into the filthy water swirling at the drain.

Not until 10 A.M. is Clayton able to get his first shot. It will be a risk since it is raining intermittently, and the sky remains leadenly gray. Clayton stands restlessly on the back of an open truck that carries the camera and crew. It is the first vehicle in the procession. Behind the truck Daisy drives with Gatsby in the Buchanan blue car, and Tom, Nick and Jordan are in Gatsby's. A few of the crew wipe away traces of rain off the cars. It is supposed to be a clear day, and Slocombe hopes to maintain this illusion on the screen by overexposing the film to make the background look brighter. It is the only possible way to save the morning's shooting schedule since the company must be gone by noon.

On a signal by Clayton, the truck moves off, and one after the other the antique cars enter the gloom of the bridge. The procession will go to Manhattan, turn around, and come back in the Queens-bound lane.

During the storm, David Merrick arrives, and one wonders if he has ever been up this early for one of his stage productions. It is a situation on which he thrives—a crisis. He can hear the fire bell ringing. He is a friend of Mayor John Lindsay and contemplates whether to call him and ask if the scene could be done on Wednesday if the weather is better. Never more at ease than when things around him seem to be going to pieces—and he has something to do—Merrick goes over the ramifications of losing a day's work: how much would it cost the company. He is determined to keep the film's budget at $6.5 million. Most producers on a movie do what they have to, getting together the package of stars, director, script and crew before the shooting and then are rarely on the set during the production. Merrick is on the set every day, bad weather or not, visible in the adversity in his tailored suit and a steadfast stiff upper lip which never seems to move the moustache that has been grown over it.

The rain becomes an annoyance rather than something unendurable. The crew bears it well, no longer seeking shelter from it, standing in the open section of the street near a policeman directing traffic away from the entrance to the bridge.

Merrick stands with them. He is not given to talking much about himself, which is at first unexpected since he

155

is the master of publicity on Broadway. The publicity has always been to keep one of his shows running, never about his personal life. All that is really known about him is that he is a lawyer and is now married to a beautiful, sensitive fashion designer, Etan and they have an infant daughter.

That morning in the rain, he talks freely about his shows, the first success a musical, *Fanny*, back in 1954 kept going by a massive sticker campaign; then John Osborne's *Look Back in Anger*, the first work of the British Angry Young Men, having a woman charge up on the stage to denounce the hero, Jimmy Porter, who is a brute to his wife; *Hello, Dolly*, the long-running musical, in which, although he often fought publicly with her, he considers Pearl Bailey the best Dolly; and then his first movie, *Child's Play*, which had not been a financial success.

"I've had eighty shows," he says, "and fifty were hits." Someone notes that *Sugar* has closed, or is about to. "I never go to closing nights," he says, and pauses before adding almost with genuine sadness, "this will be the first summer since I started on Broadway that I won't have a show running in town."

"There's not that much difference in producing a film," he adds. "You're dealing with actors and a story. The extra thing is the camera in film, and you need one to interpret Fitzgerald's prose.

The caravan comes off the bridge, gone almost a half hour. Clayton's truck leads the way. The cars snake around the steel girders and end with Clayton's still in the lead, followed by the cars with the actors. On the second return trip, the caravan is met by a barrage of cameras. Some are owned by friends and family of the crew; others are with the local, uninvited press, the largest single piece of equipment belonging to a local television station. There had been no advance publicity that the company was going to shoot on the bridge that morning. An alert television crew had read off the police teletype that the lower level of the bridge was going to be closed Sunday morning for a filming stint. As the caravan waits to make its third tour of the bridge, the cameras begin advancing towards the car in which Mia and Redford sit, the holders of the cameras pushing forward with the stealth of trained guerrillas. The most insistent are the three-member television crew. Mia looks up, and there is the lens of the shoulder-held camera poking through the open window. Redford is furious. He jumps out of the driver's seat and comes around to the front of the car.

"Get them out of here," he yells. "Ax them."

The camera and microphone record Redford's outburst.

Clayton sides with him. Cameras are everywhere; if one looks at them subjectively, they present a fantastic ballet of clicking shutters and fingers frantically pushing down buttons.

One of the T.V. crew, equally incensed at what he considers violation of his right to get a legitimate story—it is a public street—threatens to use Redford's off-screen performance on the 11-o'clock news.

"Look, everyone is a bit tense. We've been up in Newport and had nothing but rain, and here we are today with the same shit."

"I've gotten awards for getting the story. . . ."

"Everyone's a bit testy, on edge. We're heading for London in the middle of the week."

"If they try to stop me, that's when I really go after the story."

"Who the hell is he?"

Redford wants an accounting of every camera. It's an impossible task. It seems everyone has a camera now.

Mia and Redford stand by the car, an umbrella concealing them from the television camera.

"Look, you've got an interview with Merrick, and look at the old cars! Aren't they a story?"

"Yeah, but who does he think he is?"

The T.V. people go as quickly as they came; the camera is there, moving past open car windows like a piece of artillery going into battle, the operator shouldering its weight, and then it disappears.

It turns out the television crew was lenient. The bad

piece of Redford footage is not shown that night; instead, there is a rather harmless clip about the antique cars and the Roaring Twenties re-created on a wet Sunday morning in New York.

It is not much better in the afternoon. The rain persists, and the company reorganizes after lunch, or tries to, under the Queensborough Bridge, where the scene of Myrtle buying a dog will be shot. This eliminates the possibility of any modern buildings getting in the scene.

It is chaos. The traffic crawls past the company, which has taken over one side of the underpass for its equipment, crew and actors. There is really no way to control the flow coming up First Avenue, or the pedestrians who stop and ask what is happening, some of them legitimately seeking shelter from the steady rain that gives the East Side a porous grayness compatible for a flight across the moors.

In the scene, Myrtle, who is in the front seat of a car between Nick and Tom, spots a dog peddler walking under the bridge. She gets Tom to stop and lean out the window to pick a puppy from a basket held by a woman.

Clayton tries to rehearse the scene, and it is complete anarchy. Production assistants have no idea what they are doing. Commands are shouted and ignored. Faces strike blank poses and keep them. Hands fidget at belts. Toes of shoes peck at the wet cement. Annabel, who has notified friends she is pregnant by director Mike Nichols, is, for the first time on the film, reduced to tears of frustration: at the lousy weather, her condition, being unable to find a toilet, missing a hot meal and getting wet. "It's barbaric," she says. "Sure they get paid better in this country, but look at the hours they work and under what conditions! They're treated like slaves."

The workers of whom she speaks stand by the soot-covered stone arch of the bridge as if they are laborers at the base of a pyramid waiting for construction plans. Clayton comes over and consoles her. It is a fifty-fifty chance the production will suffer a collective nervous breakdown in the next few minutes. Clayton does not panic or shout, but the signs are there: the hands attending to the fringe of hair, the lips twisting into his quirky smile. He remains in the midst of the turmoil, resisting it silently, doing the only practical thing: waiting for it to pass, delaying the necessity to act until the last possible moment.

Barricades are put up to keep the spectators back from under the bridge. It is futile. The people walk around them and into the street to get closer to the camera. Annabel is no longer teary. She is numb and seals herself off from the chaos with a detached reserve one associates with the British, realizing now how much it must have been an historical defense mechanism.

The rains swell the gutter with debris. The coffee is cold, the food soggy. And suddenly, order returns. Where moments before everything was confusion, movement without a purpose, everyone now recalls what he was supposed to do and goes about doing it with the expected professionalism.

"Do you see now why more pictures aren't shot in the streets of New York?" a veteran grip says.

The snarled traffic, the impossibility of keeping spectators back from the shooting, the noise, the confusion of working on the pavements of a crowded city explain it.

Not surrendering to the adverse conditions, the company works through the afternoon, and the next day in the seclusion of the cemetery at Trinity Church under clear skies and a sun that is almost successful in penetrating the haze over Manhattan, rediscovering that moviemaking can be a rather pleasant job.

The scene in the churchyard is approached leisurely, as if the energy generated by cast and crew for shooting at the Queensborough Bridge has abated. Without undue haste, the crew moves among the tombstones. On the steps of a large memorial Nick and Jordan sit discussing Gatsby, who, Jordan reports, has been having his elaborate parties in expectation that Daisy might wander into one. She tells Nick that Gatsby wants him to invite Daisy to his house for tea. But does Daisy want to see him, Nick asks, and Jordan replies that his cousin will thank him and thank him.

In the book, this scene takes place between Nick and Jordan in a carriage in Central Park, but doing a period film in contemporary New York, with the skyline covered by television antennas and buildings not there in the 1920s is almost impossible unless it is re-created in a sound stage. It is easier to transfer this scene to the serenity of an old cemetery.

Sam is almost phlegmatic in the scene, loose to a point of nonchalance. Lois is tense and has with her for confidence-building her friend and acting coach, who stands as close as he can to the camera without being in the way, staring directly at her during the scene as if he is trying to transmit confidence to her by the intensity of his concentration on her every movement. Clayton is also very solicitous, and between takes goes to her and whispers instructions, smiling, his hand touching her shoulder reassuringly.

The next day none of the principals works. It is a scene of antique cars driving up to the entrance of the Plaza Hotel. A number of extras in costumes are used. The point of view of the camera is from the entrance of the hotel to the driveway where the cars stop, again eliminating any of modern midtown Manhattan.

At the end of Tuesday's shooting it becomes a problem of getting crew, cast and equipment to England for resumption of filming at Pinewood Studio on Friday, July 20. Redford and Mia are not scheduled to begin work immediately. He goes off camping, and she returns with her children to her home on Martha's Vineyard.

There are major problems of transportation. Five antique cars already established in the film—Gatsby's yellow Rolls Royce, Jordan's car and the three belonging to the Buchanans—have to be shipped by air to London at a cost of $10,000. Clayton and his crew want to use in London the equipment they had in Newport, so the camera and lenses have to be packed up immediately after shooting ends on Tuesday and dispatched by air to London. A great many cartons have already gone: things for Wilson's garage and Myrtle's apartment. Not all arrived promptly. Some became temporarily lost in the mail system that is rapidly disintegrating on both sides of the Atlantic; others are held up by customs.

The Cartier jewels must go, too, and assigned to carry them across the Atlantic is Greg Martin, Redford's stand-in, who, accompanied by a private guard, takes them on a night flight at the end of the week. Martin says it was an uneventful trip until near the end when he carried his package to the upstairs lounge in first class of the Boeing 747 and showed a stunned stewardess the contents of the package. Martin is met at the airport by another guard. The jewels are taken to Pinewood where they are kept in a safe in the production office, or in the gatekeeper's cottage at night where there is a twenty-four-hour watch over them.

There are other less important problems, no less annoying and amusing only in retrospect.

Some puppies had been brought over from London to be used in the scene where Myrtle picks one through the car window. Because of immigration health requirements, dogs brought into London for the first time are put in quarantine for months. Presumably, by having British dogs used in the United States, which has no such requirement, they could be brought right back to London without being kept for six months in isolation. Unfortunately, Karen Black did not pick out one of the London puppies. A search was begun at once in London to find one similar in appearance. The one chosen is somewhat longer than its cousin in the States.

Most of the crew goes to London on a morning flight Wednesday. In those last hours on Tuesday the production office on the East Side looks like a frantic evacuation with the enemy at the gates: boxes half-packed, papers falling out of them, file cabinets ajar, phones ringing incessantly before someone answers.

Hank Moonjean oversees these last moments. Though there is still more than two months of shooting to be done in London, he knows the difficult part is really over, the party scenes with the hundreds of extras. "I really feel 90 percent of the picture is over, and we only have 10 percent left to do in London," he says.

On the sidewalk, New Yorkers group in front of the show window to get one last look at the beautiful yellow Rolls Royce.

It is the car that gives Moonjean his last traumatic experience in New York.

Arrangements had been carefully made to fly the antique cars to London. Widths had been measured, pounds estimated. Everything is set. Moonjean calls the exporters. He is told the plane that will take the cars to London is in Lima, Peru.

Julia Lisberger hears the vocal explosion and looks up, doubly startled because Moonjean rarely raises his voice. The other office workers stop packing boxes to look at Moonjean, who is now threatening law suits, injunctions, wars to secure the plane which the exporter says will take at least two weeks to get to New York.

There can be some delay with the other cars, but the yellow Rolls Royce will be used immediately.

The outburst works. A series of calls is made. A plane is procured, and the next day Gatsby's Rolls Royce is in the air along with cast and crew bound for London.

Chapter VII

British Journal

July 20

Pinewood Studio is a forty-minute drive west of London past Heathrow Airport through the fabled English countryside where some of the old village life is retained in the pubs and stone cottages not posted with cigarette and beer advertisements and without television antennas poking through the quaint gabled roofs.

The studio was once an estate, and near the main gate are horse stables from the prior ownership, which are doll house in size and have been used in many costume epics. The main offices are in a long, two-storied block painted a dull, deep red color. Over the main entrance is a beautifully carved heavy dark wood fireplace frame, and it gives the visitor a sense of past grandeur as does Tom, the uniformed guard, who meets arriving cars, opens the back door and salutes smartly. Tom is retired from the British military, and his bearing and manner will make one always aware of his past.

Part of the original estate is the studio restaurant in a wing off the corridor of the main offices, and it looks on English gardens, cut and trimmed into lovely squares of grass and flowers. The gardens have served the studio for many a dueling scene and lovers' walk through the countryside of an older England. What the studio lacks is the size of the old Hollywood studios. Pinewood is not overwhelming. Its sound stages are grouped in several annexes, and once the maze of connecting corridors is figured out it becomes an intimate, easily traveled lot.

It has an air of neglect until *The Great Gatsby* company moves in. There has been no film shooting there for several weeks, and the waitresses in the restaurant are eager for human contact—let alone tips. Their pleasantness helps overcome what one is offered to eat: overcooked, mushy brussel sprouts, cold canned beans and grilled sole deformed at the edges by heavy fried batter.

The *Gatsby* production office is in something called the garden suite, a very small one-story stone block behind the main offices in a clump of bushes, reached by a sidewalk that goes past a pool built into what had been the tennis courts.

The pool is in the shape of a *T*. At the wide end there are steps up from the water on both sides to a covered cabana where a love scene takes place between Gatsby and Daisy, and where George Wilson will stand holding a gun pointed at the man in the pool. There is no water in it now; the cabana curtains are drawn back and in protective plastic coverings. Jack Clayton and Theoni Aldredge are both partial to blue and white. The curtains are in these colors and have a simple, broken line design at the bottom that is very much Greek.

The *Gatsby* company has made other alterations to the back of the main offices. There is a new facade behind the pool that is the back of Gatsby's mansion. A wing has been added to the restaurant. It is the living and dining rooms of the Buchanan home. At the other end of the main offices is the front of the Buchanan home, propped up by a scaffolding of metal poles.

Few workers from the American side of the production have come over to London. David Merrick is here and will stay to the end of the shooting, using his nights to see plays he hopes might be worth bringing to New York.

Hank Moonjean is again the first person to get a crack at the day-to-day decisions. Gene Rudolf, the American art director, has been brought over to assure the details of the interior sets stay American, down to ashtray and wall decorations. But there is a new production manager, Peter Price, this being his first film as one, and a new production secretary, Miss Jean Hall. It is to their office the inquiries or complaints now come from the world outside the studio before they are channeled into the right offices.

There is definitely a more relaxed and, at least on the surface, a more orderly process in operation. Gone is the frenzy of Newport and the feeling of pending disaster behind every dark cloud off the Atlantic Ocean. The call sheets are much more detailed as to who will be where at what time. The minutes of the pre-production meetings are even typed up so the Americans who arrive in mid-July know exactly how many days of work there will be on the sound stages, on the back lot, on location and in night shootings. Incredibly, the production arrives in Pinewood only four days behind schedule. These will be made up in England, most probably, because shooting schedules are notoriously flexible and padded, with more days scheduled than needed so the production can be brought in near or under the announced deadline.

It is also a more regulated work week: basically 8:30 A.M. to 5:30 P.M., five days a week, with tea breaks in the morning and afternoon, and lunch from 1 to 2 P.M. As the minutes said rather wistfully, under the topic "Abnormal Conditions," none are envisaged.

The talk in the office over coffee, tea and digestive biscuits is of the things that happened in getting from America to England: Karen picking out the wrong dog; the jewels coming first class with Greg Martin; the shipment of the antique cars; and, always, of what it was like in Newport, as if those who were now veterans of those days had shared an adventure like those who survived D-day.

Rudolf, bearded and in jeans—very much the American of the West in his dress, though he is from Bergen County, New Jersey, the bedroom for commuters to New York—reminds everyone how difficult it is recreating the look of the twenties on film. "So much of that era has been lost. The buildings are gone, and there are very few books or photographs to go on," he says. The production was so intricately researched, he says, that since there were no ice-cube-making refrigerators in the 1920s, each day the prop department had to chip ice from big blocks to fill the cocktail glasses for the parties.

Clayton is effusive in praise of Rudolf, and has brought him over two weeks before the rest of the company to work on the sets being prepared by British workers. The director is fairly adamant that it was not his decision, but the studio's, to shoot the rest of the picture in England. He is still so taken with the efficiency and loyalty of the American crew he has left behind that he pays for his own full-page ad in *Variety* and *The Hollywood Reporter* praising every American worker on the film by name.

Outside, the weather is familiar. Rain squalls are coming in from the direction of Gatsby's pool. With the brilliant light gone, replaced by a depressing grayness, the studio, as any of them can, does look like a junk yard of rusting machines, unused props and backdrops faded and torn. Still, even under the most adverse visual circumstances, it remains many worlds and times. There is the set of a medieval Swedish town, and next to it a propellorless Sptfire fighter plane from World War II, grounded since the filming of *The Battle of Britain*. In Studio E is a vulgarly furnished 1920s flat on Riverside Drive, New York, the kind of place where rich men put up their mistresses and let them decorate it to their own taste, concerned only where the bed and bar are located.

Into this room of mauve colors, beads and china dolls raised off the studio floor by a complex series of springs and steel bars come Myrtle, Tom and Nick, continuing the scene they had begun under the Queensborough Bridge less than a week ago.

It is not a difficult day of shooting, purposely kept light to allow those crew and actors new to each other to settle down in a new studio and to adjust to their jet lag.

The jokes are many; the absence of tension is noticeable, though it is a cramped set and the camera does not have much room for maneuvering when the trio enters the door.

"There's a lot of laughing going on for a first day in a new studio," Bruce Dern says. As has often happened, Dern comes up with the correct analysis of the situation off camera, giving almost always a good reading of the emotional levels at which the production is existing at that moment. Sometimes his reportage is dubious, but

166

most often it approximates the truth. He has made the most astute observation, that the principals in the film are essentially loners, including himself, and while they are unfailingly polite to each other on the set, some even dining at each other's homes, there is no sense of genuine closeness. They exhibit the warm surface manners that are an accommodation to an impermanent situation.

July 23

Above the sound stages, the Valley of Ashes is the sign and the eye framed within the glasses. It is an old sign, and its panels are broken off, its letters fading. As you get closer, you see it is railroad freight cars on a siding atop a bank of soot and gravel. Where the road splits, dividing the ways leading to West Egg and East Egg, a line of telephone poles goes off into infinity behind mounds of ashes; small fires burn on the sides of them, which gives off dark smoke, and stray dogs scale the shifting sides. There is Wilson's garage; two red pumps stand in front of it, a rusted corrugated tin fence is at one side and junk is scattered across the ashes out front. A stairway on one side leads to the second-floor apartment. The grime has irretrievably obscured the color of the building.

One remembers his childhood in the Great Depression, how very much this looks like the entrance to New York City from New Jersey, the highway going through wastelands of tin shacks and piles of debris, with fires burning. Men lived there, came out into the polluted day, urinated against the fence, began tending to gardens planted next to the shacks. As they worked and the air became more unmoving, holding in the darkness of a day deprived of the sun, they would take on the coloration of their surroundings and become as gray and undefined as the shapes around them.

It could have been Fitzgerald's Valley of Ashes. On first reading it is rather unclear what the author is trying to describe. It is a stretch of industrial waste, and the building housing Wilson's garage is the only structure in it. Across from it is a railroad track on a mound of ash. But then he begins describing shapes, how ashes change into hills and wheat fields, and they take on the shapes of buildings and men. It is the author's most surrealistic piece of writing in what is a realistic novel. It works beautifully because he makes his Valley of Ashes something threatening, a place of dangerous passage between the security of Long Island and the city itself, in some ways no less threatening but still with promise of exciting adventures and great parties. By making his description vague, Fitzgerald increases the ominous power of the Valley of Ashes, giving it the mystery of a dark cave one comes across in childhood.

Above his valley he puts the eyes of Doctor T. J. Eckleburg. By not describing it specifically as a signboard, he makes it more than that, the all-seeing eyes of the judge over hell.

These eyes are believed to have first appeared on the dustjacket prepared by Scribner's for *The Great Gatsby*. They were to be Daisy's looking down on a Manhattan street, alive with dazzling lights. Fitzgerald later wrote his editor Maxwell Perkins, "For Christ's sake don't give anyone that jacket you're saving for me. I've written it into the book."

When Perkins read the completed novel, he wrote Fitzgerald to praise the use of Dr. Eckleburg's "great unblinking eyes, expressionless, looking down upon the human scene. It's magnificent!"

On closer inspection, the Valley of Ashes is a movie set. The freight cars have only one side. The shack on the railroad embankment at the end of the road is a false front built to scale so that a normal-sized human standing next to it is as tall as the second floor. The mounds of ashes are also false—hollow plaster shapes covered with fake ash.

It has taken six weeks to build it with an assist from the first *Cleopatra*, the one that was to star Joan Collins and Peter Finch. A bank of the Nile had been built and left after the movie was abandoned. It is now the side of the Valley of Ashes on which the railroad track runs.

John Box, the production designer, says this was the most difficult set to conceive on film.

The first week's shooting in England takes place in the Valley of Ashes. In one of the first scenes in it, Tom and Nick pull up outside the garage and Tom asks Nick if he wants to meet his girl. Inside, Wilson is working on a wrecked Ford. He discusses with Buchanan the possibility of selling him his car, and while they talk Myrtle comes down the stairs. Tom nudges Nick to indicate she is his girl. Tom whispers into her ear that he wants to see her in the city and she agrees to meet him.

In the book Myrtle is described as being in her midthirties and quite plump. "If she were thirty-five years old and fat, why would Tom be attracted to her?" Karen says. Everyone agrees with her that Myrtle in this film should be younger and prettier than described in the novel. This makes it easier for Karen Black to play the role. She is an attractive young woman, not a classic beauty, but then she is not being asked to play Elizabeth Taylor roles. She gets offered so-called kookie parts, usually like the one she had in *Portnoy's Complaint*, which require an actress with a strong stomach to say some of the dialogue handed her in the name of art.

"Myrtle is everything at once," Karen says. "Full of life, volatile, very strongly determined in an emotional way. She is loving, a life force, but she keeps running into walls. She cares, but she is not carried along by life.

"She can't tell you why she loves Tom. She doesn't recognize his being. She's not philosophical about the relationship. To her he is a dream come true. They have similar attributes. They are both emotionally free and given to violence. And they are strongly sexual. Her life is very vivid, not at all dreamlike. She's certainly in love with Tom. He's a promise of something better in life.

"Her husband, George, is sweet. They like each other's sweetness."

Asked to elaborate on the relationships between Myrtle and the two men in her life, Karen says, brushing it aside, "If the relationship is not in the script, I don't have to know about it."

She says she is not an intellectual type of actress. "It's being, not thinking that is important. You can get any number of actors who can tell you the reasons for doing something, but still not be the character they are playing. In the acting process you don't have to know why to walk into a room. You just do it. With Jack Clayton you don't have to know about the characters. You just do it, and he will indicate to you the difference between what he wants and what you are doing."

"I have a very simple approach to acting," she adds. "I like all the parts and I like working. I have a good time."

One of her favorite scenes in the film is the one being shot now when Myrtle comes down the stairs to greet Tom and Nick, and she moves sensuously, her reddish hair in a slightly messed array of curls, as if she were coming from a pleasant romp in bed with a favorite lover. She goes over to Tom, and when her husband's back is turned, moves against him sexually, obviously. It says immediately a great deal about the rock bottom of their relationship.

Between takes she sits on the top of the stairs holding an opened pack of cigarettes. She begins dropping one after another on Sam who stands below her. At first he shrugs them off, as though they were bothersome bugs on a summer's night. Finally he looks up.

"This is what I must do to get your attention," she says, pouting, her eyes pinched at the bridge of her nose, her stare slightly ajar, disconcertingly. It is a smile that has often been turned on to prevent someone from getting angry.

When another angle of the scene is being worked out in the garage, Scott Wilson, who once he gets into the part for the day cannot be blasted out of it, wanders off by himself while Sam, Karen and Bruce go upstairs to the apartment. It is a damp, raw morning and Karen, wrapped in Clayton's windbreaker, smokes continuously, almost for warmth.

"I wasn't happy with that scene," Karen says.

"Why didn't you ask for another take?" Bruce asks.

She doesn't answer immediately.

Bruce begins to bait her, his favorite pastime with actresses. "Jack doesn't like actors."

"He does so," she replies quickly coming to his defense. "He's great with actors. The best . . ."

Sam smiles through it as if he were watching a scene in a different theater.

"Isn't she an adorable nut?" says Charlie Parker, the makeup man. "She's one of the most intelligent actresses I have ever met and totally unpredictable. She came to work one morning carrying a bag that weighed a ton. She got it to her dressing room, dumped the contents over the floor and left them there."

July 25

A disaster!

After shooting in front of Wilson's garage for two days, someone discovered the word "oculist" in the Eckleburg signboard is spelled wrong: with two *c*'s. The first reactions of panic are that it will take two days to reshoot the scenes and that Clayton is looking for Box.

July 26

The inevitable confrontation takes place in the cabana of Gatsby's pool. The witnesses to it are the participants, Jack Clayton and John Box, and because rumor and gossip are natural viruses on a movie set, there are soon many versions of what happened. But the accepted one is told by Box, since he is the only one willing to talk about it.

They meet near the shiny pillars around which are tied the blue and white Grecian curtains. Clayton picks a wrench off the ground and begins striking it against the pillars, shattering the plastic surface, according to Box.

"I took three steps forward," Box says in understated fashion, like a man at Dunkirk knowing he will survive but not quite sure how. "I wanted to watch what he was doing. It was not without interest to me.

"He said to me, 'This could have been your head.' "

The rage was over a real issue, which makes it rare on a movie set, where much is made over nothing: disturbed egos, imaginary slights, staged conflicts to jockey for better position. With the director this agitated, the vibrations reach everyone, making cast and crew edgy and cautious. One approaches Clayton as if walking across a sea of eggs.

It is too bad the spelling mistake occurred since nothing should take away from the magnificence of the set.

Construction on the Valley of Ashes had begun in April about the time workers were putting up the sides of Nick's cottage in Newport. The places where it could be located on the back lot of Pinewood were fairly well limited because it had to be where there were no trees. The embankment from *Cleopatra* was a good spot since it blocked out the trees and fields beyond it. The book does not specify whether the train tracks run across the top of the ash pile. Box thought it would do no visual harm to have it there.

The design of the Valley was aided by photos uncovered during the preliminary research for the film. They are of sections of Queens and what was probably the inspiration for Fitzgerald as he rode to Manhattan by train from Long Island.

"The photos show telegraph poles, flat roads and a lot of garbage alongside it," Box says.

In Fitzgerald's description of the Valley there is a dingy yellow brick building containing three shops: one an all-night restaurant, the other empty and the third Wilson's garage. The building is near enough to the signboard to be in the direct line of its "persistent stare."

Box and his aides eliminated the two other establishments, keeping only Wilson's garage in the building, and put the Eckleburg sign directly across the street from it. Recalling the architectural principle that nothing should be arbitrary, Box used this when it came to placing Wilson's garage in the Valley of Ashes.

"It would have to seem natural to the audience that the garage should be where it is, dictated by the logic of having the signboard and the railroad tracks across the street. The audience could not think we had placed the garage there arbitrarily," Box says.

In the long, narrow set with its distant line of utility poles and mounds of ash, Box has the road where it divides to East and West Egg at Wilson's garage.

"In dramatic terms, why not have the road split there, though the book does not make such a specific reference to any division taking place there," Box says. "I thought it would be especially poignant during the funeral procession to have the road divide at that point."

"The toughest thing about the set was designing the Eckleburg sign and getting the glasses right," Box adds. "The sign is such an abstract thing in the book. It was bloody difficult to realize it in relation to the Valley of Ashes, and then how decrepit to make it.

"The audience, I hope, will not forget those two eyes and those glasses."

Spelling is an occupational hazard to him, Box says. "Have you ever noticed what bad spellers sign painters are? I'm a notoriously bad speller. But the spelling of that word is a minute detail compared to other problems with the set, for instance, the gas pumps and getting them right.

Box was not the only bad speller on the production. "Occulist" had passed everyone's detection for days, even when the scenes were being shot. The mistake was picked up by an alert Hank Moonjean. He had received a letter from the States in which the word oculist had been mentioned. Out of curiosity, a trait essential to supervisors of a movie production, Moonjean looked up the spelling.

Oblivious to the distress caused by the sign across the street, Karen Black is in the bedroom of the apartment over the garage, heard before she is seen, her voice in a credible rendition of Puccini.

"It's gotta be a tape," an electrician says.

"Nah, it's her. She goes on like that all the time when she's not working," a friend answers.

"You're kidding."

Upstairs, Karen is sitting curled into a sensuous ball on the bed. She wears a slip and a tantalizingly distracted smile, grubbing cigarettes from anyone who passes.

"My husband's coming next week," she tells everyone.

She is notified she will not be needed for some time, and she returns to her dressing trailer parked by the food caravan and the shack where the crew eats. She sprawls on a couch, picks up a guitar and begins playing a lovely tune that sounds vaguely French. It has the bittersweet quality of an ache for unrequited love.

"That's really nice," someone says to her when she finishes. "Who wrote it?"

"I did."

There is no false pride in the statement; the assumption is one must know she has some talent. She reaches for another cigarette. Before she puts it into her mouth, her tongue curls into a tubular shape and she makes a peculiar sucking noise. The illusion created by the song is destroyed. She inhales deeply and smiles.

July 27

When Nick accompanies Tom and Myrtle to the Fifth Avenue apartment where Buchanan keeps her, he meets Catherine, Myrtle's sister, and the downstairs neighbors, Mr. and Mrs. McKee—he is a photographer—and he gets drunk. He falls asleep, and when he awakens in the early evening a party is in progress. Fitzgerald does not describe it: he suggests one is happening. People are coming and going, plans are being made, people lose each other, the author says, without trying to describe how they look, what they said, how they act. The guess is Myrtle's friends must reflect her taste.

Clayton has given Myrtle her own party by filling her apartment with people who make a terrific visual comparison with the other parties in the film, and, like the guests at those, they reveal something of the social backgrounds and aspirations by how they dress and comport themselves in a crowd.

It is at this party that Tom breaks Myrtle's nose, after being alone with her in the bedroom, presumably to have sex, and when they come out, after she shouts the name Daisy to him.

The implied sex going on behind the door bothered

174

Fitzgerald, and in letters to Maxwell Perkins he continually fretted that this scene would have censorship problems. Perkins reassured him it was not obscene.

It was Clayton's decision to have the actors in the party be Americans who live in England because they have found work on the stage or in television, or have married British. Before he went to Newport, Clayton saw the extras and had those with speaking parts read for him. Twenty-five were chosen, including Katheryn Leigh Scott as Catherine, Paul Tamarin as Mr. McKee and Beth Porter as Mrs. McKee.

"All had retained their American accents," says Jeannie Sims, Clayton's efficient, loyal assistant on almost all his films. She is genuinely fond of actors, and from her social life with them in Chelsea she knew many of those who tried out for the film.

"How would you describe the guests at Myrtle's party?" Jeannie says. "I'll just repeat what Bruce Dern said when he walked off the set the first day: 'Weird . . . weird . . . weird. . . .'

"It is hard to describe them. They're off-beat people, and somewhat pretentious. They wear garish clothes and are vulgar in their speech, at least more so than Gatsby's guests. They drink a lot and are trying to become the kind of people who would get invited to a Gatsby party. Catherine has been to one. She says so in the book. The McKees desperately want to go to one.

"These people are basically show-offs and social hustlers. They read the popular press and know what's going on."

The Myrtle party is shot over three days in Studio E. On the last afternoon before the actors get to their dressing rooms, Jeannie distributes to each a bottle of champagne, a gift from Clayton.

At lunch in the studio's main restaurant, the French doors are opened to the well-tended hedges and gardens, and David Merrick sits at a table that looks out on them, not staring at nature outside but the more exotic world of show business inside. Extras from a slapstick science-fiction comedy make one of their last appearances in the

175

dining hall. The actors have not been paid in a month, so the story is told, and the production has been suspended.

Merrick's views of actors are well known. He eats by himself, rarely with any of the cast, but he sees everything that happens in the room, his mind a cataloguing encyclopedia. He is in demand from the British press who knows he will come up with something controversial, and he freely grants interviews. A master of publicity, Merrick believes anything said during an interview is game just as long as it builds interest in the product being sold.

He is now very much against having come to London to shoot the rest of the film. He says American unions are right in calling *The Great Gatsby* a runaway production, that the film should have been completed in America. Merrick's contention is that the cost of the sets in England is much greater than had been expected because of inflation and the drastic devaluation of the dollar which has made it a second-rate currency in Europe.

"They built Nick's cottage in Newport for $20,000, and it cost $100,000 to build Gatsby's pool here."

The $100,000 figure also covered the Buchanan house sets built on to the production offices at Pinewood.

Merrick is also upset by the quality of the British building workers at Pinewood. He says the better carpenters and construction laborers go to London where they can get higher salaries.

Others on the production dispute Merrick's contention. By the end of the production, they say, a million will still have been saved by coming to London.

In the press, Clayton is often made the villain for leading the "runaway" production to London. The reasons given are that London is his home and he wanted to use a British crew.

"I take the responsibility for having said at one point in the early production meetings that a million and a half dollars could be saved by coming to England," Clayton says, "but I never insisted we come here to shoot the interiors. All I insisted from the first is that I have one camera crew throughout the whole production."

July 30

It is quiet in the Valley of Ashes. There is no wind, and the dirty clothes on a line attached to the shack at the end of the road are motionless. A stray dog sniffs at a piece of burnt rubber tire and lifts his leg.

The sign is as it was, double *c*. A model with the correct spelling has been wheeled into place across the street as if to tell the world that a mistake has been made. However, the scenes will not be reshot. Clayton has come up with a way to explain the error to those few in the audience who would notice it. Nick is in the garage talking with Wilson and makes a reference to the spelling mistake by saying Eckleburg might be a good optician but he is a lousy speller.

"Anyway, Clayton wanted to have a scene in the film between Sam and Scott since they are both such good actors," Jeannie Sims says, "and this is a way to do it."

"But why even bring it to the attention of the audience?" Box says. "How many would ever notice it?"

"If I could go up and claim those four Oscars," he adds, "I guess I have to take credit for the spelling."

July 31

It is incredible, but Theoni Aldredge has never won a Tony, Broadway's equivalent of an Oscar, though she has done eighty-two shows, including ballet and opera, since she left the Goodman School in Chicago in the early 1950s. She repeatedly is nominated for a Tony, and last year both she and her husband, actor Tom Aldredge, were up for awards, she for the clothes in *That Championship Season*, and he as the lead in *Sticks and Bones*. He didn't win either.

But Theoni is more than just the designer on *The Great Gatsby*. She is also one of the seamstresses and works along with Erica Eames and Ray Beck in the wardrobe department, several small, stuffy second-floor rooms with a view of the blank walls of an adjoining sound stage.

There is really not enough help to work on the costumes, hats and shoes still to be used in the film, nor is there an outfit for every extra. Improvisation helps. Instead of every woman getting her own hat, the same hats are reused by adding bows or taking flowers off.

Theoni never complains about the shortage of help. She is pleased with what she has been able to do with what she thinks is a relatively small budget, a quarter of a million dollars.

August 2

"I wonder if my eyes are supposed to be opened or closed in the scene," Karen Black says, discussing clinically her death in the film.

It is Clayton's wish that the audience not see Myrtle being struck by the car. The scene begins when Tom, who has Nick and Jordan as passengers in his car, stops outside Wilson's garage when he notices a crowd gathering at the entrance. He pushes through and sees Myrtle dead, stretched out on a work bench, a bright, naked bulb over her head, a blanket pulled up to her neck. Her husband, grief-stricken, is in the corner of the room banging his head against the wall. Visually, it is one of the more dramatic moments in the film because those in the audience unfamiliar with the book should be surprised and engrossed by the sudden tragic turn in the story.

Karen now is in the chair before the mirror in Charlie Parker's makeup room. She is sunk low and is chain smoking. Her feet are on the table and she calls attention to bony lumps at the base of each of her big toes.

"I broke my feet when I was dancing on my toes before I was ready for it," she says. "I studied piano, voice, opera, everything when I was a child," bringing up images of a pretty, talented girl being led by her mother to music lessons, an unwanted weekly intrusion into an otherwise pleasant life in Park Ridge, Illinois, where she was born.

She sinks lower into the chair, her dress riding up her stocky dancer's legs. "I've learned to live with my body. I love my appendix scar."

"She's an adorable nut, isn't she?" Parker smiles over

her shoulder, their faces in the mirror softened into blurs by the lights around it.

Canadian-born Parker has been in Britain thirty years where he has made a living as a makeup man. He has learned how to coexist with the temperaments of his actresses.

Love is seemingly universal on a movie set. It is a word to describe any kind of relationship that develops, and the adjectives describing it get more extravagant as the film progresses. Parker has worked with actresses intimately, as can only those who dress and make them up, and he has earned the right to be indifferent to the theatrical charms of an actress. But he seems genuinely fond of Karen, as do most of the crew, and he is not concerned if her brand of kookiness is real or not. He even goes so far as to let her put on her own makeup base, which she does expertly, dabbing the thin brush into the reddish paste, applying it to her lips.

She stops, the brush in midair, her smile beginning at the corners of her mouth. She wants something and Parker knows it. She thinks her mouth should be split at the corners in her death scene.

"Jack wants you pale and beautiful," Parker says. "He doesn't want your face bloody."

"In the book," she says, "Fitzgerald wrote that Myrtle's mouth was ripped at the corners."

Parker shrugs.

"I'm going to ask Jack." She puts on her shoes and leaves.

It is now a test of will among the director, makeup man and actress as to how Myrtle should look in the scene, and it is not a minor issue, for at stake is the power one has to exert some influence in a rather dictatorial system in which, theoretically, the director is chief.

Parker supports Clayton's interpretation. He also does not want to alienate the actress, and his scheme is to make the split lips look so grotesque that Karen will decide on her own that Clayton is right. His hope is that Clayton will refuse her request, which he does not. He refuses to make an issue of it, and she returns from the Valley of Ashes triumphant. Her look needs no words to tell what the answer is. She sits down, puts her feet on the dressing table and kicks off her shoes.

"Would you like to relax and think of nothing," Parker says. "Put your head back and settle down."

Karen slips slowly down into the chair, wiggling to get her body to fit comfortably into its confinement.

"Concentrate. I'm not joking," Parker says sternly, fatherly, with no harsh threat implied in it.

"You have to tell me what I'm to concentrate on," she says.

"Do exactly as you are told. Don't move. Breathe through your mouth." Parker is applying a clear substance to the corners of her mouth and it is hot. She fans her mouth with a tissue.

"She's crazy crackers," Parker says, shaking his head. "How can you not help but love her? She's so adorable. She's so professional."

She sticks her tongue out at him.

"I should grab it!"

She makes her familiar sucking sound.

He applies a red line to the corners of her mouth. It is only a suggestion of a tear in the flesh.

"It feels alive," she says, pointing to the job he has done on her mouth.

"It's a real cut."

She does not flaunt her modest triumph. She says to the semidefeated Parker, "I follow directions very easily." A hand mirror is on the table and she lifts it to her mouth so that she can see the pale red slits in the corners. "I love it. Great! I'm going to be marvelous dead."

She is asked if she has ever been afraid of being typecast, of getting only off-beat roles. "Sometimes," she says. "I do get offered weird stuff, a lot of caper pictures. But people know I can do almost everything on the screen."

Parker resumes lightening the color of her face, making her a grayish white. He also puts a smudge of dirt on her cheek and forehead.

"Jack says I should be pale," Karen says, as if unconcerned about the other details of her face as long as she won on the lips. "You give a little and get a little."

An unsuccessful attempt to interview her has gone on while she is being made up. The interviewer has tried to be patient with her, but the questions he has asked her have made her give hesitant, overly cute answers. When it comes to the craft of acting, she does not want to be misquoted or misunderstood, and she does not want to give away too much about how she does a role. Her knowledge of Fitzgerald's description of Myrtle's face in death shows she has read and retained her character from the original source.

"I don't like evaluations of the characters I play or how I do them. It's for the birds."

Asked if there are any questions she would have liked to have been asked in an interview and never had, she replies, "All my interviews have been good," making it obvious she thinks this one has been the exception. She stops at the door to tell the interviewer, "You shouldn't try to dig too deep to get to know me."

She walks with Parker past flats from movies long forgotten. It is night, and the huge sound studios are locked. In the cracks of the pavement leading to the Valley of Ashes wild flowers grow. There is a halo of light over Wilson's garage, the only structure in the Valley illuminated, and outside its door cars are parked and extras wait for the signal to push inside to look at the body on the table.

Because of what it represented to him, the horrible geographical transition between the two worlds, it was inevitable a death would take place in the Valley of Ashes.

When she gets to the garage, Karen dutifully climbs on the table and pulls the blanket over her body and closes her eyes. In the scene Clayton has the camera on a track from the gas pumps outside to the table inside the garage near a car on which George Wilson has been

181

working. The camera picks up Tom at his car and follows him through the crowd to the table.

Before he starts shooting the scene, Clayton studies Karen's face with the intensity of someone coming on an expected masterpiece in a museum. He huddles with Robin Grantham, Parker's assistant, who goes over to her and makes the smudges on her cheeks darker. Nothing is done to the mouth wounds. From a distance, and with the overhead light shining down on her face, they are almost unnoticeable, fading already into her pale skin. It is difficult to know who has won. Probably everyone has forgotten an issue had been made over it.

In the corner of the garage after the take, Clayton is talking with his camera crew, and Scott Wilson, in dirty dungarees and a stubble on his chin, is still banging his head against the wall, a grief-stricken expression on his face. No one bothers him. Someone hearing the thud suggests he is going to knock himself out if he stays in character much longer.

Scott is into himself even more than the character he is playing. In his free time on the set, he sometimes plays chess with Waterston; more often he is off by himself moving unobtrusively among the cameras and sets, a sad countenance. He is single and a loner, and a very bad interview which did harm to his family has made him suspicious of revealing more than he has to when speaking to journalists. Though he is consistently polite, one leaves from an encounter with him not knowing much more about him.

"I don't put myself into categories," he says. "I'm not the most outgoing person in the world. As an actor, I'm very intense."

Scott would probably not call what he does method acting. It is a close approximation of it—total involvement in character, the need to perform a psychic purification ritual before appearing in front of the camera, brooding, introspection. The young Marlon Brando and the late James Dean made a cliché of this type of acting; it remains the one authentic American acting school since World War II.

"I never planned on being an actor," he says of the not-too-distant past when he left college in Georgia, bummed to California and fell into acting. "But once I started I knew that's what I wanted to do. I can't describe the rewards I get from acting. You'd have to experience them to know what I'm talking about, of the great feeling of satisfaction you get.

"I read the script before talking with Jack. And then I read the book," Scott says. "George Wilson has a great love for Myrtle, and he's willing to overlook her affair with Tom Buchanan to keep her. He wouldn't know what to do without her. He even says to her, 'Let's go west together.'

"He is the one common man in the movie. He's the only one seen getting his hands dirty. He should be a sympathetic character in the film. It's Jack's idea to make him so, and he's right about it. Why should the only guy in the film who works for a living be made the asshole?

"Besides," he smiles, "poor people are closer together than the rich. They know how to produce babies, not money."

When Myrtle is killed in the car accident, Scott believes Wilson snaps. "Most murders are crimes of passion." He should know something about the psychology of murderers, having played one of the two killers in Truman Capote's *In Cold Blood*.

"In that film I wanted the audience to dislike what the killer represented, but also to understand him and why he did it. It's the same thing with George Wilson. The audience should be torn by Wilson's murder of Gatsby, and hopefully will have a little sympathy for him."

One thinks of what he said as he continues to smack his head against the wooden post, not heavily, but jarringly enough to make his look seem that of a punch-drunk fighter.

"It was Jack's idea to have me bang my head against the post," he says. "Jack's incredible. He has respect for actors, and they appreciate that. Actors respond to it."

The scene is started again. David Tringham tells the

extras to come more swiftly into the garage. The headlights from Tom's car pick out the people by the gas pumps. He sees something has happened to agitate them, pushing towards a disaster as crowds do naturally, attracted to it by some ancient chemical urge to see death and destruction up close. Tom leaves Nick and Jordan behind, and pushes the people aside to get into the garage, with the assurance of one who knows people are in the habit of uncomplainingly getting out of his way.

Dern once said that in the novel Tom Buchanan is a young man under tremendous stress because the only two women he has been able to make it with are being taken away from him. Now, as Buchanan stops at the table, and the dead Myrtle is in front of him, he knows the truth of it. Dern says, "the only woman with whom he has had a street-level communication is gone. He could express certain things with her that he never could with Daisy. Tom is a spoiled young man, and he doesn't get that flattering treatment from Daisy. Not only does Myrtle go out of her way to please him, to make him feel like a big man, but he gets satisfaction from having the power to make her over into someone else. He puts her up in an apartment and gives her money to buy clothes. She has a nice life when she's with him. He's making it happen for her.

"After she dies, his natural impulse is to go back into his own marriage, to try to make it work. The saddest thing for him is suddenly to realize his closest friend is gone. Myrtle is really his best friend."

When he was working on Coppola's script in the spring of 1973, Clayton elected to make every character in his film sympathetic. "I guess I love people more than Fitzgerald did. Nothing is really changed in the film from the book except some of the characters are a little more human."

Dern says, "I play Tom Buchanan more sympathetically than he is in the book, and Jack Clayton made him that way in the script. Tom is not a heavy.

"I found things in Tom to make it clear why Daisy would marry him. He has a sense of humor and a tremendous amount of energy. He is also charming with a certain amount of animal in him, and spoiled girls find this appealing. He's quick-witted, but not necessarily bright. He's learned to think on his feet without becoming ponderous. At thirty-five he finds he doesn't have to work any more. He's robbed of an energy outlet so he plays polo, follows golf and baseball, and has a love affair.

"Of the two men involved with the women in his life, he thinks George Wilson is pathetic. Gatsby he hears about through his parties before he meets him, and he believes he has made his money illegitimately. Then when he finally meets him, he sees he's a little vulgar and doesn't really have any class. He becomes suspicious of Gatsby when he sees how outrageous his conduct is with Daisy and suspects she is snowed by him. But he doesn't know she is having an affair with him until he is told it in the Plaza suite.

"After Gatsby is dead, Tom feels he has been through something heavy with Daisy and he doesn't know quite what. But he does know he has beaten a big guy, and it was the first time he was seriously challenged by anyone in his life.

"And at the end he still does not know that Daisy was behind the wheel of the car that killed Myrtle."

Dern says Buchanan is the hardest role he has ever played. "It's having to contain him as a person. He's had it all at a very young age, and he knows he is a superior person. The biggest thing I pulled off in playing Buchanan is showing a self-control and maturity, and not losing my temper. I didn't put any fake energy into the characterization. It's such a well-written role that the boundaries are set out for Tom."

There remains one rather unpleasant aspect about Tom Buchanan in book and script. He does not stand apart from his class and its attitudes, but represents them, and Tom Buchanan is a racist, very much an American of the 1920s when, at the tail end of Social Darwinism, the theory of the survival of the fittest was still applied to those who were the richest. It makes no difference Buchanan can mouth racist theories at the breakfast table and take seriously a book that expounds the theory that the Nordic race is responsible for everything great in civilization. His social stature had nothing to do with intellect. It comes down to his wealth.

"Sure, Tom could be called a racist," Dern says, "but in his society blacks were the suicide group. How many blacks did he come in contact with? At Yale there were no blacks on his athletic teams. He was a man of his time and class, and he was probably more a pig than a racist."

But Fitzgerald remained certain about the artistic worth of Tom Buchanan as a literary creation. He wrote to Perkins that Tom was the best character he had ever written, and one of the best in American fiction.

August 3

Greg Martin accidentally wounds himself while preparing for Gatsby's death scene in the pool.

He is floating on a rubber raft to which squibs, small explosive pellets, have been attached. Martin wants to see if both man and raft would sink together to the bottom when Gatsby is shot and the raft is hit by bullets. Before he can conduct the experiment, one of the squibs accidentally goes off against his right wrist, opening a wound and numbing his hand. A doctor is called to drain the wound of chemicals, but his hand remains numb for several days, and when the bandage is removed there is a small black mark under the skin.

August 6

Nothing is done to make them more liveable, and by inattention they remain quarters for transients. A minimum number of pieces of functional furniture are in them: dressing table and mirror, a few chairs, a couch with a covering that is worn yet not shabby. The walls are bare.

These dressing rooms are in a block off Stage E, and it is here the actors come to change their clothes for the next scene or to rest when they are not required on the set. Some bantering goes on across the narrow corridor before doors are closed. They are friendly with each other without giving any sense of intimacy to their relationships. They, too, are transients cut off from home for long periods of time, never really adjusting to it. They react predictably to being severed from familiar surroundings. They are at times restless, irritable, prone to quibble over unimportant matters and sometimes to snap at the crew. Except for Mia, London is not their home, and they do not seem particularly fond of the city. They spend most of each day away from it, and when they return to it in the evening it is often too late to go to the theater. Having to get up early, if not as early as when they work in Hollywood, they must go to bed at a reasonable hour, which precludes too many late hours at nightclubs.

They complain London is a boring town.

The pace at Pinewood is much slower than they have come to expect on movie sets in America, and there is some grousing that the film could be finished sooner if less time were taken with setting up the lights and if there were fewer tea breaks. Like students at private schools waiting for the first holiday of the fall semester they show some of the traditional symptoms of being homesick, if not for a specific place, at least another country.

Waterston is most articulate about the sensation of being in a strange city and not really being a part of it, though he had been in London earlier in the year to do *The Glass Menagerie* with Katharine Hepburn. He tells about an experiment in which a man was kept in a room without light or sound for days, and he compares the feeling of what this man must have gone through (being cut off from all sensual experience) with how he has felt in his first few weeks in London.

Waterston also confirms what Dern had said about him in Newport, that he has not yet learned what role to wear in public as an actor to disguise his real self. "I don't know what part is mine yet, so I stay by myself. It's much easier," he says.

When he is not working on the set, Waterston is back in his dressing room either playing chess or sleeping. He has the ability of the untroubled young to flop on a bed

187

and go to sleep immediately, and he is now taking a nap when he is called back to do a scene in the study of Gatsby's mansion, which is not in the book.

It is the first meeting between the two men when Nick finds out who Gatsby is. In the book Nick is sitting with Jordan at a Gatsby party talking with a man who is about his own age of their experiences in World War I. The stranger asks Nick if he would like to take a ride in a hydroplane he had purchased. Nick agrees, and in a passing conversation says he has never met the host of the party. The stranger, bemused, identifies himself as Gatsby, confessing he is a bad host for not having told him.

Clayton believes the audience would not accept this scene because they would be looking at Redford, the movie star, not Gatsby, a shadowy, unknown person to Nick, and they would say it is impossible for Nick not to know who Redford is.

Clayton changed the scene to the study and has Nick summoned there by Gatsby, who is at the window looking down on the party as Nick enters. What transpires between the men in those first seconds is embarrassing to both since they can say only banalities to hide the initial reaction to each other and the purpose Gatsby has for the meeting. Gatsby does most of the talking. He says he does not like parties and that as neighbors they should get to know each other better. A telephone call breaks off what has become a trying experience for Gatsby since he is too inhibited to blurt out that he wants Nick to arrange a meeting for him with Daisy.

Redford is a conscientious student of any role he undertakes, and early in the production he typed up some ideas about his concept of Gatsby. Interestingly, what appealed to him in the character, as well as bothered him, is that Gatsby is such a mystery both to those with whom he comes in contact and to the reader, who never really learns how Gatsby made his wealth—whether he is a criminal.

In his memo, Redford made twelve suggestions, most

of them line changes in the script, and then went into some detail about Gatsby.

"CHARACTER GATSBY" Successful gestures. Personality. Way of putting feet down as though they were secure there. Understanding smile. One of eternal reassurance. Concentrates on *you* with an irresistible prejudice in your favor. Picks words with care. Movement—absence of rigid sitting in youth—love for sporadic games—restlessness, breaking through punctilious manner. Smile—What is Gatsby: He must be clear. The confused image is dangerous. This does not mean that the mystery should be lost. The mystery is a large part of the attraction of Gatsby. How much of Gatsby is real and how much is an abstraction of our fantasies about wealth, power and romance."

From his initial conception, Fitzgerald was never that certain of Gatsby's character either. This was evident to Perkins after his first reading of the novel. He claimed Gatsby was too vague, that the lack of physical details about his appearance made him seem older than the text indicated, which is only one or two years more than Nick, who is thirty.

Fitzgerald answered him, "I myself didn't know what Gatsby looked like or was engaged in." He asked Zelda to draw pictures of how she thought Gatsby should look. He took Perkins's advice and made the changes. "I've brought Gatsby to life," he exclaimed in a letter to his editor in February, 1925, after having finished the galleys.

Fitzgerald had said Gatsby was modeled on a Long Island bootlegger he had met, but in the summer of 1925 he was still uncertain about Gatsby and wrote to author John Peale Bishop, "You are right about Gatsby being blurred and patchy. I never at any time saw him clear myself—for he started as one man and then changed into myself—the amalgam was never complete in my mind."

As he worked his way into the role in Newport and those first weeks in London, Redford became somewhat more definite about Gatsby's character:

"He's a strange amalgamation of various types, and it would be a mistake to go for all of them in getting his character on the screen. The best piece of writing in the book is Tom Buchanan. Fitzgerald didn't give Gatsby that clear an explanation. He has too many inconsistent sides. He's cool and distant. He's mysterious and eager to make people feel important. He's someone who play-acts the role of the great host. And at times, Fitzgerald made his character too foolish.

"Gatsby is an essence of something. He's intangible. He represents an attitude rather than being a character. The script has corrected much of this.

"Gatsby is now the embodiment of everything thought necessary to be successful. The attractive part of him is that he is a total romantic.

"The lasting impression you get of *The Great Gatsby* is of romance and enterprise, and a contempt in the story for basing everything on winning or losing. The book shows what a catastrophe is done to values when winning is made everything."

How much of what he knows about Gatsby can he get on the screen? Redford's basic intelligence makes him quite capable of presenting a rational, clear interpretation of Gatsby. The mystery remains in the transmission of an idea how to play Gatsby from the mind to the hands, legs and face of the actor, of being able to turn oneself into somebody else while still being the same actor physically as he has been in a dozen other films. It is the magical part of acting that can never really be satisfactorily explained away: how Laurence Olivier can convincingly be both Heathcliff and Hamlet.

What Redford has said about Gatsby can be seen now in the way he stands at the window holding back the curtain to better observe his creation below of which he wants no part. He is anxious about how the young man ushered into his study will respond to his home and party. His mansion is "the monument he has built for his passion for Daisy," Redford says, and when he lets the curtain fall against the window and turns to greet Nick he is shy, ready to do anything so as not to offend his guest.

One forgets it is Redford moving from the window to the desk. He is now a man with an obsession, and the party outside does not distract from it; it only makes it sadder.

August 7

Mia is pregnant!

Under normal circumstances this would be a cause for celebration. Unfortunately, her pending motherhood will take place in the middle of a $6.5-million picture, and the response is not overwhelmingly favorable. Priorities in movies are frequently established outside human considerations. The picture comes first, and taste is not always evident in those dealing with actors. The production believes it is justified in being upset. She could have waited until the fall to become pregnant. A rumor is circulated that the production might be suspended, which is a very unrealistic alternative since more than half of the picture has already been shot. Mia says the baby is not due until March, but her counting is not accepted without verification, and a call is placed to the doctor who had examined her in the spring before she began the film to find out if she had been pregnant then. Someone makes the suggestion that Mia be talked into going away for a long weekend and coming back without the child. This is never seriously pursued, though the proposer of it claims another movie star had submitted to an abortion while involved in an expensive film with a long shooting schedule.

It is finally decided to rearrange the shooting schedule to get more of her dramatic scenes done earlier. There is no way she can get her work done in less than six weeks. The possibility of going to a six-day work week is explored and discarded because there are not enough sound stages available or workers to build the necessary sets at once.

Many of these proposals and the discussions about her condition are calculating and vulgar. The film remains the prime consideration; completing it without incident or lengthy delay is the goal. Getting there almost justifies the means, which reveals how much Marxist insights have infiltrated the most capitalistic of enterprises.

There is even a Freudian explanation offered for why she allowed herself to become pregnant now. Hating acting, yet attracted to it, preferring to be a mother more than a movie star now, she unconsciously dared to get pregnant as a form of rebellion against her servitude to movies.

Around the initial panic to her announcement, Mia is serenely pleasant. She is bothered by morning sickness and tires more quickly, but she has never been more lovely. One thinks it might be her wig and costume as Daisy that have given her a mature feminine sexuality which was absent in her earlier gamine performances. When she takes off her wig, her brown hair falling to her shoulders, replaces the 1920 clothes with caftans and jeans, and moves in a charming, hesitant step, as if expected to be reprimanded for her freedom, she is even more appealing.

But now she is again in her 1920s clothes in Gatsby's study in the continuation of a scene begun in Marble Hall, Newport, where Gatsby is showing Nick and Daisy his house. They are in the study, and Gatsby is opening a champagne bottle. It is not as easy as it seems on screen. A case of Dom Perignon is off camera and a grip, trying to help Redford, loosens the wire around the cork under the wrapping before handing it to him. Each take requires a new bottle of champagne to be opened. The first time the cork comes out effortlessly, but before he can pour it, the champagne foams over Redford's hand. He goes right on with his line; only after Clayton calls the scene does he burst out laughing. On the next take, the cork won't come out. On the third take the cork pops and the champagne flows on cue.

It is weeks later that Redford remembers he wanted to make a slight change in the scene about Dan Cody, Gatsby's patron who rescued him as a young man from the prospects of a mediocre, unadventuresome farm life in Minnesota and took him away for five years on a yacht that circled the globe three times. The voyage was an alliance of several strains in the great American dream: Cody, who went West with a great appetite for wealth and women, becoming a millionaire several times over in the silver fields of Nevada, exploiting the earth as had his ancestors—for wealth was everyone's rightful inheritance in America; and Gatsby, the romantic, dreaming of escape through material possessions, not yet knowing what must be surrendered in the accumulation of them, certain only that by having them are reveries made into life. Cody dies and leaves Gatsby $25,000. He never gets it. Cody's wealth goes to his last, great whore, Ella Kaye.

Fitzgerald said Cody filled out Gatsby from a "vague contour" to the "substantiality of a man," and now on the desk in his study Gatsby keeps a photograph of his benefactor who had, as Fitzgerald described, ". . . a hard, empty face—the pioneer debauchee, who during one phase of American life brought back to the Eastern Seaboard the savage violence of the frontier brothel and saloon."

In the scene, Nick sees the photograph of Cody and asks, "Who's this?" Gatsby replies, "Mr. Dan Cody, old sport. He's dead now. He used to be my best friend years ago."

Redford wanted Nick to continue inquiring about Cody, and Gatsby would slip right through the questions by handing champagne to Daisy and going on to his story about attending Oxford after the war.

"I couldn't remember that day for the life of me what it was about Cody I wanted to have in the scene," Redford says, "but I knew I wanted to make more of Cody. I love the background Fitzgerald gave him.

"Then it came to me a month later. There is a certain thing Gatsby does through the whole film. He doesn't answer certain questions. He is forever not answering direct questions, especially from Nick who he wants to keep away from his past.

"Gatsby is afraid he'll lose his social standing if it is found out how he makes his money. It's not like today when anyone will be accepted for what he does, including criminals, as long as the color in the hand is green."

The scene goes well through the normal number of takes that Clayton requires, which is more than his actors are used to, thinking he does too many and is being overly deliberate.

Redford notices Clayton has changed his directorial technique from Newport where he did not print many takes, often using one long master shot with the camera sweeping in for close-ups without breaking the shot. In London, Redford says, he is having many more takes printed. The reason for this, Redford assumes, is that he is now more sure of what he is getting on film than he was in Newport. There, the studio was seeing rushes daily in New York; and under tremendous pressure from the unions and the uncertainty of the weather, Clayton adopted a style that would prevent the studio from making its own choices in the final cutting of the film by limiting the number of printed takes available for it to play with. In London, he does not have to show rushes daily to the studio, the home office being an ocean away.

"The way he did it in Newport was a gamble," Redford says, "but if he pulls if off it will be brilliant."

Redford's praise of Clayton remains extravagant with one reservation, less a criticism than the cry for the help only a director can give an actor.

"I wouldn't have done this film without Clayton as director," Redford says. "He is a man of great elegance and brings to every scene a superb point of view. He knows precisely what he wants to do. But I wish he was stronger with his actors and would really direct them."

As Redford speaks one sees Clayton working with his

actors, patiently, adoringly, never raising a voice to them, being totally chivalrous with his actresses. One day he went to Mia, and making it seem imaginatively whimsical, kissed her on the forehead and said, "My day wouldn't be complete if I let it go without kissing you at least twice."

"It's the English class-consciousness in him," Redford says. "In England the artist is of extreme importance, and you have to show a deference to him."

Clayton is not a director with frequent specific instructions to his actors. He makes much more subtle suggestions about toning down or playing up a scene.

"Actors are like domestic pets," Redford says. "They need to be trained and guided into place. Jack never says, 'Don't move this way or that.' "

Dern has a different complaint. His acting style is purely American, very much spontaneous and improvised. He ad-libs dialogue. Redford says this is wrong. "You just can't do that with Fitzgerald's dialogue. It'll be a disaster." But he is in awe of Dern's sharpness and the choices he makes in his characterization.

It is Dern's contention the actors must have time to work out a scene by themselves before being directed in it. "We come on the set to rehearse, and the scene has already been blocked out by Jack and the crew. There's no time to work on the scene, and it's bad for the type of actors you have in this film, who are very spontaneous. By not giving them the opportunity to show what they can do you're only inhibiting them."

Apparently this does not bother all the actors in the film. Sam and Mia seem to have the self-control of the stage actor that comes with not having their performance broken down into endless takes. The stage actor must have his character well-thought-out and plotted. He must see the role as a total character that enters the narrative at a certain time limited by the rise and fall of the curtain. A movie actor discerns his character by scenes and moments, expressions and gestures. With the discipline they have had in stage training—Mia a more recent graduate of it—they seem to respond to the freedom Clayton has given them to work out their characters in the broadest strokes.

Independence does not seem a burden to these actors, including Dern. The issue is how much Dern is playing devil's advocate, by keeping the rest of the cast creatively alert by his criticisms. Surprisingly, the more he stirs things up, the more he is liked by cast and crew. He is a charming original.

August 8

The camera is a blank eye disconnected, and cumbersomely afloat in front of the light from the sky, moving with a semblance of grace, taking in the hand-crank phonograph machine, sliding quickly over the lovers stretched on the floor in the cabana—he in black knit trunks and a striped sleeveless shirt, she in a flowing white dressing gown—stopping at their reflection in the small, round fish pond a few feet from the swimming pool.

This is one of the scenes inserted by Clayton that does not appear in the novel. It shows the renewal of the love affair between Gatsby and Daisy. One of the best critics of his own work, Fitzgerald said a fault of the novel is that the reader knows nothing of what takes place between Gatsby and Daisy when they resume their romance. The event comes to the reader secondhand through Jordan and Nick.

"It's terrible," Redford says, "but there's no romance in the Great American Novel."

The romance is given a cinematic lyricism in this scene: the blue and white Greek drapes billow, the goldfish dart through the images of the lovers on the surface of the pond, the lovers kiss, the phonograph plays a sentimental ballad.

"Jack is directing the montage between the lovers to this point where they kiss, which is like the blossoming of a flower," Redford says.

Clayton has had this scene in mind for more than a year, before the initial rewrites of the script, according to

Jeannie Sims. But it takes him longer than he wants to get it on film. The goldfish will not stay in the end of the pond near the lovers; they continuously swim out of the scene. A barricade is put across the middle to keep the fish near the actors. Next Clayton decides the water is too light for the images and he has it darkened. This takes several hours and gives David Merrick, standing on the grass by the swimming pool, opportunity to go over again his objections to having the production moved to London.

"The pool and all this," Merrick says, pointing to the false building fronts attached to the back of the Pinewood office, "cost $100,000."

Back at the fish pond, the camera drifts over the actors and their rippling images in the water. The camera is never still if it is to take in everything important in the scene.

"Jack doesn't like to see things still in his movie," Redford says of Clayton's directorial style.

The smile, half crooked and sad, is there as he moves around the equipment, and so is the mystery about the person behind the smile; it is this to which his crew and cast respond. Because it is so bland and unrevealing, they can create their own person behind it to explain him to themselves. Of his personal life not much is known—only that he has had two wives, that he began his career in the British film industry before the war, where he worked as a gofor. After serving in the Royal Air Force with tours of duty in many foreign countries, he worked his way through almost every job in the movie industry from first assistant director to production manager before his first directorial assignment, the short film, *The Bespoke Overcoat*, which won him an Oscar for the Best Short Subject, and then *Room at the Top*, the film that secured his reputation as a brilliant if illusive director.

In a decade he has made only four feature films, and the mystery remains how a Britisher came to direct this most American of novels. One of the rumors is that Warren Beatty, who wanted to play Gatsby, had suggested

Clayton to Ali MacGraw. "I don't know if Warren was responsible for bringing up my name with Paramount, but I know I was approved for the job by Bob Evans," Clayton says.

He came on the picture in October, 1971, many years after he had read *The Great Gatsby* for the first time in 1935. "I was fifteen years old. I have an incredibly strong memory. That year I read two books: *They Shoot Horses, Don't They?* and *The Great Gatsby*. I wanted to make both of them into movies, and at one time I even tried to buy the rights to *Gatsby*."

"I was attracted to the story and the people in *Gatsby*. I love people obsessed, people with grand delusions. I'm enormously sympathetic with all the characters in the book. I like them all, even Tom.

"I'm also attracted to stories about social class. *Room at the Top* is about class. Set in England immediately after the war, it shows the tremendous change that took place in the social structure of the country, very markedly so. There's a universality to these stories. Emotions and aspirations don't change. Over the years there has been very little change in class attitudes. You can see this in the rich of Newport."

As he talks about his film, the artificial material of the floor around the pool sways to the heavy movements of the grips crossing it, and the motion is that of a boat entering slightly rough water.

"There are great physical difficulties with this picture," he says. "It should have been made in America, and I deeply resent people saying I wanted to bring the production to England. To keep it totally and authentically American, everything had to be copied, not designed, and I insisted we hire only Americans even in the bit parts to keep the look American."

A worker moves past Clayton with a fan. He plugs it in to an outlet and directs it on the curtains, which explode over the lovers. Before the fan is turned off, the curtains slowly drift over them, the shadow trailing the material.

"Fifty percent of what I do in a film is worked out in

advance, the other half is improvised in the rehearsal period. If you work over a scene too much you take out a great deal of its freshness.

"This is not a fast-tempo film. It's a film of great mood, of heat and emotion."

There is a languidness now in the way he directs the lovers to shift their bodies to embrace, to be in a better position to study features long forgotten and untouched. Daisy lifts her arms, and the silk spreads like butterfly's wings. The wind from the fan sets the material in motion once more.

How lovely it is to be beautiful and wealthy, to have everything before you, to believe, as does Gatsby as he envelops Daisy, that the past can be reclaimed. It is an exquisite scene that shows how emotion can expand in wealth-bought moments of leisure.

But how far can money take you? Can one ever escape the consequences of the pursuit?

That evening in a health club in the basement of a fashionable hotel in Park Lane, three American businessmen, naked, their bodies pink and sweaty, sit in a row in a sauna discussing the troubles of Spiro Agnew. They are sympathetic, having voted for his political party from habit and self-interest, or what they believe it to be since money and what it can buy eventually makes allies of those who have made money the means and goal of life. These men are practical, not profound. They do not question the values of the business world. However, over the summer they have seen their version of the American Dream tarnished by Watergate. The lack of confidence in America is gauged in the continuous decline of the dollar in international trading.

"They shouldn't bring this out," one of them says, his buttocks making a sucking sound when he shifts them on the wet wood. "Look what it's doing to our image."

The redness from the dry heat makes their paunches look baby smooth; only their faces give way to the years and their newfound sadness. They try so hard to remain innocents, hoping a little corruption can be contained as long as the system is basically sound. But is it? Watergate is creating a new generation of doubters.

"Every businessman has done something a little dishonest," another says without conviction.

The dry heat in the box has cleared the air of everything but a suffocatingly confused morality.

August 9

It is an important confrontation scene between the lovers in Gatsby's bedroom. It is another scene to show what the lovers do in the present. Gatsby not only wants to reclaim the past, to obliterate it, but also to have Daisy explain precisely why she would not marry him, why she abandoned him for Tom Buchanan, a man she does not love.

Daisy tells him about her wedding day, how it began with her drunk and Jordan Baker dumping her into a cold tub of water to sober her up for the ceremony. She breaks down and, sobbing, gives a perfectly logical explanation for her action.

". . . rich girls don't marry poor boys, Jay Gatsby. Haven't you heard? Rich girls don't marry poor boys."

It is a long, intricate scene for Mia. She begins it on one side of the room before a full-length mirror, walks to Redford who sits in a chair on the other side, kneels and begins crying. She releases the tears on cue, and quickly stops them when the take is over.

"It's such a difficult scene," Mia says. "The mood changes frequently in it. It's hard to say what Daisy is doing at that moment. You can interpret the scene so many ways. I think she is saying to Gatsby, 'Look, it's your fault. You've made me suffer. You were in a uniform, and I couldn't tell who you were, if you were rich or poor. You really betrayed me by leading me on with that uniform.' But then, Daisy, is also such a selfish girl."

Mia has been working on the part for months now. It is still an intellectual and artistic challenge. She is nervous when there are strangers on the set watching her work, and becomes exasperated when photographers

200

whom she does not know impassively click off exposures while she is acting.

"I don't think I've compromised myself in how I'm playing Daisy," she says. "Jack has given me a lot of options in working out the part."

She recrosses the room, entirely feminine, and though she is extremely thin, her arms and legs almost without shape, she is tremendously sexual in an adult way, which has to do with the whole woman and the self within as much as with any specific exterior part like big breasts, ripe thighs or well-curved legs.

There are many takes. Clayton is more deliberate than usual, doing at least six takes for most of the scenes now. Repetition has not given Mia more confidence; she is even upset by the presence of the producer back of the camera by himself, his face devoid of expression. This inhibits the actors because they cannot read if he approves of their performance.

Redford, too, is bothered by the abundance of strangers and photographers on the set this day and he agrees with Mia to ask Clayton that only essential personnel be allowed to stay.

"I always thought I would like to play Daisy," Mia says. "I saw her as a collage of personalities that when come together present a certain life-style. After I was given the role I read and read everything, Fitzgerald's novels, books about him and Zelda. His descriptive passages still give me such pleasure. The last paragraph in *Gatsby* about the orgiastic future and how each year it recedes still moves me to tears. The books that were most helpful were the biography *Zelda* by Nancy Milford and Fitzgerald's *The Beautiful and the Damned.*

"In getting Daisy down as a character I tried many kinds of walks, hand motions and voice levels until I felt right doing it. What must come out in acting is what comes most naturally, and you know what that is from the inside out. I did not have to look at myself in a mirror to see how I walk and move to know if it is right. It felt right and I knew the character of Daisy had emerged from within me.

"In the first script Daisy was to be Southern and I wanted to do the role in an accent. But Jack felt the point in using the accent would be difficult to make on the screen.

"Some of the difficulty with the role and the script is that Fitzgerald's dialogue is very flowery. It is prose written for the printed page, not to be spoken, such as 'You remind me of a rose' or 'Is this where you live, absolutely dearest one?' "

Redford concurs with her about Fitzgerald's dialogue. It was Clayton's decision to use as much of it as possible, figuring that it is too well-known to be tampered with, which would set him up for charges of destroying a masterpiece by purists who have never had to speak dialogue written to be read.

"It's too literary and stilted," Redford says, "and Gatsby often gets the worse lines to say."

The scene goes well between Mia and Redford, and in the breaks they talk about how to improve it. There is an admiration between them for the skills each brings to the camera and each other's temperament. If all actors have them, they keep theirs under control. Scenes are done without emotional flare-ups, the safety valves in movie work for insecure persons.

Later Redford tells friends in New York that Mia is probably the most professional actress he has ever worked with, and his judgment is supported by Annabel, who is usually sparing in her praise. She says Mia can pick up a scene effortlessly, even after a break in the continuity, coming back to it with the same body motions and voice level.

It is not an easy time for Mia. She suffers from morning sickness. There is talk of renting a cottage nearer the studio so she will not have to endure the hour ride from her home in Surrey each morning. This is not done. She often comes now from bed to the studio in her nightgown, knowing there will be long waits before she is called on the set, and she can go back to sleep in her dressing room.

Her pregnancy is the grist for gossip on the set. A movie company without something to fantasize about is a company in trouble, and though *Gatsby*, amazingly for the pressure on the production, has been relatively free of problems that disrupt and delay shooting—a knowledgeable New Yorker says he knew the film was free of major troubles when he read nothing adverse about it in the gossip columns—Mia has given them something to talk about in the interminable moments between scenes when a set is being relit or redecorated and boredom breeds malicious rumors.

Because she has survived in a profession with a high mortality rate (and how many of her generation in Hollywood, still young, have been able to keep a career going?) despite a well-publicized disastrous first marriage and a string of unsuccessful films, Mia is one of those who attracts friends who want to be there when she falls. Behind her back these people say she is cold and calculating, which goes against the evidence on the set, where she is nothing less than friendly with the other actors and crew down to the lowest-paid grip. It is only a new phase, they say, as if actresses cannot stop role-playing off the set. But better for those who work with her, if this is an act, that she is gracious rather than bitchy.

"I don't think any of us are like the characters we play in the film," she says. "I know I'm nothing like Daisy. She believes money can shield you from life. It's hard to believe a person like Daisy can still exist in the world. Maybe they still do in the South. The way to play Daisy I gleaned from Fitzgerald, not from my own life.

"Daisy is not meant to be a sympathetic character," she says, and then on reflection quickly changes this harsh judgment.

"When I read the part, my heart didn't swell to a sympathetic character. I'm naturally a sympathetic person, and I respond to the sadness of messed-up, lost people. But I realized that they probably could not be anything else but the kind of people they are. They do not have many options. The more you understand them, the more you realize they are trapped. In one way the people in a

203

ghetto are better off than they are. At least they have something to aspire to, a way of life that is better off materially.

"If the drive for money is taken away from them, it would be interesting to see what Fitzgerald's characters would do."

When she is working, Mia invariably has lunch in the studio commissary, taking a big window table that becomes her special place from where she welcomes anyone from the production to eat with her, most often Sam and Lois, but frequently Annabel. She changes from her costume, putting on a comfortable caftan or, later in the filming, as her pregnancy advances and shows, her nightgown with a coat around her shoulders. She leaves her wig on, and this confuses friends, Candace Bergen, for example, who does not recognize her and walks past without speaking.

"Candace! It's me, Mia!" she says with the glee of one used to surprising friends.

She is also cordial with actors and staff of the other films being shot in Pinewood, and one of her luncheon guests is Michael Dunn, the dwarf, who is working on *The Abdication* with Liv Ullmann and Peter Finch. She has a sturdy appetite but eats with the eclecticism of a child, pushing aside unwanted mounds of food that do not please her, devouring what tastes good: a cool glass of wine, smoked salmon, a dessert with fresh cream.

She is both a good storyteller and a listener at the table; being both salty and elegant in her language depending on the subject and guest. There is the suggestion of the hedonist still within her, that has been pushed aside for a newer self, the well-mannered, aristocratic young woman who reads good books and enjoys classical music.

"I can't get through Hardy or Henry James," she says, "but I really enjoy Solzhenitsyn."

Without much in the way of a formal education, she has made herself well-read. She is a product of a number of fashionable convent schools and was never a good student at any of them. "Learning was presented so dully at those places. I did all the right things. Crammed for my exams. But my mind kept wandering. I hated school. I just barely graduated. I knew I would have to learn on my own, and I read voraciously." She prides herself on the friends she has made in the intellectual community where she is esteemed as something other than an actress. A close friend is author Thornton Wilder, one of the many older persons with whom she feels more comfortable than with some of her contemporaries.

She had the best and worst of a Hollywood childhood. Her parents were part of one of the world's most insecure businesses. Her mother is Maureen O'Sullivan, still most famous as the first Jane in the Tarzan films; her father was the director John Farrow, who made a number of sturdy B movies—among them the thriller, *The Big Clock* in the late 1940s—but who never came up with the big one to put him in the first rank of directors.

"At the end of his life my father was not poor, but fairly broke. He couldn't get work in films and was doing television shows. He died of a stroke ten years ago, just after my mother had a hit on Broadway in *Never Too Late*. Our family was always very close. My brother and sisters are still my best friends."

She is proud of her mother who has kept a career going longer than most actresses of her generation. "My mother is a survivor," she says, "and she has kept her sense of humor."

As a child of the business she knew very little else in her early years. From the time she could dream and try to act them out she wanted to be an actress. "I was always putting on neighborhood plays. I loved make-believe. In nursery school I was always a terrible audience. I came alive only on the stage."

Her career was established early, at eighteen, in the popular television series "Peyton Place," in which she played the sensitive waif Allison. She stayed with the show two years until she became a victim of amnesia in the script, strayed off and was written out. She enjoyed doing the series only for the first year. "They brought in so many new characters and plots that the audience became confused. And they had us doing two segments at once. I was commuting between sets at 20th on roller skates."

She has done very little television since "Peyton Place," and now sees that medium as awesome in the way it eats up talent. "You can burn yourself out quickly in television." Still, she is one of the few still working from that first generation of young television actresses. "A lot of the people I first worked with in television got sifted out between the ages of twenty and thirty."

She began her own movie career after the end of the studio system to which her parents belonged. "In those days the studios protected their people and allowed them to make mistakes. They made so many pictures that they didn't have to carry a stigma if one of them failed. The only place today where you can experiment like that is on the stage. I don't want to make a lot of films. I'd like to keep doing one a year, which wouldn't take me away from my family for very long.

"The stage is first with me now. The theater is the place to learn. I want to do Shakespeare and Chekhov and then I'd like to do a farce. There's not enough time to do everything I want on the stage. Still I know the stage is where people go who love acting, and in Great Britain you get marvelous opportunities to work on the stage with great actors. Over here actors do movies for money."

The glass of red wine has beads of condensation on the edge when her lips touch it, and she savors the liquid, her big round eyes rising over it. The eyes are those of a child with wonderful expectations of life, and it is those eyes which attract one to her first; they disarm you with her sense of duality of innocence and coquettishness.

A grip summons her back to the set. Without her glasses on, she walks as if she expects to ram into something. She is almost past John Box at the table nearest the entrance when he says to her, in complimenting her on the scene she is doing with Redford, "I'm glad I didn't meet a girl like Daisy when I was young."

The next day she continues the same scene, not allowing anything that might have happened in the interval, or her morning nausea, to interfere with her performance; she picks up the same physical motions and voice inflections of the agitated Daisy who wants to keep both husband and lover, and believes she can do this if one does not force her to make a choice.

As Mia and Redford work on the scene, Bruce Dern, in track clothes and sweaty from his daily run, stands behind the camera and at the break, yells, "I'm not going to stand around watching some asshole make love to my wife." Redford is the first to laugh.

At lunch Mia continues to talk about her childhood in Hollywood and says she does not make moral judgments about those days. She is a woman who does not live in the past.

"In my dreams I'm always flying. I feel as if I have no brakes. They say if you dream about flying you won't change. But until recently my life was always changing. I had remained fluid, maybe a little too fluid," she says in obvious reference to stories about her life-style as the heroine of the flower children in the 1960s.

Is the serenity she now exudes also fluid, subject to change? Some of her composure must be attributed to her interest in philosophy, in particular Eastern religion with the emphasis on meditation. She was one of the first celebrities to travel to the Far East to partake of the spiritual healing of Transcendental Meditation. Unlike the later camp followers of that religious vogue in Hollywood, she retained her interest and faith in it, using that which has been helpful to her.

"I've read a lot about religion in the past few years, and I've learned there are no conflicting truths."

Her goals in life are now clear, she says. What then is important to her life, the essential ingredient? Is it her family, her way of life in England that is so different, less hurried than what she knew in Hollywood and so much more reflective? "I can see myself doing something else, being someone other than an actress. There is something even more important to me than my family, but I don't want to talk about it."

There is a sincere finality in the way she says it that closes off further discussion of this point.

Her eyes, however, hold on to the moment, the question and the promise.

When she returns to work in the stifling second-floor wardrobe room, a string has broken on a Cartier pearl necklace and Ray Beck and Erica Eames are diligently restringing the pearls.

August 13

Today Gatsby dies.

It is the end of the story, really, and when Scribner's was preparing *The Great Gatsby* for publication, Fitzgerald wrote to his editor pleading that the advance publicity not tell that Gatsby gets killed, that this foreknowledge would ruin the book's suspense for potential readers.

It is an extremely hot day for the murder. The weather has been spectacular for the past few weeks—the sky cloudless, the air warm without the depressing humidity of New York or Chicago. The English crew is not used to such weather, and they bare their chests to the sun as if the pleasurable sensation of warmth is new to them. On lunch break they swim in Gatsby's pool behind the production office. They are a much more docile group of workers than the Americans in Newport, who were efficient, independent and garrulous. The British are more responsive to chains of command and divisions of power; yet they are not necessarily better workers. There is not much camaraderie with those above them in hierarchy. The creative division between them and those who design, photograph, direct and act in movies is respected. Eventually, they get things done, but they seem to be conditioned to tea breaks, shorter work days and lower pay. If not inspired laborers, they are good, decent men, and they frolic in the pool with gratitude, as if they were sons of the grounds keeper allowed to use the master's pool.

It is cleared now. At the end of the pool farthest from the cabana, two cameras are on platforms in the water. Clayton, bare-chested, wades into the shallow end, oblivious that his jeans are getting wet.

In his striped two-piece bathing suit, his head resting on his folded arms, Redford is on a rubber raft drifting in the water near the cameras. The point of view is a long shot of the cabana and a hand, holding a gun, protruding between the curtain and the white column.

Before the first take, Scott Wilson, in a gray work shirt and soiled overalls, paces by the goldfish pond. He is spaced-out, his eyes focusing into himself and his conception of his character, George Wilson, not on the crew and spectators ringing the distant end of the pool for this climactic moment. Jeannie Sims goes to those she thinks might want to talk with Scott and suggests they don't "while he is getting into his role." He seems to be there already, relentlessly circling the pond, the gun in his hand jerking nervously, his eyes bloodshot.

The barrel of the gun comes through the space between column and curtain, and it recoils when the first bullet is fired. Redford leisurely rolls off the raft and stays submerged a few seconds. Another take. Another roll. After each take Redford swims to the side of the pool and dries himself off. He is a most unconcerned victim, dying indifferently. Those unfamiliar with filmmaking among the spectators do not realize he is not in the scene. "I'm not even into my role now," he says.

He is in the scene after lunch. Before he gets back on the raft, a black girdle containing pellets which will explode with a substance resembling blood when detonated is strapped around his lower chest, concealed by the top of his bathing suit. The girdle pinches his skin and pulls his red chest hairs. Someone suggests he shave his chest for the scene. Redford snickers and takes his place on the raft. Greg Martin wades to him and gives him a capsule which, when he bites, will give off a liquid simulating

209

blood pouring from his mouth. The pellets will be set off from a panel worked by a man behind the camera. Next to it is a bottle of fake blood called Kensington Gore.

In the scene Gatsby, exhausted from the events of the previous night (having spent the early morning hours with Nick telling him what had happened in the car that Daisy was driving and then waiting fruitlessly for her to come to him for help), is into his own reveries, still holding to the dream. He hears something in the cabana. He raises himself and starts to turn when the gun is fired. His body jerks, and the blood erupts through the cloth of his bathing suit and gushes from his mouth before he slips off the raft and sinks slowly to the bottom.

There is pain in having the pellets explode against his skin. "It's this sensation," Redford says, slamming his fist against the chest of the man next to him.

On the second take, Redford is in the process of rolling off the raft when the third pellet goes off belatedly, stunning his right arm with its sharp impact. Clayton sees Redford is in some pain and asks him solicitously, in the same voice of concern he used with the worker in Newport, if he wants a doctor. Redford brushes it off, rubs his arm and climbs back on the raft.

On the third take, the pellets on both Redford and the raft go off at once, so that both sink together before Redford has a chance to roll clear of it.

"What are you doing?" someone chides the emerging, bemused Redford.

"I'm coming up just to breathe," he says.

Take after take is called; two cameras record the scene, one a close-up of the bullets crashing into Gatsby's body, the other the full scene of the body being struck, pulled up by the impact and then falling into the water. In the cutting room both angles will be used to show Gatsby's death. It is not a pleasant experience for Redford to have the pellets open repeatedly against his chest. He goes through each take with equanimity, even seeing the humor in getting paid for having your body smacked by detonations.

It is almost an idyllic end for Gatsby—the Grecian curtains flapping in the breeze, the water clear and calm, the columns of the cabana impersonal and stately. When he hears the footsteps, and calls "Daisy," how really near is his dream.

Nick believes Gatsby had lost the dream when she did not call him during the night. He realizes Gatsby has "paid a high price for living too long with a single dream." From the novel one remembers how Nick sees the pool—leaves scattered across its surface, driven by the wind towards the drain—and the blood. In the pool now, the imitation blood quickly loses its color and hardens on the surface, like wax melting from the heat of a candle.

The tragedy is completed. The list of the Buchanan victims is finished. Wilson turns the gun on himself, puts the barrel in his mouth and fires.

"Gatsby dies because he's a schmuck," Redford says. "He had the strength of will to get him where he is, but the fatal mistake is that he believed you can repeat the past."

August 16

On the veranda the Buchanans are entertaining Jordan Baker and Nick Carraway, he for the first time in their home. Tom is talking about a book that has impressed him, *The Rise of the Colored Empires.* He warns that the white race faces the possibility of being submerged by the blacks. Low-key racism over the morning coffee. Daisy does not take ideas seriously. She gently mocks her husband, saying to Nick that the black people have to be beaten down. A telephone rings and Tom goes to the sun porch to answer it. Up to then an engaging participant in the conversation, Daisy loses her lightness, excuses herself and follows her husband, almost running. Jordan, whom Nick has just met, and knows from the newspapers as a promising golfer—but one who reputedly cheats in the big matches—whispers to him that Tom has a girl friend.

The actors have been together now for several months, and the personality differences and the moments of tension produced by them have been buffeted down and rounded off, so that now, though they could not be considered close friends, they are pleasant with each other and work well together, a tiny repertory company with a definite run.

When they are not acting they go into the sun porch, where the whiteness of the curtains and furniture covers makes it seem cooler, and they talk about things they have experienced independently the previous night—read in the newspapers or seen on television. It is the kind of talk that is not meant to be shared, but rather to be used in social intercourse where manners are more significant than substance.

Mia is now very much the homebody, because of the distance she lives from London, and her present condition makes her one even if her inclination is not in that direction. She reads a great deal and well, has become versed in classical music, talking with knowledge about her husband's recordings and his plans to do the symphonies of Shostakovich. Over several days she has off from the film, she goes with Previn to Salzburg where he conducts the London Symphony Orchestra—triumphantly, according to the British press—and the couple's picture, both smiling shyly at the airport, makes most of the papers.

Lois is now much more at ease, no longer very lonely. After having moved from a hotel which she detested to a flat in Chelsea, she has decided she likes London. Bruce Dern, the irreconcilable Californian, has a calendar on which he marks off the days until he can get back to his beach house in Malibu. On his free time he runs in the parks of Mayfair near Claridge's Hotel where he and his wife stay. Sam Waterston remains the most formally polite and enigmatic. The persuasive Ivy League upbringing prevents him from being nothing less than correct in most social situations, but he still remains in them somewhat reserved and standoffish. He is liked by everyone because his passion for privacy has not made him rude. Nevertheless, he can be strangely insensitive at times, which comes from not really knowing well those with

212

whom he has social intercourse. He sees people as if through a glass wall. He is separated from his wife and has his young son with him for the summer.

It remains hot outside, and Clayton's pulse is under siege by the weather. He chain smokes and sips from a glass of watered-down cognac. He is again wrapping wet compresses around his wrist.

On the lawn in front of the terrace the crew is chasing a flock of doves to a precise spot so that they will be in the background of the scene. The herd instinct is at work in the birds, and they are complacently driven into a circle directly behind the breakfast table.

Dern's imagination is as free as ever. A butterfly floats in front of his face during his lines. Unperturbed, he makes use of the butterfly, pays attention to it as if it belongs there and, acting annoyed by its presence, swats at it with his hand while continuing his lines.

There are other annoyances. Pinewood is fairly near Heathrow Airport. There is a continuous roar from jets taking off and landing, the noise preceding the appearance of the planes over a line of trees. There is also a thump-thump coming from behind the bushes where the production crew of *The Abdication* is working on a set.

"Better get over there and stop them while we're shooting," David Tringham says sternly to no one in particular. The thumping continues.

A constant problem on the filming has been the quality of the sound system. This should have been expected because of the many crowd scenes in which the actors' voices are lost in the general hubbub of other voices and shuffling feet. But the actors complain they have never been in a picture where there have been so many wild tracks, that is, repeating the lines in a clear tape after a scene is finished, or where they have had to loop so many scenes, which is doing over the lines in a studio while synchronizing their voice to the scene being shown on a screen. Dern is adamant on this point; he is against anything that might possibly keep him in London one minute after he finishes his role.

Now, because the shoes on the stone terrace make

noise that is picked up by the sound boom, the actors are wearing cloth wrapped around their shoes.

August 17

Tomorrow, Saturday, is Redford's thirty-sixth birthday. Since it is a normal day off, the event is celebrated today on location, an old farm a half hour from the studio where scenes of Wilson walking through stables are done. Also shot are scenes of the five principals—Daisy, Gatsby, Tom, Jordan and Nick—in two cars going over a country road from Long Island to New York City.

There are those who claim in the past few years Redford has become very conscious of aging, which explains his reluctance to being photographed or appearing live on television, the most devastating machine devised to give away someone's age. It is too simplistic an explanation. Redford has always backed off from most types of publicity, even when he was ten years younger. He will do publicity but is selective about it. It is not so much his age as it is his passionate desire for privacy for himself and his family that is at the heart of this reluctance to allow himself to be exploited, and this, more than anything specific, has helped to create his image as a rather aloof, cold individual. He is almost childish in finding ways not to be on time for a session with a photographer, even after he has agreed to do one. He can seriously weigh for hours whether to do an interview. In fact, he is almost never less than amusing and intelligent in his interviews when he gets around to doing them. His craving for privacy, not, as some have said, a desire to enhance his image as a loner of integrity in a business of moral bandits, makes him the scourge of publicists.

The birthday party is given in the courtyard of the stables beyond a stone bridge over a dark green, stagnant fish pond. Redford stays on the set longer than he has to, cutting pieces of his birthday cake and pouring wine. He pays close attention to Mia's twins and Sam's son, making sure they are the first to get cake.

Mia gives Redford a thoughtful gift, a bound copy of the Nobel Prize speech Solzhenitsyn was never able to give in Oslo at the award ceremony.

It is a particularly annoying day for Mia. Her pregnancy has finally made the London newspapers. It was agreed that when inquiries were made by British journalists they would be told that there is always conjecture that Mia is pregnant or getting a divorce—a response that tells nothing, and leaves it up to the reporter to guess the truth. Now that this story is blown, the second cover is used. Mia was never quite sure of her condition, which for the past several weeks has been impossible to keep secret on the set since the wardrobe department continues to let out her clothes.

August 21

It is Jack Clayton's idea of a practical joke. The scene is the Buchanan dining room. Tom and Daisy are at each end of the long table. Gatsby is on one side, Nick and Jordan on the other. Soon they will go to the Plaza Hotel, having nothing better to do on a hot summer day. A servant enters from behind Tom, goes to him and whispers that he is wanted on the telephone. In the first take, Peter Finch comes in as the servant and says to Dern that they are out of beer. At first startled, the actors quickly break up laughing.

August 23

It is a tea party on the lawn of the Buchanan mansion. There is no dialogue, and on the screen the scene will only be a few seconds. It is in the film to show the comparison of the Buchanan life-style through their parties with those given at Gatsby's and Myrtle's. The women are gorgeously dressed, and almost all carry lap dogs. The scene has become a family album for the production with the wives of David Merrick and Bruce Dern as extras, as well as Mia's son, Matthew.

In the restaurant at lunch Vanessa Redgrave, in flaming red wig and overalls, is collecting for a cause, trade unionism in the movie industry. Finch gives her a rather generous donation without in any way subscribing to the cause. She is that persuasive with her intensity for the underdog.

Tennessee Williams is also there dining with David Merrick who will produce his newest play on Broadway.

Mia is reduced to being a fan, and she borrows a pen to get his autograph. She manages to do it without being overly cute.

It is a very relaxed day. Not only is it near the end of the week, with only one more month to go on the production, but Monday is a bank holiday in Great Britain and the company has the day off.

Chapter VIII

Paris Interlude

Before the Fitzgeralds arrived in Paris in 1924 they went to Great Neck, Long Island, where Scott began work on *The Great Gatsby*, probably in 1923 in a room over the garage of a home he rented at 6 Gateway Drive.

In those first years on Long Island he drank heavily and suffered from insomnia, which plagued him for the rest of his life. There were always parties to give and to go to, and weekend guests who stayed through Wednesday. The people were fascinating. One, a Long Island bootlegger, became the model for Jay Gatsby. When the illegal liquor ran out there were wild motorcades to New York, Zelda leading the way, and once in a city that never shut down there were places to go, above all the Plaza.

There was very little work done in those years after quickly writing two major novels, *This Side of Paradise* and *The Beautiful and Damned* while still under twenty-five. He had made a lot of money early and quickly learned how to spend it, as he reported in his essay, "How to Live on $36,000 a Year."

His strain of Puritan guilt would not let him enjoy these squandered days. He wrote to Perkins that it was not reading or traveling which had brought down his daily output of words to 100, but drinking and raising hell. His bad writing habits were also blamed on laziness, self-doubt and referring everything to Zelda.

In the fall of 1923, after his play, *The Vegetable*, had a disastrous tryout in Atlantic City, putting him further in financial debt, Fitzgerald went on the wagon. While sticking to the writing of *Gatsby*, he also produced a great quantity of stories and articles that were marketable in the popular magazines. He was not proud of this hack work that came so easily to him. He knew *Gatsby* contained his claim of being a serious novelist.

That winter he deleted the prologue of about eighteen thousand words from his book, which became the short story, "Absolution." He also worked on a title for the book, and some of those proposed by him were *Ash Heaps and Millionaires, Gold-Hatted Gatsby, The High-bouncing Lover, Trimalchio, On the Road to West Egg* and *Trimalchio in West Egg.* Perkins always preferred *The Great Gatsby.*

In the spirit of self-reform after all those binges on Long Island, the Fitzgeralds decided in the spring of 1924 to go to France, which was filling up with young creative Americans, or those wishing to be, who had served in or were liberated by World War I—which had snapped the provincial strain in a country isolated from Europe by a wide ocean and political intent for more than a century. The Americans could do in Paris what they could not in Chicago, or so they believed. The war had made their youth vulnerable, and thus precious, a commodity to be exploited by their newfound romantic consciousness that had developed after the war and had to confront the fact of death in life.

"We were going to the Old World to find a new rhythm for our lives, with a true conviction that we had left our old selves behind forever. . . ." Fitzgerald wrote.

At first they did not stay in Paris, but went to the south of France, where that summer Zelda had an affair with Edouard Josanne, a handsome French aviator. For Fitzgerald, both fascinated and repelled by what sex can do to romantic love, something went out of his life and marriage, an innocence which could never again be found.

He continued to work on his novel, and from St. Raphael on August 25 he wrote to Perkins that the novel would be done the following week and the revised manuscript sent to him by October.

"I think my novel is about the best American novel ever written," Fitzgerald said. "It is rough stuff in places, runs only to about 50,000 words & I hope you won't shy at it."

In October, in another letter to Perkins, Fitzgerald was temporarily more interested in a young writer he had just read for the first time. He identified him as "Ernest Hemmingway," misspelling his name, and said his collection of short stories, *In Our Time*, was remarkable. "He's the real thing," he said of a man he would not meet until the following spring. Only toward the end of the letter did he refer to his novel, and then to say it would be sent in five days.

On October 29, Fitzgerald sent the manuscript to Perkins and in a covering letter gave him instructions on how to market it, what he thought would be a reasonable price—two dollars—and how it should be a full-sized book. He said he would be anxiety-ridden until he heard what Perkins thought of the novel, valuing his judgment even more than Edmund Wilson's.

In November, before he had received a reply from Perkins, he wrote to him saying again he believed the title should be *Trimalchio in West Egg*.

The long-awaited letter from Perkins arrived dated November 14. He called the novel a wonder. He was profuse with his adjectives: "Vitality to an extraordinary degree and glamour, and a great deal of underlying thought of unusual quality," "mystic atmosphere" and "marvelous fusion . . . of the extraordinary incongruities of life today. As for sheer writing, it's astonishing."

He agreed that having the story told through a narrator, "who is more of a spectator than an actor," gives distance to his characters, and was a correct literary device.

Scott and Zelda spent that winter in Rome where he visited a studio to see the filming of *Ben Hur*. He also drank badly and got in a fight with a taxi driver that ended with Fitzgerald in jail arguing with the police and being beaten up. He read proofs on the novel that winter. Correspondence continued between him and Perkins on how the book could be tightened. Fitzgerald did the final revisions on the galleys in Capri.

Publication date was April 10, and Fitzgerald wrote to Perkins that *Gatsby* was a man's book. "Supposing women didn't like the book because it has no important woman in it. I wrote it over at least five times and I still feel that what should be the strong scene (in the hotel) is hurried and ineffective."

He wanted to be in Paris for the publication, but the car in which he and Zelda were driving from the southern coast of France broke down in Lyons. The next day Fitzgerald cabled Perkins: "Any News?"

When he received the initial word it was disappointing. The editor told him sales had not been good in the first ten days. He fretted that the slim size of the book might be working against it.

On April 24, 1925, Fitzgerald answered Perkins, blaming part of the book's problem on its title, which he said is only "fair." He also returned to his concern that the novel does not have an important woman character, a judgment disputed by critics ever since. "Women control the fiction market at present," he said, and added, "I don't think the unhappy end matters particularly." He then talked about giving up serious writing and going to Hollywood. "Anyhow there's no point in trying to be an artist if you can't do your best."

Back in Paris he tracked down Hemingway in a Left Bank cafe where he would go in the afternoon to write at a rear table, using the city as a background for his creative work the way Fitzgerald was never able to do. It was the summer of 1925, the summer for anyone who wanted to be a writer to be in Paris, and the two men, both under thirty—Hemingway the younger by several years and not having yet published his first novel—began an intense friendship that ultimately brought out the worst in each, especially Hemingway who never acted towards Fitzgerald at crucial moments in his life with the graciousness and affection expected for the one man most instrumental in bringing him to the attention of Scribner's and Maxwell Perkins.

But that was later, when Fitzgerald's drinking had made him an unproductive lush incapable of producing the major novel everyone expected from him immediately after *The Great Gatsby* and before Hemingway be-

220

came the internationally famous writer and celebrity who instructed men in how to be more manly. Now they drank together in small cafes of St. Germain and Montparnasse and talked about their works in progress, Fitzgerald impatiently waiting for a favorable reaction from Hemingway to *The Great Gatsby*, Hemingway talking to Fitzgerald about his first completed novel, *The Sun Also Rises*. They were young and believed in writing as a career, and together they created for generations the ideal of what the Literary Life can be in a city congenial to the artistic temperament.

Since Hemingway and Fitzgerald, there has not been a similar literary friendship that has so persisted in the imaginations of those who want to be writers. What made this relationship even more magical was that it took place in Paris, and long after they had gone—Fitzgerald back to the United States, Hemingway to Key West—writers who wanted to live as they had in this city came to where they had sat in the outdoor cafes to be in communion with them, believing that imitation of their lives—even to drinking excessively and going to Spain to chase the bulls—would make them writers.

Those wanting reaffirmation of a faith in a Literary Life still come to Paris, scorning the worry of successful writers about movie sales and subsidiary rights, living in poverty and believing that having your words printed is worth more than anything a publisher can pay. The young are exhilarated by this knowledge.

There are those who come again, some too late, remembering what it was to be young on the first trip to Paris: the Seine at night and the old men fishing in the dead water; the faded books and cheap prints in the stalls across from Notre Dame; the Cezannes at the Jeu de Paume; the view of the city from Sacre-Coeur; and how all this had inspired one to believe in his talent—to rise in the morning and open the shutters onto the cobbled streets to watch the women carrying long loaves of bread, to smell the rain that was on the leaves, to know that day there would be something worth putting on paper and someone to read it.

221

They still come, but there is a new city, threatening, crowding in the small streets of the Left Bank. It is the city of high-rise apartments and office buildings, plunging like knives into the soul of the city, like the office building over the Montparnasse railroad station and the administration office of the University further along the Seine. From the top of Notre Dame one can see the new city on stilts moving to encircle and crush what had been there in the summer of 1925, when men felt compatible with the smallness of the city and its provincialism that came from its division into distinct districts, each with its own cafes and character.

Still, it is not all gone. Paris remains a city for those with a dream of creating, whether it be a poem, short story, novel, song or painting. Because of whom it attracts, it remains a city of strangers.

At first they did not like the Americans who lived in their adopted city. "This city is full of Americans—most of them former friends—whom we spend most of our time dodging, not because we don't want to see them but because Zelda's only just well," Fitzgerald wrote. The Americans, he added, "seem to be incapable of any sort of conversation not composed of semi-malicious gossip about New York courtesy celebrities." Still, he said, "I've gotten to like France."

It became a bad year for Fitzgerald. Hoping that his novel would quickly sell 75,000 copies, by June only 15,000 in hard cover had been sold, and by October, less than 20,000.

The Fitzgeralds stayed on through the next year, spending part of the summer on the Riviera with Gerald and Sara Murphy. But Paris must end for everyone. It comes time to move on, trying to keep within one the spirit of the city, the memory of the youth that brought one there.

Fitzgerald stayed in France through December, 1926. The perfect male friendship of the previous summer had become strained, permanently altered. There was a boxing match between Hemingway and Morley Callaghan, a young Canadian writer, in which Fitzgerald was the referee. According to Hemingway, he let the fight go on until he was beaten, humiliated by Callaghan. He could not tolerate being anything less than his idea of the complete man before other men, especially Fitzgerald, with whom he had a most curious attraction, an almost continuous flirtation. When it became too intense, possibly suspect, he went for Fitzgerald's psychic jugular vein, mocking his drinking in the short story, "The Snows of Kilimanjaro." The love-hate of Hemingway for Fitzgerald could be brutal, cruel.

Fitzgerald could never speak less than well of Hemingway, even after the fatal boxing match, groveling to remain his friend, and continuing to write extravagant praise of his work to Perkins, as if that friendship of the summer of 1925 was the most meaningful relationship he had known.

But even in Paris one can stay young and promising for only so long, as most Americans who go back to remember learn when they see the young still crowding the Left Bank cafes, thinking only of their future, rather than the dangerous encirclement by ugly tall buildings in the distant haze—closer this year than the last, and closer still next year.

In December of 1925, from Paris, Fitzgerald wrote Perkins, "I wish I were twenty-two again with only my dramatic and feverishly enjoyed miseries. You remember I used to say I wanted to die at thirty—well, I'm twenty-nine and the prospect is still welcome. My work is the only thing that makes me happy—except to be a little tight—and for those two indulgences I pay a big price in mental and physical hangover."

One day, Paris must die in everyone.

Chapter IX

The Last Month

August 28, 29

The antique cars go through the Valley of Ashes one last time. It is a gray, overcast day, one of the few without sunshine in the closing month of summer. Wilson's garage looks as if it has been closed indefinitely. Across from it piles of old rubber tires are burned to give off clouds of black smoke. Some of the crew wear bandanas around their noses and mouths.

A car gets ready to pass Wilson's garage. It is the funeral procession for Gatsby. Parked to one side is the hearse, the coffin in the back, a single spray of flowers over it. It will not be used in this scene, which is a close-up of Nick and Gatsby's father, Mr. Gatz, in the back seat of a car provided by the funeral director. They are the only mourners to attend the service of a man who kept so many amused through the nights of summer.

The camera is in the front seat; Chic Waterson, the operator, is crouched behind it and Clayton is on the running board. He gives the cue, and the car moves past the stray dogs foraging on the side of the ash embankment, the burning rubber, the box cars on the siding, the signboard announcing excursions up the Hudson River and the eyes of Dr. Eckleburg.

A local Lutheran minister was invited to lunch at the studio restaurant where his brains were picked on the proper procedures for a Lutheran burial service. For his expert testimony, Jeannie Sims says, he was awarded a free meal.

"Nowadays they're just pleased to be wanted, for anything," someone says.

At one of the breaks in the shooting, Tony Harvey, the director of *The Abdication*, peddles a bike on the set with his star, Liv Ullmann, on the back hugging his waist, a puzzled look on her face as if she half-expected to fall off. They are looking for Clayton and have just missed him as the car disappears through the smoke around a bend in the road, going to West Egg. Behind the artificial mounds of ashes it is a desolate cow field, ready after *Gatsby* leaves to become something else: a royal court, an air-force base, a jungle.

With the car gone, the Valley of Ashes is empty except for the smoke and bleakness. Then up the road from the production office come several dozen mentally retarded persons, most of them young and in wheelchairs, being pushed by attendants. Their arms are bent, trying to point; their lips open, growls and groans coming out; and their eyes are heavy, squinting in the weak light. The attendant treat it as a normal movie-studio tour, giving a running commentary that is extraordinarily not to the point. The caravan of the deformed does not stop at the Valley of Ashes; it proceeds around another bend where wild flowers grow through cracks in the cement.

The next day the burial of Gatsby takes place in St. Pancreas Cemetery in North London.

It is neutral in appearance, nondenominational in faith—Christian perhaps, with possibly a few Jews buried behind the rows of crosses. At the entrance wild berries grow over a wall. A man picks some.

"They taste the better for them," a studio driver says, chuckling at his example of black humor.

The burial takes place on a plot of ground in a circle of the road. The company had tried to find a Lutheran cemetery; instead one had to be faked, and false tombstones with German names—Brunner, Vanberg, Burger, Bultman and Deile—were placed around the hole that had been dug for Gatsby. Out of the camera's range, machines are set up to blow smoke into the burial area. On the screen it will appear the mist of morning.

Almost late for the funeral is David Merrick, who arrives in a striped and somber suit. "Have I come dressed properly for the funeral?" he asks. Clayton laughs. It is impossible to know if the joke is appreciated, the smile genuine or polite. After the calamitous beginning of their professional relationship in Newport, they act as if they had learned to accept each other, which shows the splendid advantages of having a benign neutrality toward each other. It is the proper way to act on a movie company where anything—including devout hatreds or sexual liaisons—rarely lasts beyond the last take. In fact, one suspects the truth is that Clayton now respects, even likes Merrick.

Merrick sits in a canvas chair with his name on it. "It was over my dead body we came here," he says, not intending it to be a pun. He has recently given an interview to *Variety*, repeating his complaint that nothing was saved by moving the production to London.

"There is the VAT tax, which is 10 percent added to the value of almost everything, and the dollar is devalued," he says. "And John Box underestimated the construction costs over here. We're way over budget on that item. Anyone will tell you that 40 percent of the workers in the studio are useless; the other 60 percent not much better, and of them only 10 percent pretty good.

"Beside, even if we saved $300,000 here, it was not worth the trouble it caused us with the unions."

The only mourners at the burial are Mr. Gatz and Nick. The minister is on the edge of the open grave, the father and friend back from it, where the smoke curls from the woods. There has been some discussion as to whether the coffin at Lutheran Suviz services is in the ground or suspended over the grave. Clayton decides it is not worth pursuing, and the coffin goes into the ground.

The minister's voice intones, ". . . that we may at length fall peacefully asleep in Thee, and awake after Thy likeness; through Thy mercy, O our Lord, who livest and reignest with the Father and the Holy Ghost, one God, world without end. Amen."

When the service is almost completed, Owl-Eyes arrives, making his apology to Nick for being late. "My God! They used to go to his house by the hundreds," he says after Nick makes note of the scarcity of mourners. Owl-Eyes takes off his glasses, wipes them, and says what

226

Dorothy Parker did when she heard Fitzgerald had died. "The poor son-of-a-bitch."

August 30, 31

He is wearing a tweed cap and dark glasses when he enters the baggage area of Heathrow Airport. He is in a good mood, relaxed and smiling, giving the impression of being content as he always does when he has been alone with his family for any length of time.

Redford has been called back from a five-day vacation with his family in Scotland to do the shirt scene, which Clayton says is one of the most impossible to direct in the film.

It is a fifteen-minute ride from the airport to the studio, and after growling that he had better work immediately after he was called back a day early, he settles into the back of the car and talks about his trip. He had been in Scotland once before, when he was a broke young painter waiting in England for transportation home and had hitched a ride to Scotland. In a village pub there he had played darts and won a bet, and now, a decade later, he was again in the village, wondering whether he should enter, to cross the threshold to his past. He finally did and found the man he had played darts with had remembered him, had cut out newspaper articles about his fame as a movie star and could not believe this famous person would ever come back to visit the village.

Another place Redford is fearful of returning to is a house in Florence where he has left some of the paintings he did in Europe after quitting college. It is as if he can still quarrel with himself whether he had made the right choice in becoming an actor, one of such fame and power that he now finds his private freedom of action too often curtailed. Today, these paintings might still tell him if there was an alternate course of artistic expression for him. In his conversations, Redford often brings up situations to show you can never go home again, as if he really wants to believe it rather than being truly convinced of it.

On his vacation, he says, he has reread a number of

227

Fitzgerald short stories and finds many terrible, especially "The Diamond as Big as The Ritz." His comments are perceptive about the structural weaknesses of some of Fitzgerald's work and the repetitiveness of the theme of aging young men who realize they will never live up to their initial promise, a condition haunting Fitzgerald as drink continued to erode his talent.

Redford does not have to wait. He goes to work immediately on the shirt scene, which takes place in a mirrored alcove of Gatsby's bedroom.

The scene is based on life. Fitzgerald knew of a Long Island bootlegger who bragged that he never wore the same shirt twice. Fitzgerald put it into the book to show Gatsby's idealism and bad taste, and after Gatsby shows the shirts to Daisy, Fitzgerald has her break down and cry.

"The conception of a man throwing shirts around to impress a woman he wants back can be written, but it is almost inconceivable to film, and not because it is difficult to do visually. Gatsby has acquired all this money to get Daisy back. He is not a miser. The gesture of tossing the shirts is to say to her, 'This is what I've got for you.' It's the mood of a young boy," Clayton says.

"Anyway, I like scenes that are impossible to do."

Redford's instincts are to play down whenever possible Gatsby's boyishness. He does not want the character to be too foolish. But the scene is played the way Clayton wants it done and the way Fitzgerald wrote it.

There are seventy silk shirts of all colors in the drawers, and Redford begins to throw them one by one. The open glass-paneled doors catch this image and duplicate it so that there is one long line of Gatsbys heaving shirts.

On the first take one of the shirts floats over the lens and the scene has to be stopped. Then, after each take, and there are many, the shirts must be refolded and put back in the drawers. Everyone pitches in, including Mia and Sam Waterston. As the shirts continue to drop over the camera Clayton asks Redford to throw them higher.

The scene is continued the next day, and between

takes, Mia, tired by her pregnancy, rests on Gatsby's bed talking with Annabel about raising children. It is not a very heavy conversation; it centers on the value to motherhood of Pampers, which Mia cannot find in England. In mid-conversation she is called back to the alcove. She takes her seat in front of the shirt drawers and convincingly turns on the tears.

This is one of Annabel's favorite scenes. "It shows Daisy responding to Gatsby's naiveté. It also signals the resumption of their romance."

The camera is now on a close-up of Daisy. Off screen, Redford continues to throw the shirts. Clayton tells Mia to hold the shirt away from her face when she begins to cry. On the next take she holds the shirt exactly where Clayton shows her. Redford's aim, however, is not accurate. One hits her in the face.

"I thought you were a great natural athlete," she says to him.

There is excitement at the window table during lunch. Mia has been talking with Sam and Peter Finch about doing Chekhov's *Sea Gull* on Broadway for a limited run, possibly next year, and she is caught up by the expectations of it.

"I'm fairly quick at learning scripts. I break them down to scenes, and I read a play over and over."

As she talks, one reflects on her complexity, of her varied personalities over the years, of her interests from politics to literature and of her passion to guard her private life. She does this even when she is telling things that make one think she is giving away secrets.

"The actors I admire are those like Paul Scofield, professionals who have built long careers by perfecting their acting craft. And you have to have guts to survive. I come from a large family with brothers, and you have to learn to compete to survive. People say I've changed, that I'm into a new phase, but I still have my priorities, my goals. I could work much more if I weren't so involved in raising a family. With my new child in March, I'll have four children under the age of four."

Sam Waterston arrives, sits down and orders lunch. He

says to Mia, "By the way, have you seen the morning papers? Michael Dunn died."

The thirty-nine-year-old actor was found dead in his hotel room, presumably of natural causes.

She does not answer. She puts down her fork and sits rigidly. For a moment tears brim under her eyes. Just when they should run down her cheeks they are stopped, and though still watery, her eyes begin to clear and she says almost defiantly, "I expect people my age to die."

September 3

The Plaza Hotel scene, the longest—six pages—and probably the most pivotal in the film. The five principals are gathered in a replica of a Plaza Hotel suite, authentic to the wallpaper and door knobs. The major confrontation of Tom and Gatsby over Daisy takes place in the dazzling whiteness of this room. Everyone knows it is an important scene and treats it as such. Not officially, but in fact, it is a closed set with only Annabel and the necessary crew watching the rehearsals.

Writing to Perkins on December 20, 1924, Fitzgerald said, "The Hotel scene will never quite be up to mark— I've worried about it too long & I can't quite place Daisy's reaction. But I can improve it a lot. It isn't imaginative energy that's lacking—it's because I'm automaticly (sic) prevented from thinking it out over again because I must get all those characters to New York in order to have the catastrophe on the road going back & I must have it pretty much that way."

Bruce Dern thinks the scene is not necessary in the film. By then the audience should know which way Daisy will fall when pushed, he says.

Clayton, trying always to keep the script faithful to the book, says, "I plan to do this scene basically in three master shots. It's an impossibly written scene in the book. You can't have Tom and Jay in the room arguing over Daisy without a fight. By nature Gatsby should lunge at Tom and try to kill him.

"The problem, though, is how to break the scene," he says.

What Coppola and Clayton have done is to compress

the scene. As written by Fitzgerald, it rambles at the beginning with a discussion about the heat in Louisville when Daisy and Tom were married, which leads to reminiscences of those at the service about someone fainting, a man named Biloxi. Instead, the scriptwriters go immediately to the conflict of the scene.

Gatsby uses his favorite phrase, "old sport," which prompts Tom to ask sarcastically where he picked it up. Oxford, Gatsby says, where he studied a few months after the Armistice, an opportunity given to officers who had served in France. Daisy accuses Tom of trying to start trouble. Tom goes off on his tangent about people scorning such traditional institutions as family life, and that soon everything will go overboard and there will be intermarriages. Gatsby butts into the monologue to say Daisy has never loved him. Tom laughs, "You must be crazy." Gatsby replies quickly, "She only married you because I was poor and she was tired of waiting for me." Tom charges that it's a lie. She loves me and I love her, he says. "Sometimes she gets foolish ideas in her head and doesn't know what she's doing. Once in a while I go off on a spree and make a fool of myself, but I always come back. . . ." Gatsby pleads with Daisy to tell her husband she has never loved him. Daisy tries but, exasperated, says to Gatsby, "Oh, you want too much. I love you now . . . isn't that enough? I can't help what's past." She begins to sob. "I did love him once, but I loved you, too." At that moment Gatsby must know he can't recapture the past, but he persists. "Daisy's leaving you." Tom knows she never will and shouts at Gatsby, "She's not leaving me! Certainly not for a common swindler who'd have to steal the ring he put on her finger."

Here Fitzgerald continues the scene, with Tom, going into some detail about Gatsby's shady moneymaking ways and then showing the reader that Tom is convinced he has won Daisy. Almost too gentlemanly, Tom suggests Daisy and Gatsby go back together. "Go on. He won't annoy you. I think he realizes that his presumptuous little flirtation is over," Tom says.

Clayton has the actors arranged before the camera:

Gatsby and Tom facing each other, Daisy and Nick between them sitting on a couch, Jordan in a chair near Gatsby. They have fake beads of perspiration on their faces.

"I know some of Fitzgerald's dialogue is terribly stilted," Clayton says, "but I wouldn't change anything important."

In this scene, most of the sentences have been lifted verbatim from the book, and they play well in the mouths of the actors. The scene is time-consuming, taking several days, but it goes smoothly, much better than anyone had anticipated.

In the beginning of the scene, Redford does digress from the script. When he tells Tom he went to Oxford as an officer after the Armistice, he asks him if he had been in the war, knowing he hadn't.

"I talked it over with Clayton," Redford says, "and I added that sentence to show some of Gatsby's hatred of privilege."

It is not often Redford makes an issue of changing the dialogue this far into production. Dern is much more apt to improvise.

"When we were rehearsing in Newport," Mia says, "I was afraid Bruce would be improvising every other line, and you can't do it with Fitzgerald."

This is the only major alteration in the dialogue from the script. Dern picks it up without hesitation, answers him abruptly and then tries to put Gatsby off balance by asking him what kind of row he is trying to start.

To end the scene more effectively, Clayton has decided to have Daisy bolt from the room and have Gatsby chase her, which breaks the tension more naturally and avoids the logical conclusion, which would be to have the two men go after each other.

What is missing is the coda to the scene Fitzgerald gives. It's Nick's interior monologue when he realizes, while driving back to Long Island, that it is his thirtieth birthday. It is one of the saddest observations about growing old.

"Thirty," Nick thinks, "the promise of a decade of

232

loneliness, a thinning list of single men to know, a thinning briefcase of enthusiasm, thinning hair."

September 5

Douglas Slocombe is in a traditional pose, holding his lens to the sky for a reading on the light, waiting for a patch of blue into which the sun can move. Behind him an antique car with Tom and Nick waits to be driven up to the front of the Buchanan house. It is the continuation of the scene shot at Hammersmith Farm in Newport where Nick comes ashore in a rowboat and is met by Tom who has been playing polo.

It is fall now in England, and each morning there is a misty fog that rarely lifts before noon. There is pressure to go inside the studio and do a cover shot. But Peter Price, the production manager, resists, playing a hunch after hearing the weather report on BBC radio that the weather might clear earlier. He advises the company to stay on the location, which is the driveway and the false front of the Buchanan home.

Price watches the sun break through and feels justified. All agree he has been a calm, efficient manager.

Until the sun arrives, the actors find things to do. Mia is working on a New England quilt for her children. She has cut out squares from old Christmas cards and is sewing colorful cloth patches to each. Lois comes over and offers to help.

The greatest transformation among the actors—and there has not been that much—is in Lois. Many of her overt symptoms of anxiety have been overcome, repressed. This is noticeable when Francois Moullin, one of the American A. D.'s from Newport, makes a surprise visit to the set today—he has been vacationing in Europe —and Lois is the first to go over and give him an affectionate hug. The friction between them has been removed, the cause forgotten. Nothing is forever in show business, not feuds, not loves.

Lois is quite frank about her insecurities. "I don't want to be discarded in two years. I don't want to get my acting jobs just because I'm photogenic, and nothing else. I was excitable back in Newport, too quick to react to things. I knew the film was going to be big, but it was even bigger than I had expected and I said things I shouldn't have. I hadn't learned how to keep my guard up, like Mia and Bob. Now I watch everything, trying to learn."

Mia is oblivious to those around her. She concentrates on the quilt. She has brought a box of jelly beans for the crew, a gesture that further endears her to them. It takes some persuasion to get her away from her quilt to talk about Daisy.

"I'm not sure if Daisy really loves Gatsby," she says, shrugging her shoulder.

On the lawn inside the circular driveway, Redford is by himself practicing how old people walk in imitation of someone on the set. He has the motion down perfectly. "I think there's a weakness in the joints," he says. "They lose their spring."

A new schedule is handed out from the production office. The film will finish in two weeks, a week under schedule. Mia's pregnancy has been a good thing; it's induced the company to speed up the shooting, which the actors feel has gone on much longer than necessary by about a month.

"You know shooting schedules are padded," someone says, "so they can go back to the studio and say, 'Look how we brought the picture in under time.'"

"It's really an unusual company," Lois says, infected by the return of her confidence. "Everyone really likes each other."

Overhearing this remark, Annabel says with conventionally mature wisdom, "Why, does she believe that!"

The absence of any overt hostility is taken as a sign of friendship, an era of good feeling. Most everyone knows, however, that this is as transparent and fleeting as the celluloid on which the story is shot.

Mia reflects on what she has said about the love between Gatsby and Daisy. She has no illusions about the duration of friendships formed on a movie company.

"It would be fatal if the audience did not believe they were in love. What kind of love it is is up to the audi-

234

ence to decide. The kind of love it is doesn't take away from the intensity of the feeling they have for each other. It's an elusive book. The characters are so very strange and elusive."

She talks again about her idea of doing Daisy in a Southern accent. "Scottie asked if I were going to do her with one. Instead, I'm trying to do it with a Southern attitude."

Redford, walking past, adds, "You do roles in attitudes. It's difficult not to play attitudes. You try to do them boldly, differently."

The sun comes out, and Clayton does the car scene in record time while Douglas stands back-to-back to him, facing the pale sun.

When the scene is finished, time is altered. It is now the afternoon for the Plaza Hotel. Gatsby and Nick are standing by the car underneath the balcony waiting for the others in the party. Mia runs to the railing to inquire whether she should bring something to drink. She moves away, returns and drops a rose, which lands in the back seat of the car, almost dropping on Gatsby's hand.

There is a great deal of commotion behind the camera with people milling about during the rehearsal. Redford asks people to move out of his eye line when he looks to the camera. "The people aren't supposed to be there. It's disturbing," he says.

There is also a voice coming from *The Abdication* behind the trees. The voice is indistinct, far off, annoying. "Is that John Box?" Redford quips.

The scene is ready to go again. Mia steps to the balcony and asks Annabel, "Do I say 'shall we take' or 'shall we bring' anything to drink?"

"Take," Annabel says, consulting the script.

"Daisy goes for too long a stretch in the book being fey," Redford says. "It becomes monotonous."

The rose flutters to the car seat. Gatsby, startled, looks up.

The scene continues. The sun does not go away.

September 7

The feeling that the production is coming to an end,

235

first noticed when the crew and actors started to talk about their next projects, has been made official. Today the crew gets its two-week notice. It does not mean the production will not run over. But it would be financially easier to finish within this time. The threat of imminent unemployment is unnerving; yet it is tempered by a sense of relief, of one who knows an affair has gone on too long and lost some of its first beauty.

September 9

A British newspaper columnist refers to Redford as the Howard Hughes of actors, insinuating he is a recluse to the press. The reputation is not really justified. Redford today has consented to talk at the National Film Society in its theater on the south bank of the Thames. When he goes on stage some minutes late (and not unexpectedly, his reputation for being tardy having preceded him across the Atlantic), the auditorium is filled.

It is a curiously uneven session with the public. Redford can be a fantastic interview if the questions are good and lively. But the woman interviewer, attractive, vaguely elegant in the way British women can be when they are well-spoken and not aggressive, has not really prepared herself to be anything but conventional. Her questions are predictable, her information about Redford sounding as if it had been gathered from stale press releases. If she has seen his movies, she does not really know what they are about. As well as he possibly can be, Redford is receptive to her questions, but few relate to the other. He is often left with a thought not thoroughly explored because her response is not to what he has said but to the next question on her list.

Nor are the questions from the audience much better. They are asked with deference to his status; the questioners act as if they are in front of a member of the royal family and are struck awkward and shy. An older man is more strident. He wants to know what other actors Redford likes.

Redford replies, "I don't like talking about other actors," and the forceful way he says it reveals a hurt from the past. "I like actors who have paid their dues, who know what it's like going to an open audition. It's like a cattle call. It's a humiliating experience. It's hard for those of us who have achieved some success in the business to forget what all of us have had to go through at one time or another."

He talks about his early stage training and says, "I really prefer film. I couldn't say that for years," referring to the superior attitude of those who work on the stage. "I used to act with my back. I resisted all the traditional techniques of the craft, and I don't like to rehearse. Sometimes rehearsal is needed for blocking out a scene, but film is a media for spontaneity."

Someone asks him about growing up in Hollywood. Did he have any favorites? "When I was very young I thought Bambi was the greatest." After the laughter subsides, he says, "There was nobody I worshipped in those days. I guess I liked Errol Flynn and Spencer Tracy. They looked like they were having a good time."

He is asked about *Downhill Racer,* his fine film about an American ski jock. "I wanted to make a film about an athlete who is a creep, who is tolerated because he wins." Commenting about his career as an athlete in high school and college, before he dropped out, he says, "I discovered one day that the sport life is boring and had become very narrow. I no longer liked team sports. I didn't like what team sports bred in you. I didn't want to feel like I had to win or lose all the time. I prefered individual sports, like skiing and tennis, with you up against the elements."

About whether his films have the potential for a wide audience, Redford says, "It's hard to decide what is commercial. I had no idea *Butch Cassidy and the Sundance Kid* would be such a success. I knew, though, I enjoyed it. If you begin making films for other people it can be a disaster. Unfortunately our society is structured for success, and the films I wanted to make haven't made much money."

Asked if he watches his old films, he replies, "It doesn't please or excite me to see myself on the screen."

Inevitably, Watergate comes up and Redford says, "The United States is in for a rugged time. The key to my country's future lies in the past, when we had courage and hope." He could have been talking about Jeremiah Johnson and the pure experience of a mountain man coming to terms with himself in the wilderness, or unconsciously, he could have been Gatsby, going back to the past, trying to recapture it.

"I'm interested in the forces that overwhelm the individual," he says.

Again, Gatsby?

September 11-20

For the next eight shooting days there is the impression that the schedule—once such a fixed agenda, having been rearranged and tightened—consists now of doing pick-up shots and finishing off scenes started earlier; the actors, with their ambitions and their egos, are like colts in the starting gate ready to bolt for new races.

Dern wants to go home to Malibu to await his next picture, a western with Kirk Douglas for Paramount. Lois will stay on in London for a while before going back to New York to study acting for six months, her self-imposed time limit before taking on another acting assignment. Waterston, too, will go back to New York to look for another play or film. "It doesn't seem possible, but I've been around Broadway eleven years," he says. Until the baby is born, Mia will be content to remain in the countryside, tending her children, reading. Redford has a new film, *The Great Waldo Pepper*, a story about barnstorming pilots. He has six weeks off before the filming begins, and he thinks about going somewhere uncharted by tourists, possibly southern Turkey, for an adventure, what the wilderness provides him in Utah.

On the first of these eight days the company goes to Windsor Park near the royal family's castle for a scene of Gatsby and Nick driving to New York for their luncheon date when Gatsby will try to prepare Nick to set up a meeting with Daisy.

It is warm and sunny. The early morning haze is gauze-like over the gently sloping fields, and one expects deer to wander unmolested into the camera's range. There is a languidness to the company's pace. As a working unit it is unwinding; the tension that held it together dissipating. People are arrayed over the ground; some of the men are shirtless, sunning themselves; others play cricket.

There is something eternally young about Redford's fascination with sport. He has a natural inquisitiveness about games, and he goes over to one of the crew to ask how to hold the bat and position himself for hitting the ball in cricket. Soon he is taking his swings with the rest of the men. Redford really does consciously stand apart from those he must work with on film. But on occasions such as this he displays moments of camaraderie which gains him their respect. If one can honestly respond to a presence of power rather than a concrete person on the set, the crew does like Redford.

Before the scene begins, Redford goes off with Waterston to discuss their approach to it. Gatsby's yellow car is attached to a small truck with the camera in its open back. Because of the noise, the actors know this dialogue will have to be looped in the studio.

Redford has some definite ideas about the scene. When he first read the script he wrote down this observation. "Buildup is missing. False starts and unfinished sentences before his surprising outburst. Maybe it needs a couple of stabs at small talk, generated by Nick before the thing gets going."

As it is written, the scene begins in the car parked in Gatsby's garage. He turns to Nick and bluntly asks, "Look here, old sport, what's your opinion of me, anyhow?"

Redford believes there should be a longer buildup. "What the audience has seen so far in the film, Gatsby hasn't been with Nick that much for him to come right out and ask him such a personal question." He thinks the audience should be told the two men have had other contacts, and this could be done by bringing in Jordan's name.

On a legal pad, Redford wrote out the way he would like the scene to play:

GATSBY: I believe you're taking Miss Baker to tea this afternoon.

NICK: Yes. Why? How did you know?
Gatsby pauses. ("There should be awkward silences in this scene," Redford says.)

NICK: Do you mean to tell me that you're in love with Jordan Baker?

GATSBY: No, I'm not. But she has kindly consented to speak to you about a certain matter.
(Here, Gatsby asks Nick what he thinks about him.)

What Redford has done is to take Fitzgerald's scene the way he wrote it and rearranged it.

Redford takes up his revisions with Clayton and has them rejected.

Next, Redford wins a point. The script has Gatsby say to Nick that he is from the Midwest. What part, Nick asks? San Francisco, Gatsby replies.

Redford wants this deleted. "Saying this makes Gatsby look silly. He isn't a stupid man." The actor gets his way with a well-taken point.

He wins one more point. Where Gatsby is telling Nick about his war experiences, the script has him say, "I was promoted to major, and every Allied Government gave me a decoration. Even Montenegro—little Montenegro, down on the Adriatic Sea. Look. . . ." He reaches into his pocket and pulls out a medal to show Nick.

Redford has inserted the sentence, "I distinguished myself in a battle in the Argonne Forest and was promoted to major." This establishes what Gatsby did in the war, and makes him more an authentic hero, as Fitzgerald must have intended by having that line in the book.

Shades of Newport. Another extravaganza. A wedding party in the Terrace Room of the Plaza Hotel, built in

Studio D. The authenticity of tables, chairs, china, wallpaper and light fixtures has been checked by the art department. Dozens of extras have been hired, many of them British because there are no speaking parts except for the principals in the scene. Now the extras are sitting at tables sipping champagne or dancing in front of the long table where the bride and groom sit.

It is the continuation of the Plaza suite scene, not as Fitzgerald had written it. He ended his scene with the people leaving the room more quietly than could have been expected.

Here Daisy, followed by Gatsby, dashes down the stairs and pushes her way through the dancers while Tom walks along the balcony behind the wedding party, calling to Gatsby that he knows about his illegal business dealings with Wolfsheim, that their Chicago drugstores sell alcohol over the counter.

Again using almost the exact dialogue from the book, Clayton has Tom shout, "But the drugstores are just small change. . . . He's got something new with Wolfsheim, something big . . . something that everyone's afraid to talk about."

Gatsby turns and glares at him. Now he could kill his adversary.

Clayton shoots the scene in two parts. The first point of view is of Tom moving along the balcony; the second is of Daisy and Gatsby in the crowd. The extras are so diligent about looking as if they are guests at a wedding party that they forget to react naturally to the scene and do not look up when Tom begins ranting. David Tringham has to go among them and ask them please to notice Dern when he begins talking.

He is the connection with the other *Gatsby,* the one no one wants to mention because it was done badly, made into a routine gangster movie which began with Gatsby in the back seat of a getaway car firing a machine gun.

"It never happens to one," Howard Da Silva says.

"It's weird to be in a movie you did twenty-five years ago."

Da Silva was then George Wilson, more recently Benjamin Franklin in the stage and screen versions of *1776*, and now for two days in London, Wolfsheim, Gatsby's notorious partner.

He is in his dressing room in his underwear, stretched out on the couch reading a newspaper, waiting to be called on the set, a basement restaurant catering to sporting clientele where he will play a scene with Gatsby and Nick.

Da Silva is one of those actors you know even if you don't know his name because, subtly, unexpectedly, he has made a lasting impression on audiences by giving distinguished performances in films one remembers only for his work in them. He is a character actor who has survived; and almost ageless, he remains young, kept that way by his inordinate interest in what is around him. He has just returned from a visit to China, and arriving in London immediately wants to know what he should see on the stage.

"I've forgotten the other picture. It was done entirely in the studio, and it was not very expensive. When I was first mentioned for Wilson they said I was too strong an actor. Wilson is someone compulsively drawn to his wife and dependent on her. He is a child-man.

"I had a feeling about Alan Ladd that he never got the chance to display his real acting gifts too often on the screen. His innate quality was one of sadness.

"I don't even remember Wolfsheim from that picture, but I do remember him from the book as an interesting reference, the man who fixed the World Series. His function is to make Gatsby more mysterious.

"When I met Clayton to talk over the part with him, I was immediately drawn to him. This is also the first time I've worked for Merrick. I like Merrick," he says as if he expected someone to jump out of the closet to dispute it. "He stays on his side of the fence. He's known in the business as a hard bargainer and a man with complete integrity. I like his total, rather magnificent body of work he has produced on Broadway."

Of the two actors he works with in the scene, he has never performed with Redford. "I liked *The Candidate*, though. It's the closest thing we have to an American black political comedy. And he has such a wicked smile."

He has worked with Sam Waterston. "I directed him in a play off-Broadway called *Thistle in My Bed*. Sam becomes pregnant in it."

In this scene, Wolfsheim disturbs Nick's midwestern sensibility by describing a gangland killing that had taken place outside the restaurant several years earlier. Gatsby stops the story, afraid Wolfsheim has mistaken Nick for some other potentially shady associate. Gatsby is called away from the table and Wolfsheim shows his erudition by saying to Nick what a fine fellow Gatsby is. "He went to Oggsford College in England. You know Oggsford College?" To impress Nick of his own class, he shows him his cuff links made of human molars.

When Gatsby returns and tells Wolfsheim everything has been taken care of, Wolfsheim excuses himself. "I belong to another generation. You sit here and discuss your sports and your young ladies and your . . . as for me, I am fifty years old and I won't impose myself on you any longer." He leaves and Nick asks Gatsby if Wolfsheim is a dentist. No, Gatsby answers, he's a gambler and fixed the World Series of 1919.

Just as they are ready to leave, Tom, who has been eating at a rear table, comes over, and Nick introduces him to Gatsby. He asks Nick how a struggling bond salesman can afford to eat where big-business types hang out. Nick says he has been having lunch with Mr. Gatsby, and when they turn he is no longer there. "Well, you're free now, Nick," Tom says.

Dern does some peculiar things with that last line, rolling his eyes and leering as if he were Groucho Marx chasing a pretty girl. It is the first time Redford has been outspokenly critical of what an actor is doing in the film, and he tells Clayton he cannot understand what Dern is trying to do with his mocking mannerisms.

"We have to work this as an ensemble piece of film or it won't work at all," Redford says.

The scene continues as Dern wants to play it. Redford, watching off camera, looks puzzled.

It is Saturday, and the *Evening Standard*, the afternoon paper, is filled with football and racing results. The item is one paragraph on the bottom of the second page. Betty Field, the Daisy in the Alan Ladd version of *Gatsby* is dead of a cerebral hemorrhage suffered while walking alone on the beach at Cape Cod.

Of her performance in *Gatsby*, *Variety* said, "A bit of illumination of the brittle and faithless jazz-age type is delivered in irritating snatches by our old friend, Betty Field."

One already misses her acting dependability.

Clayton has changed his mind. Much of the dialogue between Gatsby and Nick in the car in Windsor Park will now be done in the studio in Gatsby's garage. Gatsby now tells everything he wants Nick to know about him as they are getting into his Rolls Royce, even showing him the Montenegrin medal, and when he closes the door asks Nick what he thinks of him.

Redford is uneasy. The scene is tried a number of ways, standing outside the car, then inside. He takes his jacket off.

"I know what they're doing," says a reporter from an international magazine who is trying to impress everyone with his expertise about filmmaking. "Redford is trying to look relaxed in this scene."

It is not worth telling the reporter it is not a take, only a rehearsal, and Redford has taken his jacket off to keep it freshly pressed for the actual filming.

Later, Redford, still on edge, asks Clayton to have the set cleared of strangers, referring to two young women who nobody seems to know. Clayton, obligingly, does what his star asks and tells Hank Moonjean to get rid of them. He interprets "them" to mean everyone, and Moonjean asks the reporter to leave, too.

The reporter, stuttering, is hustled into an alleyway as the sound-stage door is lowered and the red light signifying a take is turned on.

Mia is sitting on a stool doing close-ups for inserts. She is truly beautiful. Her eyes are open, clear and expressive with desire; her wig does not have a strand of hair out of place; the jewels are dazzling; the dress exquisite. The glamor stops at her feet. She is wearing sloppy, mismatched slippers.

"For Daisy, it was just another summer," Redford says.

She is now in the Palm Court of the Plaza Hotel. Gatsby is dead and it is as if nothing has happened in her life to disturb the money-bought composure. She is going to Europe with her husband. Where else to make one's final social appearance in New York than at the Plaza!

Before Nick comes home, in the novel, he is walking down Fifth Avenue on an October afternoon when he meets Tom who is by himself. Nick refuses to shake his hand. Accusingly, he asks Tom what he told Wilson to get him to kill Gatsby. "I told him the truth," as he knows it, he says. Wilson came to his home waving a gun and threatening to kill him, and he told him Gatsby had run over his wife.

This scene is transferred now to the Palm Court where Nick and Jordan are having their final lunch, and the Buchanans come in with their child and nanny in tow. Daisy is brought back for a reprieve to re-emphasize the point of her coldness. She rushes over to Nick, tells him about her new house and, leaning close, whispers an invitation for him to visit when she gets back from Europe. "You know how I love to see you at my table," she says.

The action takes place at a table near the main entrance to the dining room. Though much of it will be shot in a close-up of Nick and Tom, there has to be movement in the background, and this keeps the assistant directors busy lining up the extras and inspecting each one. The extras are held back until the right moment, then tapped on the shoulder when, smiling and chattering, they cross behind the two men.

It is a breathtaking set, brilliantly lit and decorated. So much care has gone into getting everything right for the atmosphere and dress of the 1920s that it is unfortunate much of it will only be a blur. The dramatic focal point is the two men, and the camera must not stray from them until Daisy arrives to end the scene.

"They don't make movies like this anymore," a grip says, as have many others who have worked on the film and were overwhelmed by the sets and the numbers of extras.

The scene really belongs to Nick and the gesture he makes when Tom offers his hand to be shaken and it is rejected. One remembers what Redford said once: "It's exciting for actors to get to do gestures written down by Fitzgerald."

With this gesture Nick makes his second judgment about the rich. The first was the morning after Myrtle's death when he calls to Gatsby across the lawn that he is worth more than the whole damn bunch of them and waves a salute to him. And now, by turning aside the handshake, he denounces Tom and what his world stands for.

Waterston is absolutely first-rate in the scene, but as usual he does not reveal what he is thinking about his character at that moment or the choices he has made in playing the scene. He has a confidence about his craft that cannot be shaken.

Clayton is not satisfied with Mia's dialogue as it is written in the script. At the last moment he changes it and hands her the revisions on a piece of yellow paper. She sits in the corner going over the words, saying them to herself, breaking down the sentences to find the internal rhythms.

Now she is ready for her entrance. The magnificent coat designed by Theoni Aldredge conceals Mia's pregnancy, which has become an obsession with the company. The theory now is that the audience, if it sees any signs of her pregnancy in the film, will never accept her as Daisy. But if determination and skill can overcome an audience's predisposition to judge her performance by her pregnancy, then she will certainly carry off her role.

She sweeps down on Nick. Her voice, which as Fitzgerald wrote it, has the sound of money, saying banal things, now has the sound of icicles falling off a roof on a winter's night. For those who would embrace her and make her a life's pursuit, the only possibility is death.

When she finishes the scene, she is like a little lost girl standing in the huge set that loses its definition because it is unfinished where the camera will not go. She says, as she has almost every day she has worked, when it appears the day is over, "Can I go now?" saying it like a child timidly asking a favor from an adult.

She is dismissed, and when she goes the presence of Daisy is still in the room.

What has to be made clear in this scene is what Fitzgerald has Nick think when he leaves Tom on Fifth Avenue. The Buchanans are people who "smashed things and creatures and then retreated back into their money or their vast carelessness, or whatever it was that kept them together."

It is time for Redford to go.

First he has to do a scene with Mia, who is called back for one shot with him in the car, which occurs after she has thrown him the rose and they are getting ready to drive together to the Plaza Hotel. It is a daylight scene and supposed to be hot and muggy. But it is raw and rainy, much like the weather that came off the ocean in Newport earlier in the summer when there was still an absence of warmth in the air and the drizzle penetrated as harshly as a winter's sleet.

The only way to simulate a nice day is to have the car protected, and Clayton comes up with the idea of erecting a tunnel of plastic over it, lighting the interior and getting the scene done quickly. There is no dialogue and the scene is shot rapidly as the rain pelts the plastic.

Then Redford has to return to a small, cold studio, not too far from the dressing-room block where he has been looping for several days in his free time. It is a painstaking process, and he has already been doing it for hours. When he finishes he will have done 160 loops, which he contends is almost all his scenes in the film.

"It's difficult to get up emotionally for the scenes when you're looping," he says.

Earlier in the day he was in London shopping for gifts for the director, his co-star and a few secretaries. He seems pleased in having thought of doing it, not from any sense of a performance of duty, but in getting pleasure from giving gifts to people admired and liked. He has already bought several hundred T-shirts from Marks and Spencer and had the film's title and logo silkscreened on each as a gift for the crew.

It remains puzzling, though, for one who has worked so hard to stay apart from cast and crew during the production to act in his last hours on the film as if it were Christmas Eve, with such a sense of anticipation going about playing Santa Claus. Perhaps Redford, too, in the well of the self where insecurities remain that drove him into becoming an actor, has a need to be liked.

The atmosphere in the corridor and the dressing rooms is like a prep-school dormitory hours away from a holdiay recess. The banter is unrestrained. If they were the kind of people to pull them off, it would be a time for pranks.

Dern, who has a cold, is in his sweat suit prepared to jog around the back lot in the night rain. "I can't break my schedule of running every day, not even now," he says.

That afternoon, in the lobby of Claridge's, he had been stopped by King Constantine of Greece who is shopping in England for a place to live, apparently accepting his dethronement as a permanent status. The King had been watching Dern run in a nearby park and asked him about his exercise program.

For the first time in weeks, Lois Chiles is displaying temperament. She is being kept at the studio to do a voice-over, and she wants to go home, arguing to herself before presenting her points to the director that she can do it later.

Neither Dern nor Redford will stay for the rap party on Monday, the 24th of October. They both plan to fly back to the States tomorrow, the 21st, as soon as the rushes of their last scenes have been shown, approved by Clayton and they are cleared to go.

Lois wins her case, and she is excused for the night. In the back seat of a studio car speeding through the near-empty streets of the London suburb, she talks about acting, and in mid-sentence realizes that when she started the film she was not nearly as open as she is now.

"I learned acting comes from within," she says. "You have to feel the part. Jack didn't have to direct. He just looked at us with that fierce glare, and we knew what he wanted. I really believe we all worked well together, that we learned from each other.

"Now I've got to go back to New York to study," she says with the determined confidence that was not part of her in the cavernous dressing room in Rosecliff where she berated assistant directors and wanted star treatment, which had caused resentment in the other actors, who had paid their dues.

Before he is called to the set, Redford looks at the last batch of colored slides taken by a photographer assigned to the picture. He is killing those he does not like, and his judgments are quick and critical, calling out his rejections in the darkened room. He has developed a marvelous sense of how he should look in photographs—if not yet in roles that are really right for him—that would advance his career artistically rather than maintain it at a certain level of popularity.

The last scene is of Gatsby in the rain in the bushes outside the Buchanan house, waiting to speak to Nick after he drops off Jordan. Originally this scene was to have been done in Nick's cottage. Gatsby was to have gone there, awakened Nick and told him what really happened on the road.

This was the reason the cottage set contained a fully dressed bedroom that was never used, to the dismay of Gene Rudolf and his art department. Waterston had a good reason why this scene would never be effective in the bedroom. Would Nick, now so involved in the conflict between Gatsby and Tom, and a witness to the night's tragedy, go home and immediately go to sleep?

Redford has a reservation about the scene. He does not want Gatsby to have to spring from the bushes as if he were a furtive thief. The vigil outside the Buchanan house waiting for the light from Daisy's room should be in the open, he says.

Someone comes to his dressing room to tell him the camera is being set up as if the shot would be of him coming from the bushes. Redford, irritated, borrows a wool topcoat and goes to Clayton to reiterate his objections.

The rain is merciless now. A lean-to with a plastic roof is improvised for the crew, and a bottle of liquor is passed among them. The last image they have of him is in his pink suit and white shoes, wearing a raincoat until the take begins, standing in the rain, near, but so distant.

In the notebook he kept early in the production when he was working out his character, Redford wrote: "Somehow one feels in the end of *Gatsby* that something is missing. Something not enough—they say the story is great but isn't and is it enough? I find that curiously there is a blank in the area of Gatsby's and Daisy's affair."

September 24, The Last Day

"There's no alternative but to shoot," Clayton says.

"But it's hard to keep the concentration," Annabel adds.

So it has to come to this on the last day in one of the last scenes: Kensington Town Hall with Nick sitting at a desk going through records, other clerks moving about, fans whirling in a room of Wedgewood blue and white Georgian twirl designs. It is supposed to be a bond office in Wall Street.

The company has taken over the second floor. Business as usual goes on in the first-floor offices, though cables are draped over the stairs, making it a hazardous passage for anyone walking to the second floor. The oldtimers in the building survived the blitz; a day with a movie company should be simple.

It is almost a rerun of the opening days. Douglas is taking a very long time to light the scene; Clayton has a cold, and Sam is smiling enigmatically.

"What should I be doing with my hands at the desk?" he asks, not so much to elicit information as to say something during the interminable wait.

Ramon comes into the room and shows a bandaged finger. It is an accidental cut that has required five stitches. His wound gets almost as much attention as the scene being shot, concentration being that difficult in the closing hours of *The Great Gatsby*.

Clayton tries shooting the scene through a ticker-tape machine near Nick's desk. He then does Nick in close-up. Sam finds something to do with his hands. He fumbles with the pages of the book on his desk.

Wandering among the play-acting American capitalists is an authentic one, David Merrick, who has missed very few days of the shooting, being a presence seemingly without creative power on the set, yet one acknowledged to have power and to have made important decisions behind the scenes.

"The social implications of this film pleases me. Both Jack Clayton and I are politically somewhat to the left, and this film gives a picture of the rich the way we see them. They leave nothing but carnage around them.

"I'm sure this film will find a tremendous audience in the grass roots. They'll find out the film really has nothing to do with fashion and big parties. They'll see how bitterly anti-wealth and capitalism *Gatsby* is," he says.

"As long as it makes money, it can spout the philosophy of Mao," someone chimes in.

In the afternoon the company returns to the studio to do inserts. A newspaper in the production office is opened to a story that Metro-Goldwyn-Mayer, for all intents, is going out of the movie business and into Las Vegas hotels, a suitable end for a great movie company which in its years of decline produced consistently bad movies.

Behind the office, the drain has been opened in Gatsby's pool. It is empty, and the blue and white cabana drapes are tied back and put in plastic coverings.

Around four o'clock, the last shot is done, of Nick holding Gatsby's medal in his hand.

Rap parties are inevitable and deadly. They are everything from cauldrons of badly bruised egos functioning under imaginary hurts to last nights at summer camp with everyone drowning in sentimentality, pledging to write.

"They're worth going to," Annabel says. "Someone always gets killed driving home drunk, or there's a fist fight."

Fisticuffs would not be expected at this gathering. No one has shown evidence of feeling that strongly about anyone else, in love or hatred, to bring such an explosive end to the production. The only one showing emotion is Lois. Her eyes are red and wet, and she tells everyone how sorry she is it is over.

Someone came up with the wonderful idea of having the party in the Palm Court set. Everyone connected with the film has been invited by a letter from Clayton. The party is his gift, and at six o'clock the bar is opened and waitresses from the studio restaurant begin circulating with trays of hors d'oeuvres already getting cold.

There is a three-piece band. Music from the twenties used in the film is requested. The musicians play raggedly and off tempo. "Charleston" sounds like "Ain't She Sweet." Even the old-timers don't try to dance to it. The band goes into "What'll I Do," playing it as a half-remembered tune, dropping notes carelessly so that it goes from a waltz to a two-step.

The wives of the crew have come to see the stars, and they are dressed in what they believe is Hollywood chic:

skirts too short for the age of the wearers, platform shoes giving too much elevation, a touch too much makeup and earrings too large.

The center of attention is Mia, who the British know better than they do Redford. She is comfortably, totally pregnant, her condition well displayed in her floor-length casual skirt.

Bruce Dern has left her a job to do. She goes to the bandstand and reads a letter from Dern. He has given $100 to be raffled off among the crew. The winner turns out to be the assistant auditor, Paul Cadiou, and someone yells, "Fix!"

There is no genuine socializing between workers and the brass. Clayton, Merrick and the actors are at one large table near the bandstand.

The hostility between producer and director is gone. Clayton has said to Merrick how much he likes him now and has seen how he has grown to like the movie business. He told him how he had worked with Producer Alexander Korda, and was sure he was a genius as were David Selznick, and by reputation Irving Thalberg, and he was willing to put Merrick in that esteemed group. Clayton urged him to continue producing films.

The crew with wives and girl friends sit towards the back, showing proper distance and decorum. How much England is still a class society. Bred into these decent people is an automatic bow to those who they believe are in a higher social class. On a movie set those at the top are the actors, director and producer. Only when Clayton brings on an old vaudevillian who does a rousing tap dance, do the workers relax. They cheer the performer as if he were a familiar face from their own pub.

The crew says it's the best rap party they have ever had at Pinewood, even better than those given on the James Bond pictures. But the men don't seem happy to be there, chafing as if they were forced to be in a church wearing starched collars.

There is a dance with Mia, and she says, "We must do a picture again, soon," and it breaks your heart. No one

253

has to say the party is over. It's a fact. The bar is closed, and what food remains is soggy, cold and unpalatable.

The last to go is Jack Clayton. The rage that has always been in him, there during the labor crisis in Newport, erupts one last time and he systematically begins to smash out the windows in the main corridor, first with a bench, and then with his bare fist.

EPILOGUE

The plane is 35,000 feet over the Atlantic Ocean. The two men who have brought the suitcase with them through customs have it on the floor between them. They are drinking champagne and talking with a young American businessman about his fabulous job which has brought him wealth, a home and family in southern California, an obese body and a slight puffing when he walks up the stairs to the Captain's Lounge.

Everything in first class reeks of money: the food, the expensive wine, the smiles of the hostesses, the system that has enabled the plane to be in the sky at that moment, a civilization in pursuit of riches.

It is alone in space. A cloud bank has cut off the plane from earth.

Inside the suitcase are the Cartier jewels, going home to America.

OTHER BERKLEY BESTSELLERS
FOR YOU TO ENJOY!